METAPHYSICS

By ARISTOTLE

Translated by W. D. ROSS

Metaphysics
By Aristotle
Translated by W. D. Ross

Print ISBN 13: 978-1-4209-8185-8
eBook ISBN 13: 978-1-4209-8211-4

Cover Image: a detail of a portrait of Aristotle by Luca Giordano, c. 1653.

Please visit *www.digireads.com*

CONTENTS

Book I

1

All men by nature desire to know. An indication of this is the delight we take in our senses; for even apart from their usefulness they are loved for themselves; and above all others the sense of sight. For not only with a view to action, but even when we are not going to do anything, we prefer seeing (one might say) to everything else. The reason is that this, most of all the senses, makes us know and brings to light many differences between things.

By nature animals are born with the faculty of sensation, and from sensation memory is produced in some of them, though not in others. And therefore the former are more intelligent and apt at learning than those which cannot remember; those which are incapable of hearing sounds are intelligent though they cannot be taught, e.g. the bee, and any other race of animals that may be like it; and those which besides memory have this sense of hearing can be taught.

The animals other than man live by appearances and memories, and have but little of connected experience; but the human race lives also by art and reasonings. Now from memory experience is produced in men; for the several memories of the same thing produce finally the capacity for a single experience. And experience seems pretty much like science and art, but really science and art come to men through experience; for 'experience made art', as Polus says, 'but inexperience luck.' Now art arises when from many notions gained by experience one universal judgement about a class of objects is produced. For to have a judgement that when Callias was ill of this disease this did him good, and similarly in the case of Socrates and in many individual cases, is a matter of experience; but to judge that it has done good to all persons of a certain constitution, marked off in one class, when they were ill of this disease, e.g. to phlegmatic or bilious people when burning with fevers—this is a matter of art.

With a view to action experience seems in no respect inferior to art, and men of experience succeed even better than those who have theory without experience. (The reason is that experience is knowledge of individuals, art of universals, and actions and productions are all concerned with the individual; for the physician does not cure man, except in an incidental way, but Callias or Socrates or some other called by some such individual name, who happens to be a man. If, then, a man has the theory without the experience, and recognizes the universal but does not know the individual included in this, he will often fail to cure; for it is the individual that is to be cured.) But yet we think that knowledge and understanding belong to art rather than to experience, and we suppose artists to be wiser than men of experience (which implies that Wisdom depends in all cases rather on knowledge); and this because the former know the cause, but the latter do not. For men of experience know that the thing is so, but do not know why, while the others know the 'why' and the cause. Hence we think also that the master-workers in each craft are more honourable and know in a truer sense and are wiser than the manual workers, because they know the causes of the things that are done (we think the manual workers are like certain lifeless things which act indeed, but act without knowing what they do, as fire burns,—but while the lifeless things perform each of their functions by a natural tendency, the labourers perform them through habit); thus we view them as being wiser not in virtue of being able to act, but of having the theory for themselves and knowing the causes. And in general it is a sign of the man who knows and of the man who does not know, that the former can teach, and therefore we think art more truly knowledge than experience is; for artists can teach, and men of mere experience cannot.

Again, we do not regard any of the senses as Wisdom; yet surely these give the most authoritative knowledge of particulars. But they do not tell us the 'why' of anything—e.g. why fire is hot; they only say that it is hot.

At first he who invented any art whatever that went beyond the common perceptions of man was naturally admired by men, not only because there was something useful in the inventions, but because he was thought wise and superior to the rest. But as more arts were invented, and some were directed to the necessities of life, others to recreation, the inventors of the latter were naturally always regarded as wiser than the inventors of the former, because their branches of knowledge did not aim at utility. Hence when all such inventions were already established, the sciences which do not aim at giving pleasure or at the necessities of life were discovered, and first in the places where men first began to have leisure. This is why the mathematical arts were founded in Egypt; for there the priestly caste was allowed to be at leisure.

We have said in the *Ethics* what the difference is between art and science and the other kindred faculties; but the point of our present discussion is this, that all men suppose what is called Wisdom to deal with the first causes and the principles of things; so that, as has been said before, the man of experience is thought to be wiser than the possessors of any sense-perception whatever, the artist wiser than the men of experience, the master-worker than the mechanic, and the theoretical kinds of knowledge to be more of the nature of Wisdom than the productive. Clearly then Wisdom is knowledge about certain principles and causes.

2

Since we are seeking this knowledge, we must inquire of what kind are the causes and the principles, the knowledge of which is Wisdom. If one were to take the notions we have about the wise man, this might perhaps make the answer more evident. We suppose first, then, that the wise man knows all things, as far as possible, although he has not knowledge of each of them in detail; secondly, that he who can learn things that are difficult, and not easy for man to know, is wise (sense-perception is common to all, and therefore easy and no mark of Wisdom); again, that he who is more exact and more capable of teaching the causes is wiser, in every branch of knowledge; and that of the sciences, also, that which is desirable on its own account and for the sake of knowing it is more of the nature of Wisdom than that which is desirable on account of its results, and the superior science is more of the nature of Wisdom than the ancillary; for the wise man must not be ordered but must order, and he must not obey another, but the less wise must obey him.

Such and so many are the notions, then, which we have about Wisdom and the wise. Now of these characteristics that of knowing all things must belong to him who has in the highest degree universal knowledge; for he knows in a sense all the instances that fall under the universal. And these things, the most universal, are on the whole the hardest for men to know; for they are farthest from the senses. And the most exact of the sciences are those which deal most with first principles; for those which involve fewer principles are more exact than those which involve additional principles, e.g. arithmetic than geometry. But the science which investigates causes is also instructive, in a higher degree, for the people who instruct us are those who tell the causes of each thing. And understanding and knowledge pursued for their own sake are found most in the knowledge of that which is most knowable (for he who chooses to know for the sake of knowing will choose most readily that which is most truly knowledge, and such is the knowledge of that which is most knowable); and the first principles and the causes are most knowable; for by reason of these, and from these, all other things come to be known, and not these by means of the things subordinate to them. And the science which knows to what end each thing must be done is the most authoritative of the sciences, and more authoritative than any ancillary science; and this end is the good of that thing, and in general the supreme good in the whole of nature. Judged by all the tests we have mentioned, then, the name in question falls to the same science; this must be a science that investigates the first principles and causes; for the good, i.e. the end, is one of the causes.

That it is not a science of production is clear even from the history of the earliest philosophers. For it is owing to their wonder that men both now begin and at first began to philosophize; they wondered originally at the obvious difficulties, then advanced little by little and stated difficulties about the greater matters, e.g. about the phenomena of the moon and those of the sun and of the stars, and about the genesis of the universe. And a man who is puzzled and wonders thinks himself ignorant (whence even the lover of myth is in a sense a lover of Wisdom, for the myth is composed of wonders); therefore since they philosophized order to escape from ignorance, evidently they were pursuing science in order to know, and not for any utilitarian end. And this is confirmed by the facts; for it was when almost all the necessities of life and the things that make for comfort and recreation had been secured, that such knowledge began to be sought. Evidently then we do not seek it for the sake of any other advantage; but as the man is free, we say, who exists for his own sake and not for another's, so we pursue this as the only free science, for it alone exists for its own sake.

Hence also the possession of it might be justly regarded as beyond human power; for in many ways human nature is in bondage, so that according to Simonides 'God alone can have this privilege', and it is unfitting that man should not be content to seek the knowledge that is suited to him. If, then, there is something in what the poets say, and jealousy is natural to the divine power, it would probably occur in this case above all, and all who excelled in this knowledge would be unfortunate. But the divine power cannot be jealous (nay, according to the proverb, 'bards tell a lie'), nor should any other science be thought more honourable than one of this sort. For the most divine science is also most honourable; and this science alone must be, in two ways, most divine. For the science which it would be most meet for God to have is a divine science, and so is any science that deals with divine objects; and this science alone has both these qualities; for (1) God is thought to be among the causes of all things and to be a first principle, and (2) such a science either God alone can have, or God above all others. All the sciences, indeed, are more necessary than this, but none is better.

Yet the acquisition of it must in a sense end in something which is the opposite of our original inquiries. For all men begin, as we said, by wondering that things are as they are, as they do about self-moving marionettes, or about the solstices or the incommensurability of the diagonal of a square with the side; for it seems wonderful to all who have not yet seen the reason, that there is a thing which cannot be measured even by the smallest unit. But we must end in the contrary and, according to the proverb, the better state, as is the case in these instances too when men learn the cause; for there is nothing which would surprise a geometer so much as if the diagonal turned out to be commensurable.

We have stated, then, what is the nature of the science we are searching for, and what is the mark which our search and our whole investigation must reach.

3

Evidently we have to acquire knowledge of the original causes (for we say we know each thing only when we think we recognize its first cause), and causes are spoken of in four senses. In one of these we mean the substance, i.e. the essence (for the 'why' is reducible finally to the definition, and the ultimate 'why' is a cause and principle); in another the matter or *substratum*, in a third the source of the change, and in a fourth the cause opposed to this, the purpose and the good (for this is the end of all generation and change). We have studied these causes sufficiently in our work on nature, but yet let us call to our aid those who have attacked the investigation of being and philosophized about reality before us. For obviously they too speak of certain principles and causes; to go over their views, then, will be of profit to the present inquiry, for we shall either find another kind of cause, or be more convinced of the correctness of those which we now maintain.

Of the first philosophers, then, most thought the principles which were of the nature of matter were the only principles of all things. That of which all things that are consist, the first from which they come to be, the last into which they are resolved (the substance remaining, but changing in its modifications), this they say is the element and this the principle of things, and therefore they think nothing is either generated or destroyed, since this sort of entity is always conserved, as we say Socrates neither comes to be absolutely when he comes to be beautiful or musical, nor ceases to be when loses these characteristics, because the *substratum*, Socrates himself remains, just so they say nothing else comes to be or ceases to be; for there must be some entity—either one or more than one—from which all other things come to be, it being conserved.

Yet they do not all agree as to the number and the nature of these principles. Thales, the founder of this type of philosophy, says the principle is water (for which reason he declared that the earth rests on water), getting the notion perhaps from seeing that the nutriment of all things is moist, and that heat itself is generated from the moist and kept alive by it (and that from which they come to be is a principle of all things). He got his notion from this fact, and from the fact that the seeds of all things have a moist nature, and that water is the origin of the nature of moist things.

Some think that even the ancients who lived long before the present generation, and first framed accounts of the gods, had a similar view of nature; for they made Ocean and Tethys the parents of creation, and described the oath of the gods as being by water, to which they give the name of Styx; for what is oldest is most honourable, and the most honourable thing is that by which one swears. It may perhaps be uncertain whether this opinion about nature is primitive and ancient, but Thales at any rate is said to have declared himself thus about the first cause. Hippo no one would think fit to include among these thinkers, because of the paltriness of his thought.

Anaximenes and Diogenes make air prior to water, and the most primary of the simple bodies, while Hippasus of Metapontium and Heraclitus of Ephesus say this of fire, and Empedocles says it of the four elements (adding a fourth—earth—to those which have been named); for these, he says, always remain and do not come to be, except that they come to be more or fewer, being aggregated into one and segregated out of one.

Anaxagoras of Clazomenae, who, though older than Empedocles, was later in his philosophical activity, says the principles are infinite in number; for he says almost all the things that are made of parts like themselves, in the manner of water or fire, are generated and destroyed in this way, only by aggregation and segregation, and are not in any other sense generated or destroyed, but remain eternally.

From these facts one might think that the only cause is the so-called material cause; but as men thus advanced, the very facts opened the way for them and joined in forcing them to investigate the subject. However true it may be that all generation and destruction proceed from some one or (for that matter) from more elements, why does this happen and what is the cause? For at least the *substratum* itself does not make itself change; e.g. neither the wood nor the bronze causes the change of either of them, nor does the wood manufacture a bed and the bronze a statue, but something else is the cause of the change. And to seek this is to seek the second cause, as we should say,—that from which comes the beginning of the movement. Now those who at the very beginning set themselves to this kind of inquiry, and said the *substratum* was one, were not at all dissatisfied with themselves; but some at least of those who maintain it to be one—as though defeated by this search for the second cause—say the one and nature as a whole is unchangeable not only in respect of generation and destruction (for this is a primitive belief, and all agreed in it), but also of all other change; and this view is peculiar to them. Of those who said the universe was one, then none succeeded in discovering a cause of this sort, except perhaps Parmenides, and he only inasmuch as he supposes that there is not only one but also in some sense two causes. But for those who make more elements it is more possible to state the second cause, e.g. for those who make hot and cold, or fire and earth, the elements; for they treat fire as having a nature which fits it to move things, and water and earth and such things they treat in the contrary way.

When these men and the principles of this kind had had their day, as the latter were found inadequate to generate the nature of things men were again forced by the truth itself, as we said, to inquire into the next kind of cause. For it is not likely either that fire or earth or any such element should be the reason why things manifest goodness and, beauty both in their being and in their coming to be, or that those thinkers should have supposed it was; nor again could it be right to entrust so great a matter to spontaneity and chance. When one man said, then, that reason was present—as in animals, so throughout nature—as the cause of order and of all arrangement, he seemed like a sober man in contrast with the random talk of his predecessors. We know that Anaxagoras certainly adopted these views, but Hermotimus of Clazomenae is credited with expressing them earlier. Those who thought thus stated that there is a principle of things which is at the same time the cause of beauty, and that sort of cause from which things acquire movement.

4

One might suspect that Hesiod was the first to look for such a thing—or some one else who put love or desire among existing things as a principle, as Parmenides, too, does; for he, in constructing the genesis of the universe, says:—

Love first of all the Gods she planned.

And Hesiod says:—

First of all things was chaos made, and then
Broad-breasted earth...
And love, 'mid all the gods pre-eminent,

which implies that among existing things there must be from the first a cause which will move things and bring them together. How these thinkers should be arranged with regard to priority of discovery let us be allowed to decide later; but since the contraries of the various forms of good were also perceived to be present in nature—not only order and the beautiful, but also disorder and the ugly, and bad things in greater number than good, and ignoble things than beautiful—therefore another thinker introduced friendship and strife, each of the two the cause of one of these two sets of qualities. For if we were to follow out the view of Empedocles, and interpret it according to its meaning and not to its lisping expression, we should find that friendship is the cause of good things, and strife of bad. Therefore, if we said that Empedocles in a sense both mentions, and is the first to mention, the bad and the good as principles, we should perhaps be right, since the cause of all goods is the good itself.

These thinkers, as we say, evidently grasped, and to this extent, two of the causes which we distinguished in our work on nature—the matter and the source of the movement—vaguely, however, and with no clearness, but as untrained men behave in fights; for they go round their opponents and often strike fine blows, but they do not fight on scientific principles, and so too these thinkers do not seem to know what they say; for it is evident that, as a rule, they make no use of their causes except to a small extent. For Anaxagoras uses reason as a *deus ex machina* for the making of the world, and when he is at a loss to tell from what cause something necessarily is, then he drags reason in, but in all other cases ascribes events to anything rather than to reason. And Empedocles, though he uses the causes to a greater extent than this, neither does so sufficiently nor attains consistency in their use. At least, in many cases he makes love segregate things, and strife aggregate them. For whenever the universe is dissolved into its elements by strife, fire is aggregated into one, and so is each of the other elements; but whenever again under the influence of love they come together into one, the parts must again be segregated out of each element.

Empedocles, then, in contrast with his predecessors, was the first to introduce the dividing of this cause, not positing one source of movement, but different and contrary sources. Again, he was the first to speak of four material elements; yet he does not use four, but treats them as two only; he treats fire by itself, and its opposite—earth, air, and water—as one kind of thing. We may learn this by study of his verses.

This philosopher then, as we say, has spoken of the principles in this way, and made them of this number. Leucippus and his associate Democritus say that the full and the empty are the elements, calling the one being and the other non-being—the full and solid being being, the empty non-being (whence they say being no more is than non-being, because the solid no more is than the empty); and they make these the material causes of things. And as those who make the underlying substance one generate all other things by its modifications, supposing the rare and the dense to be the sources of the modifications, in the same way these philosophers say the differences in the elements are the causes of all other qualities. These differences, they say, are three—shape and order and position. For they say the real is differentiated only by 'rhythm' and 'inter-contact' and 'turning'; and of these rhythm is shape, inter-contact is order, and turning is position; for A differs from N in shape, AN from NA in order, Ⴈ from H in position. The question of movement—whence or how it is to belong to things—these thinkers, like the others, lazily neglected.

Regarding the two causes, then, as we say, the inquiry seems to have been pushed thus far by the early philosophers.

5

Contemporaneously with these philosophers and before them, the so-called Pythagoreans, who were the first to take up mathematics, not only advanced this study, but also having been brought up in it they thought its principles were the principles of all things. Since of these principles numbers are by nature the first, and in numbers they seemed to see many resemblances to the things that exist and come into being-more than in fire and earth and water (such and such a modification of numbers being justice, another being soul and reason, another being opportunity—and similarly almost all other things being numerically expressible); since, again, they saw that the modifications and the ratios of the musical scales were expressible in numbers;—since, then, all other things seemed in their whole nature to be modelled on numbers, and numbers seemed to be the first things in the whole of nature, they supposed the elements of numbers to be the elements of all things, and the whole heaven to be a musical scale and a number. And all the properties of numbers and scales which they could show to agree with the attributes and parts and the whole arrangement of the heavens, they collected and fitted into their scheme; and if there was a gap anywhere, they readily made additions so as to make their whole theory coherent. E.g. as the number 10 is thought to be perfect and to comprise the whole nature of numbers, they say that the bodies which move through the heavens are ten, but as the visible bodies are only nine, to meet this they invent a tenth—the 'counter-earth'. We have discussed these matters more exactly elsewhere.

But the object of our review is that we may learn from these philosophers also what they suppose to be the principles and how these fall under the causes we have named. Evidently, then, these thinkers also consider that number is the principle both as matter for things and as forming both their modifications and their permanent states, and hold that the elements of number are the even and the odd, and that of these the latter is limited, and the former unlimited; and that the One proceeds from both of these (for it is both even and odd), and number from the One; and that the whole heaven, as has been said, is numbers.

Other members of this same school say there are ten principles, which they arrange in two columns of cognates—limit and unlimited, odd and even, one and plurality, right and left, male and female, resting and moving, straight and curved, light and darkness, good and bad, square and oblong. In this way Alcmaeon of Croton seems also to have conceived the matter, and either he got this view from them or they got it from him; for he expressed himself similarly to them. For he says most human affairs go in pairs, meaning not definite contrarieties such as the Pythagoreans speak of, but any chance contrarieties, e.g. white and black, sweet and bitter, good and bad, great and small. He threw out indefinite suggestions about the other contrarieties, but the Pythagoreans declared both how many and which their contrarieties are.

From both these schools, then, we can learn this much, that the contraries are the principles of things; and how many these principles are and which they are, we can learn from one of the two schools. But how these principles can be brought together under the causes we have named has not been clearly and articulately stated by them; they seem, however, to range the elements under the head of matter; for out of these as immanent parts they say substance is composed and moulded.

From these facts we may sufficiently perceive the meaning of the ancients who said the elements of nature were more than one; but there are some who spoke of the universe as if it were one entity, though they were not all alike either in the excellence of their statement or in its conformity to the facts of nature. The discussion of them is in no way appropriate to our present investigation of causes, for they do not, like some of the natural philosophers, assume being to be one and yet generate it out of the one as out of matter, but they speak in another way; those others add change, since they generate the universe, but these thinkers say the universe is unchangeable. Yet this much is germane to the present inquiry: Parmenides seems to fasten on that which is one in definition, Melissus on that which is one in matter, for which reason the former says that it is limited, the latter that it is unlimited; while Xenophanes, the first of these partisans of the One (for Parmenides is said to have been his pupil), gave no clear statement, nor does he seem to have grasped the nature of either of these causes, but with reference to the whole material universe he says the One is God. Now these thinkers, as we said, must be neglected for the purposes of the present inquiry—two of them entirely, as being a little too naive, viz. Xenophanes and Melissus; but Parmenides seems in places to speak with more insight. For, claiming that, besides the existent, nothing non-existent exists, he thinks that of necessity one thing exists, viz. the existent and nothing else (on this we have spoken more clearly in our work on nature), but being forced to follow the observed facts, and supposing the existence of that which is one in definition, but more than one according to our sensations, he now posits two causes and two principles, calling them hot and cold, i.e. fire and earth; and of these he ranges the hot with the existent, and the other with the non-existent.

From what has been said, then, and from the wise men who have now sat in council with us, we have got thus much—on the one hand from the earliest philosophers, who regard the first principle as corporeal (for water and fire and such things are bodies), and of whom some suppose that there is one corporeal principle, others that there are more than one, but both put these under the head of matter; and on the other hand from some who posit both this cause and besides this the source of movement, which we have got from some as single and from others as twofold.

Down to the Italian school, then, and apart from it, philosophers have treated these subjects rather obscurely, except that, as we said, they have in fact used two kinds of cause, and one of these—the source of movement—some treat as one and others as two. But the Pythagoreans have said in the same way that there are two principles, but added this much, which is peculiar to them, that they thought that finitude and infinity were not attributes of certain other things, e.g. of fire or earth or anything else of this kind, but that infinity itself and unity itself were the substance of the things of which they are predicated. This is why number was the substance of all things. On this subject, then, they expressed themselves thus; and regarding the question of essence they began to make statements and definitions, but treated the matter too simply. For they both defined superficially and thought that the first subject of which a given definition was predicable was the substance of the thing defined, as if one supposed that 'double' and '2' were the same, because 2 is the first thing of which 'double' is predicable. But surely to be double and to be 2 are not the same; if they are, one thing will be many—a consequence which they actually drew. From the earlier philosophers, then, and from their successors we can learn thus much.

6

After the systems we have named came the philosophy of Plato, which in most respects followed these thinkers, but had peculiarities that distinguished it from the philosophy of the Italians. For, having in his youth first become familiar with Cratylus and with the Heraclitean doctrines (that all sensible things are ever in a state of flux and there is no knowledge about them), these views he held even in later years. Socrates, however, was busying himself about ethical matters and neglecting the world of nature as a whole but seeking the universal in these ethical matters, and fixed thought for the first time on definitions; Plato accepted his teaching, but held that the problem applied not to sensible things but to entities of another kind—for this reason, that the common definition could not be a definition of any sensible thing, as they were always changing. Things of this other sort, then, he called Ideas, and sensible things, he said, were all named after these, and in virtue of a relation to these; for the many existed by participation in the Ideas that have the same name as they. Only the name 'participation' was new; for the Pythagoreans say that things exist by 'imitation' of numbers, and Plato says they exist by participation, changing the name. But what the participation or the imitation of the Forms could be they left an open question.

Further, besides sensible things and Forms he says there are the objects of mathematics, which occupy an intermediate position, differing from sensible things in being eternal and unchangeable, from Forms in that there are many alike, while the Form itself is in each case unique.

Since the Forms were the causes of all other things, he thought their elements were the elements of all things. As matter, the great and the small were principles; as essential reality, the One; for from the great and the small, by participation in the One, come the Numbers.

But he agreed with the Pythagoreans in saying that the One is substance and not a predicate of something else; and in saying that the Numbers are the causes of the reality of other things he agreed with them; but positing a dyad and constructing the infinite out of great and small, instead of treating the infinite as one, is peculiar to him; and so is his view that the Numbers exist apart from sensible things, while they say that the things themselves are Numbers, and do not place the objects of mathematics between Forms and sensible things. His divergence from the Pythagoreans in making the One and the Numbers separate from things, and his introduction of the Forms, were due to his inquiries in the region of definitions (for the earlier thinkers had no tincture of dialectic), and his making the other entity besides the One a dyad was due to the belief that the numbers, except those which were prime, could be neatly produced out of the dyad as out of some plastic material. Yet what happens is the contrary; the theory is not a reasonable one. For they make many things out of the matter, and the form generates only once, but what we observe is that one table is made from one matter, while the man who applies the form, though he is one, makes many tables. And the relation of the male to the female is similar; for the latter is impregnated by one copulation, but the male impregnates many females; yet these are analogues of those first principles.

Plato, then, declared himself thus on the points in question; it is evident from what has been said that he has used only two causes, that of the essence and the material cause (for the Forms are the causes of the essence of all other things, and the One is the cause of the essence of the Forms); and it is evident what the underlying matter is, of which the Forms are predicated in the case of sensible things, and the One in the case of Forms, viz. that this is a dyad, the great and the small. Further, he has assigned the cause of good and that of evil to the elements, one to each of the two, as we say some of his predecessors sought to do, e.g. Empedocles and Anaxagoras.

7

Our review of those who have spoken about first principles and reality and of the way in which they have spoken, has been concise and summary; but yet we have learnt this much from them, that of those who speak about 'principle' and 'cause' no one has mentioned any principle except those which have been distinguished in our work on nature, but all evidently have some inkling of them, though only vaguely. For some speak of the first principle as matter, whether they suppose one or more first principles, and whether they suppose this to be a body or to be incorporeal; e.g. Plato spoke of the great and the small, the Italians of the infinite, Empedocles of fire, earth, water, and air, Anaxagoras of the infinity of things composed of similar parts. These, then, have all had a notion of this kind of cause, and so have all who speak of air or fire or water, or something denser than fire and rarer than air; for some have said the prime element is of this kind.

These thinkers grasped this cause only; but certain others have mentioned the source of movement, e.g. those who make friendship and strife, or reason, or love, a principle.

The essence, i.e. the substantial reality, no one has expressed distinctly. It is hinted at chiefly by those who believe in the Forms; for they do not suppose either that the Forms are the matter of sensible things, and the One the matter of the Forms, or that they are the source of movement (for they say these are causes rather of immobility and of being at rest), but they furnish the Forms as the essence of every other thing, and the One as the essence of the Forms.

That for whose sake actions and changes and movements take place, they assert to be a cause in a way, but not in this way, i.e. not in the way in which it is its nature to be a cause. For those who speak of reason or friendship class these causes as goods; they do not speak, however, as if anything that exists either existed or came into being for the sake of these, but as if movements started from these. In the same way those who say the One or the existent is the good, say that it is the cause of substance, but not that substance either is or comes to be for the sake of this. Therefore it turns out that in a sense they both say and do not say the good is a cause; for they do not call it a cause *qua* good but only incidentally.

All these thinkers then, as they cannot pitch on another cause, seem to testify that we have determined rightly both how many and of what sort the causes are. Besides this it is plain that when the causes are being looked for, either all four must be sought thus or they must be sought in one of these four ways. Let us next discuss the possible difficulties with regard to the way in which each of these thinkers has spoken, and with regard to his situation relatively to the first principles.

8

Those, then, who say the universe is one and posit one kind of thing as matter, and as corporeal matter which has spatial magnitude, evidently go astray in many ways. For they posit the elements of bodies only, not of incorporeal things, though there are also incorporeal things. And in trying to state the causes of generation and destruction, and in giving a physical account of all things, they do away with the cause of movement. Further, they err in not positing the substance, i.e. the essence, as the cause of anything, and besides this in lightly calling any of the simple bodies except earth the first principle, without inquiring how they are produced out of one another,—I mean fire, water, earth, and air. For some things are produced out of each other by combination, others by separation, and this makes the greatest difference to their priority and posteriority. For (1) in a way the property of being most elementary of all would seem to belong to the first thing from which they are produced by combination, and this property would belong to the most fine-grained and subtle of bodies. For this reason those who make fire the principle would be most in agreement with this argument. But each of the other thinkers agrees that the element of corporeal things is of this sort. At least none of those who named one element claimed that earth was the element, evidently because of the coarseness of its grain. (Of the other three elements each has found some judge on its side; for some maintain that fire, others that water, others that air is the element. Yet why, after all, do they not name earth also, as most men do? For people say all things are earth Hesiod says earth was produced first of corporeal things; so primitive and popular has the opinion been.) According to this argument, then, no one would be right who either says the first principle is any of the elements other than fire, or supposes it to be denser than air but rarer than water. But (2) if that which is later in generation is prior in nature, and that which is concocted and compounded is later in generation, the contrary of what we have been saying must be true,—water must be prior to air, and earth to water.

So much, then, for those who posit one cause such as we mentioned; but the same is true if one supposes more of these, as Empedocles says matter of things is four bodies. For he too is confronted by consequences some of which are the same as have been mentioned, while others are peculiar to him. For we see these bodies produced from one another, which implies that the same body does not always remain fire or earth (we have spoken about this in our works on nature); and regarding the cause of movement and the question whether we must posit one or two, he must be thought to have spoken neither correctly nor altogether plausibly. And in general, change of quality is necessarily done away with for those who speak thus, for on their view cold will not come from hot nor hot from cold. For if it did there would be something that accepted the contraries themselves, and there would be some one entity that became fire and water, which Empedocles denies.

As regards Anaxagoras, if one were to suppose that he said there were two elements, the supposition would accord thoroughly with an argument which Anaxagoras himself did not state articulately, but which he must have accepted if any one had led him on to it. True, to say that in the beginning all things were mixed is absurd both on other grounds and because it follows that they must have existed before in an unmixed form, and because nature does not allow any chance thing to be mixed with any chance thing, and also because on this view modifications and accidents could be separated from substances (for the same things which are mixed can be separated); yet if one were to follow him up, piecing together what he means, he would perhaps be seen to be somewhat modern in his views. For when nothing was separated out, evidently nothing could be truly asserted of the substance that then existed. I mean, e.g. that it was neither white nor black, nor grey nor any other colour, but of necessity colourless; for if it had been coloured, it would have had one of these colours. And similarly, by this same argument, it was flavourless, nor had it any similar attribute; for it could not be either of any quality or of any size, nor could it be any definite kind of thing. For if it were, one of the particular forms would have belonged to it, and this is impossible, since all were mixed together; for the particular form would necessarily have been already separated out, but he all were mixed except reason, and this alone was unmixed and pure. From this it follows, then, that he must say the principles are the One (for this is simple and unmixed) and the Other, which is of such a nature as we suppose the indefinite to be before it is defined and partakes of some form. Therefore, while expressing himself neither rightly nor clearly, he means something like what the later thinkers say and what is now more clearly seen to be the case.

But these thinkers are, after all, at home only in arguments about generation and destruction and movement; for it is practically only of this sort of substance that they seek the principles and the causes. But those who extend their vision to all things that exist, and of existing things suppose some to be perceptible and others not perceptible, evidently study both classes, which is all the more reason why one should devote some time to seeing what is good in their views and what bad from the standpoint of the inquiry we have now before us.

The 'Pythagoreans' treat of principles and elements stranger than those of the physical philosophers (the reason is that they got the principles from non-sensible things, for the objects of mathematics, except those of astronomy, are of the class of things without movement); yet their discussions and investigations are all about nature; for they generate the heavens, and with regard to their parts and attributes and functions they observe the phenomena, and use up the principles and the causes in explaining these, which implies that they agree with the others, the physical philosophers, that the real is just all that which is perceptible and contained by the so-called 'heavens'. But the causes and the principles which they mention are, as we said, sufficient to act as steps even up to the higher realms of reality, and are more suited to these than to theories about nature. They do not tell us at all, however, how there can be movement if limit and unlimited and odd and even are the only things assumed, or how without movement and change there can be generation and destruction, or the bodies that move through the heavens can do what they do.

Further, if one either granted them that spatial magnitude consists of these elements, or this were proved, still how would some bodies be light and others have weight? To judge from what they assume and maintain they are speaking no more of mathematical bodies than of perceptible; hence they have said nothing whatever about fire or earth or the other bodies of this sort, I suppose because they have nothing to say which applies peculiarly to perceptible things.

Further, how are we to combine the beliefs that the attributes of number, and number itself, are causes of what exists and happens in the heavens both from the beginning and now, and that there is no other number than this number out of which the world is composed? When in one particular region they place opinion and opportunity, and, a little above or below, injustice and decision or mixture, and allege, as proof, that each of these is a number, and that there happens to be already in this place a plurality of the extended bodies composed of numbers, because these attributes of number attach to the various places,—this being so, is this number, which we must suppose each of these abstractions to be, the same number which is exhibited in the material universe, or is it another than this? Plato says it is different; yet even he thinks that both these bodies and their causes are numbers, but that the intelligible numbers are causes, while the others are sensible.

9

Let us leave the Pythagoreans for the present; for it is enough to have touched on them as much as we have done. But as for those who posit the Ideas as causes, firstly, in seeking to grasp the causes of the things around us, they introduced others equal in number to these, as if a man who wanted to count things thought he would not be able to do it while they were few, but tried to count them when he had added to their number. For the Forms are practically equal to—or not fewer than—the things, in trying to explain which these thinkers proceeded from them to the Forms. For to each thing there answers an entity which has the same name and exists apart from the substances, and so also in the case of all other groups there is a one over many, whether the many are in this world or are eternal.

Further, of the ways in which we prove that the Forms exist, none is convincing; for from some no inference necessarily follows, and from some arise Forms even of things of which we think there are no Forms. For according to the arguments from the existence of the sciences there will be Forms of all things of which there are sciences and according to the 'one over many' argument there will be Forms even of negations, and according to the argument that there is an object for thought even when the thing has perished, there will be Forms of perishable things; for we have an image of these. Further, of the more accurate arguments, some lead to Ideas of relations, of which we say there is no independent class, and others introduce the 'third man'.

And in general the arguments for the Forms destroy the things for whose existence we are more zealous than for the existence of the Ideas; for it follows that not the dyad but number is first, i.e. that the relative is prior to the absolute,—besides all the other points on which certain people by following out the opinions held about the Ideas have come into conflict with the principles of the theory.

Further, according to the assumption on which our belief in the Ideas rests, there will be Forms not only of substances but also of many other things (for the concept is single not only in the case of substances but also in the other cases, and there are sciences not only of substance but also of other things, and a thousand other such difficulties confront them). But according to the necessities of the case and the opinions held about the Forms, if Forms can be shared in there must be Ideas of substances only. For they are not shared in incidentally, but a thing must share in its Form as in something not predicated of a subject (by 'being shared in incidentally' I mean that e.g. if a thing shares in 'double itself', it shares also in 'eternal', but incidentally; for 'eternal' happens to be predicable of the 'double'). Therefore the Forms will be substance; but the same terms indicate substance in this and in the ideal world (or what will be the meaning of saying that there is something apart from the particulars—the one over many?). And if the Ideas and the particulars that share in them have the same form, there will be something common to these; for why should '2' be one and the same in the perishable 2's or in those which are many but eternal, and not the same in the '2' itself' as in the particular 2? But if they have not the same form, they must have only the name in common, and it is as if one were to call both Callias and a wooden image a 'man', without observing any community between them.

Above all one might discuss the question what on earth the Forms contribute to sensible things, either to those that are eternal or to those that come into being and cease to be. For they cause neither movement nor any change in them. But again they help in no wise either towards the knowledge of the other things (for they are not even the substance of these, else they would have been in them), or towards their being, if they are not in the particulars which share in them; though if they were, they might be thought to be causes, as white causes whiteness in a white object by entering into its composition. But this argument, which first Anaxagoras and later Eudoxus and certain others used, is very easily upset; for it is not difficult to collect many insuperable objections to such a view.

But, further, all other things cannot come from the Forms in any of the usual senses of 'from'. And to say that they are patterns and the other things share in them is to use empty words and poetical metaphors. For what is it that works, looking to the Ideas? And anything can either be, or become, like another without being copied from it, so that whether Socrates or not a man Socrates like might come to be; and evidently this might be so even if Socrates were eternal. And there will be several patterns of the same thing, and therefore several Forms; e.g. 'animal' and 'two-footed' and also 'man himself' will be Forms of man. Again, the Forms are patterns not only sensible things, but of Forms themselves also; i.e. the genus, as genus of various species, will be so; therefore the same thing will be pattern and copy.

Again, it would seem impossible that the substance and that of which it is the substance should exist apart; how, therefore, could the Ideas, being the substances of things, exist apart? In the *Phaedo* the case is stated in this way—that the Forms are causes both of being and of becoming; yet when the Forms exist, still the things that share in them do not come into being, unless there is something to originate movement; and many other things come into being (e.g. a house or a ring) of which we say there are no Forms. Clearly, therefore, even the other things can both be and come into being owing to such causes as produce the things just mentioned.

Again, if the Forms are numbers, how can they be causes? Is it because existing things are other numbers, e.g. one number is man, another is Socrates, another Callias? Why then are the one set of numbers causes of the other set? It will not make any difference even if the former are eternal and the latter are not. But if it is because things in this sensible world (e.g. harmony) are ratios of numbers, evidently the things between which they are ratios are some one class of things. If, then, this—the matter—is some definite thing, evidently the numbers themselves too will be ratios of something to something else. E.g. if Callias is a numerical ratio between fire and earth and water and air, his Idea also will be a number of certain other underlying things; and man himself, whether it is a number in a sense or not, will still be a numerical ratio of certain things and not a number proper, nor will it be a of number merely because it is a numerical ratio.

Again, from many numbers one number is produced, but how can one Form come from many Forms? And if the number comes not from the many numbers themselves but from the units in them, e.g. in 10,000, how is it with the units? If they are specifically alike, numerous absurdities will follow, and also if they are not alike (neither the units in one number being themselves like one another nor those in other numbers being all like to all); for in what will they differ, as they are without quality? This is not a plausible view, nor is it consistent with our thought on the matter.

Further, they must set up a second kind of number (with which arithmetic deals), and all the objects which are called 'intermediate' by some thinkers; and how do these exist or from what principles do they proceed? Or why must they be intermediate between the things in this sensible world and the things-themselves?

Further, the units in must each come from a prior but this is impossible.

Further, why is a number, when taken all together, one?

Again, besides what has been said, if the units are diverse the Platonists should have spoken like those who say there are four, or two, elements; for each of these thinkers gives the name of element not to that which is common, e.g. to body, but to fire and earth, whether there is something common to them, viz. body, or not. But in fact the Platonists speak as if the One were homogeneous like fire or water; and if this is so, the numbers will not be substances. Evidently, if there is a One itself and this is a first principle, 'one' is being used in more than one sense; for otherwise the theory is impossible.

When we wish to reduce substances to their principles, we state that lines come from the short and long (i.e. from a kind of small and great), and the plane from the broad and narrow, and body from the deep and shallow. Yet how then can either the plane contain a line, or the solid a line or a plane? For the broad and narrow is a different class from the deep and shallow. Therefore, just as number is not present in these, because the many and few are different from these, evidently no other of the higher classes will be present in the lower. But again the broad is not a genus which includes the deep, for then the solid would have been a species of plane. Further, from what principle will the presence of the points in the line be derived? Plato even used to object to this class of things as being a geometrical fiction. He gave the name of principle of the line—and this he often posited—to the indivisible lines. Yet these must have a limit; therefore the argument from which the existence of the line follows proves also the existence of the point.

In general, though philosophy seeks the cause of perceptible things, we have given this up (for we say nothing of the cause from which change takes its start), but while we fancy we are stating the substance of perceptible things, we assert the existence of a second class of substances, while our account of the way in which they are the substances of perceptible things is empty talk; for 'sharing', as we said before, means nothing.

Nor have the Forms any connexion with what we see to be the cause in the case of the arts, that for whose sake both all mind and the whole of nature are operative,—with this cause which we assert to be one of the first principles; but mathematics has come to be identical with philosophy for modern thinkers, though they say that it should be studied for the sake of other things.

Further, one might suppose that the substance which according to them underlies as matter is too mathematical, and is a predicate and differentia of the substance, i.e. of the matter, rather than matter itself; i.e. the great and the small are like the rare and the dense which the physical philosophers speak of, calling these the primary differentiae of the *substratum*; for these are a kind of excess and defect. And regarding movement, if the great and the small are to *be* movement, evidently the Forms will be moved; but if they are not to be movement, whence did movement come? The whole study of nature has been annihilated.

And what is thought to be easy—to show that all things are one— is not done; for what is proved by the method of setting out instances is not that all things are one but that there is a One itself,—if we grant all the assumptions. And not even this follows, if we do not grant that the universal is a genus; and this in some cases it cannot be.

Nor can it be explained either how the lines and planes and solids that come after the numbers exist or can exist, or what significance they have; for these can neither be Forms (for they are not numbers), nor the intermediates (for those are the objects of mathematics), nor the perishable things. This is evidently a distinct fourth class.

In general, if we search for the elements of existing things without distinguishing the many senses in which things are said to exist, we cannot find them, especially if the search for the elements of which things are made is conducted in this manner. For it is surely impossible to discover what 'acting' or 'being acted on', or 'the straight', is made of, but if elements can be discovered at all, it is only the elements of substances; therefore either to seek the elements of all existing things or to think one has them is incorrect.

And how could we learn the elements of all things? Evidently we cannot start by knowing anything before. For as he who is learning geometry, though he may know other things before, knows none of the things with which the science deals and about which he is to learn, so is it in all other cases. Therefore if there is a science of all things, such as some assert to exist, he who is learning this will know nothing before. Yet all learning is by means of premises which are (either all or some of them) known before,—whether the learning be by demonstration or by definitions; for the elements of the definition must be known before and be familiar; and learning by induction proceeds similarly. But again, if the science were actually innate, it were strange that we are unaware of our possession of the greatest of sciences.

Again, how is one to come to know what all things are made of, and how is this to be made evident? This also affords a difficulty; for there might be a conflict of opinion, as there is about certain syllables; some say *za* is made out of *s* and *d* and *a*, while others say it is a distinct sound and none of those that are familiar.

Further, how could we know the objects of sense without having the sense in question? Yet we ought to, if the elements of which all things consist, as complex sounds consist of the elements proper to sound, are the same.

10

It is evident, then, even from what we have said before, that all men seem to seek the causes named in the *Physics*, and that we cannot name any beyond these; but they seek these vaguely; and though in a sense they have all been described before, in a sense they have not been described at all. For the earliest philosophy is, on all subjects, like one who lisps, since it is young and in its beginnings. For even Empedocles says bone exists by virtue of the ratio in it. Now this is the essence and the substance of the thing. But it is similarly necessary that flesh and each of the other tissues should be the ratio of its elements, or that not one of them should; for it is on account of this that both flesh and bone and everything else will exist, and not on account of the matter, which he names,—fire and earth and water and air. But while he would necessarily have agreed if another had said this, he has not said it clearly.

On these questions our views have been expressed before; but let us return to enumerate the difficulties that might be raised on these same points; for perhaps we may get from them some help towards our later difficulties.

Book II

1

The investigation of the truth is in one way hard, in another easy. An indication of this is found in the fact that no one is able to attain the truth adequately, while, on the other hand, we do not collectively fail, but every one says something true about the nature of things, and while individually we contribute little or nothing to the truth, by the union of all a considerable amount is amassed. Therefore, since the truth seems to be like the proverbial door, which no one can fail to hit, in this respect it must be easy, but the fact that we can have a whole truth and not the particular part we aim at shows the difficulty of it.

Perhaps, too, as difficulties are of two kinds, the cause of the present difficulty is not in the facts but in us. For as the eyes of bats are to the blaze of day, so is the reason in our soul to the things which are by nature most evident of all.

It is just that we should be grateful, not only to those with whose views we may agree, but also to those who have expressed more superficial views; for these also contributed something, by developing before us the powers of thought. It is true that if there had been no Timotheus we should have been without much of our lyric poetry; but if there had been no Phrynis there would have been no Timotheus. The same holds good of those who have expressed views about the truth; for from some thinkers we have inherited certain opinions, while the others have been responsible for the appearance of the former.

It is right also that philosophy should be called knowledge of the truth. For the end of theoretical knowledge is truth, while that of practical knowledge is action (for even if they consider how things are, practical men do not study the eternal, but what is relative and in the present). Now we do not know a truth without its cause; and a thing has a quality in a higher degree than other things if in virtue of it the similar quality belongs to the other things as well (e.g. fire is the hottest of things; for it is the cause of the heat of all other things); so that that causes derivative truths to be true is most true. Hence the principles of eternal things must be always most true (for they are not merely sometimes true, nor is there any cause of their being, but they themselves are the cause of the being of other things), so that as each thing is in respect of being, so is it in respect of truth.

2

But evidently there is a first principle, and the causes of things are neither an infinite series nor infinitely various in kind. For neither can one thing proceed from another, as from matter, *ad infinitum* (e.g. flesh from earth, earth from air, air from fire, and so on without stopping), nor can the sources of movement form an endless series (man for instance being acted on by air, air by the sun, the sun by Strife, and so on without limit). Similarly the final causes cannot go on *ad infinitum*,—walking being for the sake of health, this for the sake of happiness, happiness for the sake of something else, and so one thing always for the sake of another. And the case of the essence is similar. For in the case of intermediates, which have a last term and a term prior to them, the prior must be the cause of the later terms. For if we had to say which of the three is the cause, we should say the first; surely not the last, for the final term is the cause of none; nor even the intermediate, for it is the cause only of one. (It makes no difference whether there is one intermediate or more, nor whether they are infinite or finite in number.) But of series which are infinite in this way, and of the infinite in general, all the parts down to that now present are alike intermediates; so that if there is no first there is no cause at all.

Nor can there be an infinite process downwards, with a beginning in the upward direction, so that water should proceed from fire, earth from water, and so always some other kind should be produced. For one thing comes from another in two ways—not in the sense in which 'from' means 'after' (as we say 'from the Isthmian games come the Olympian'), but either (i) as the man comes from the boy, by the boy's changing, or (ii) as air comes from water. By 'as the man comes from the boy' we mean 'as that which has come to be from that which is coming to be' or 'as that which is finished from that which is being achieved' (for as becoming is between being and not being, so that which is becoming is always between that which is and that which is not; for the learner is a man of science in the making, and this is what is meant when we say that from a learner a man of science is being made); on the other hand, coming from another thing as water comes from air implies the destruction of the other thing. This is why changes of the former kind are not reversible, and the boy does not come from the man (for it is not that which comes to be something that comes to be as a result of coming to be, but that which exists after the coming to be; for it is thus that the day, too, comes from the morning—in the sense that it comes after the morning; which is the reason why the morning cannot come from the day); but changes of the other kind are reversible. But in both cases it is impossible that the number of terms should be infinite. For terms of the former kind, being intermediates, must have an end, and terms of the latter kind change back into one another, for the destruction of either is the generation of the other.

At the same time it is impossible that the first cause, being eternal, should be destroyed; for since the process of becoming is not infinite in the upward direction, that which is the first thing by whose destruction something came to be must be non-eternal.

Further, the final cause is an end, and that sort of end which is not for the sake of something else, but for whose sake everything else is; so that if there is to be a last term of this sort, the process will not be infinite; but if there is no such term, there will be no final cause, but those who maintain the infinite series eliminate the Good without knowing it (yet no one would try to do anything if he were not going to come to a limit); nor would there be reason in the world; the reasonable man, at least, always acts for a purpose, and this is a limit; for the end is a limit.

But the essence, also, cannot be reduced to another definition which is fuller in expression. For the original definition is always more of a definition, and not the later one; and in a series in which the first term has not the required character, the next has not it either.—Further, those who speak thus destroy science; for it is not possible to have this till one comes to the unanalysable terms. And knowledge becomes impossible; for how can one apprehend things that are infinite in this way? For this is not like the case of the line, to whose divisibility there is no stop, but which we cannot think if we do not make a stop (for which reason one who is tracing the infinitely divisible line cannot be counting the possibilities of section), but the whole line also must be apprehended by something in us that does not move from part to part.—Again, nothing infinite can exist; and if it could, at least the notion of infinity is not infinite.

But if the kinds of causes had been infinite in number, then also knowledge would have been impossible; for we think we know, only when we have ascertained the causes, that but that which is infinite by addition cannot be gone through in a finite time.

3

The effect which lectures produce on a hearer depends on his habits; for we demand the language we are accustomed to, and that which is different from this seems not in keeping but somewhat unintelligible and foreign because of its unwontedness. For it is the customary that is intelligible. The force of habit is shown by the laws, in which the legendary and childish elements prevail over our knowledge about them, owing to habit. Thus some people do not listen to a speaker unless he speaks mathematically, others unless he gives instances, while others expect him to cite a poet as witness. And some want to have everything done accurately, while others are annoyed by accuracy, either because they cannot follow the connexion of thought or because they regard it as pettifoggery. For accuracy has something of this character, so that as in trade so in argument some people think it mean. Hence one must be already trained to know how to take each sort of argument, since it is absurd to seek at the same time knowledge and the way of attaining knowledge; and it is not easy to get even one of the two.

The minute accuracy of mathematics is not to be demanded in all cases, but only in the case of things which have no matter. Hence method is not that of natural science; for presumably the whole of nature has matter. Hence we must inquire first what nature is: for thus we shall also see what natural science treats of (and whether it belongs to one science or to more to investigate the causes and the principles of things).

Book III

1

We must, with a view to the science which we are seeking, first recount the subjects that should be first discussed. These include both the other opinions that some have held on the first principles, and any point besides these that happens to have been overlooked. For those who wish to get clear of difficulties it is advantageous to discuss the difficulties well; for the subsequent free play of thought implies the solution of the previous difficulties, and it is not possible to untie a knot of which one does not know. But the difficulty of our thinking points to a 'knot' in the object; for in so far as our thought is in difficulties, it is in like case with those who are bound; for in either case it is impossible to go forward. Hence one should have surveyed all the difficulties beforehand, both for the purposes we have stated and because people who inquire without first stating the difficulties are like those who do not know where they have to go; besides, a man does not otherwise know even whether he has at any given time found what he is looking for or not; for the end is not clear to such a man, while to him who has first discussed the difficulties it is clear. Further, he who has heard all the contending arguments, as if they were the parties to a case, must be in a better position for judging.

The first problem concerns the subject which we discussed in our prefatory remarks. It is this—(1) whether the investigation of the causes belongs to one or to more sciences, and (2) whether such a science should survey only the first principles of substance, or also the principles on which all men base their proofs, e.g. whether it is possible at the same time to assert and deny one and the same thing or not, and all other such questions; and (3) if the science in question deals with substance, whether one science deals with all substances, or more than one, and if more, whether all are akin, or some of them must be called forms of Wisdom and the others something else. And (4) this itself is also one of the things that must be discussed—whether sensible substances alone should be said to exist or others also besides them, and whether these others are of one kind or there are several classes of substances, as is supposed by those who believe both in Forms and in mathematical objects intermediate between these and sensible things. Into these questions, then, as we say, we must inquire, and also (5) whether our investigation is concerned only with substances or also with the essential attributes of substances. Further, with regard to the same and other and like and unlike and contrariety, and with regard to prior and posterior and all other such terms about which the dialecticians try to inquire, starting their investigation from probable

premises only,—whose business is it to inquire into all these? Further,
we must discuss the essential attributes of these themselves; and we
must ask not only what each of these is, but also whether one thing
always has one contrary. Again (6), are the principles and elements of
things the genera, or the parts present in each thing, into which it is
divided; and (7) if they are the genera, are they the genera that are
predicated proximately of the individuals, or the highest genera, e.g. is
animal or man the first principle and the more independent of the
individual instance? And (8) we must inquire and discuss especially
whether there is, besides the matter, any thing that is a cause in itself or
not, and whether this can exist apart or not, and whether it is one or
more in number, and whether there is something apart from the
concrete thing (by the concrete thing I mean the matter with something
already predicated of it), or there is nothing apart, or there is something
in some cases though not in others, and what sort of cases these are.
Again (9) we ask whether the principles are limited in number or in
kind, both those in the definitions and those in the *substratum*; and (10)
whether the principles of perishable and of imperishable things are the
same or different; and whether they are all imperishable or those of
perishable things are perishable. Further (11) there is the question
which is hardest of all and most perplexing, whether unity and being, as
the Pythagoreans and Plato said, are not attributes of something else but
the substance of existing things, or this is not the case, but the
substratum is something else,—as Empedocles says, love; as some one
else says, fire; while another says water or air. Again (12) we ask
whether the principles are universal or like individual things, and (13)
whether they exist potentially or actually, and further, whether they are
potential or actual in any other sense than in reference to movement;
for these questions also would present much difficulty. Further (14), are
numbers and lines and figures and points a kind of substance or not,
and if they are substances are they separate from sensible things or
present in them? With regard to all these matters not only is it hard to
get possession of the truth, but it is not easy even to think out the
difficulties well.

2

(1) First then with regard to what we mentioned first, does it
belong to one or to more sciences to investigate all the kinds of causes?
How could it belong to one science to recognize the principles if these
are not contrary?

Further, there are many things to which not all the principles
pertain. For how can a principle of change or the nature of the good
exist for unchangeable things, since everything that in itself and by its
own nature is good is an end, and a cause in the sense that for its sake

the other things both come to be and are, and since an end or purpose is
the end of some action, and all actions imply change? So in the case of
unchangeable things this principle could not exist, nor could there be a
good itself. This is why in mathematics nothing is proved by means of
this kind of cause, nor is there any demonstration of this kind—
'because it is better, or worse'; indeed no one even mentions anything
of the kind. And so for this reason some of the Sophists, e.g.
Aristippus, used to ridicule mathematics; for in the arts (he
maintained), even in the industrial arts, e.g. in carpentry and cobbling,
the reason always given is 'because it is better, or worse,' but the
mathematical sciences take no account of goods and evils.

But if there are several sciences of the causes, and a different
science for each different principle, which of these sciences should be
said to be that which we seek, or which of the people who possess them
has the most scientific knowledge of the object in question? The same
thing may have all the kinds of causes, e.g. the moving cause of a house
is the art or the builder, the final cause is the function it fulfils, the
matter is earth and stones, and the form is the definition. To judge from
our previous discussion of the question which of the sciences should be
called Wisdom, there is reason for applying the name to each of them.
For inasmuch as it is most architectonic and authoritative and the other
sciences, like slave-women, may not even contradict it, the science of
the end and of the good is of the nature of Wisdom (for the other things
are for the sake of the end). But inasmuch as it was described' as
dealing with the first causes and that which is in the highest sense
object of knowledge, the science of substance must be of the nature of
Wisdom. For since men may know the same thing in many ways, we
say that he who recognizes what a thing is by its being so and so knows
more fully than he who recognizes it by its not being so and so, and in
the former class itself one knows more fully than another, and he
knows most fully who knows what a thing is, not he who knows its
quantity or quality or what it can by nature do or have done to it. And
further in all cases also we think that the knowledge of each even of the
things of which demonstration is possible is present only when we
know what the thing is, e.g. what squaring a rectangle is, viz. that it is
the finding of a mean; and similarly in all other cases. And we know
about becomings and actions and about every change when we know
the source of the movement; and this is other than and opposed to the
end. Therefore it would seem to belong to different sciences to
investigate these causes severally.

But (2), taking the starting-points of demonstration as well as the
causes, it is a disputable question whether they are the object of one
science or of more (by the starting-points of demonstration I mean the
common beliefs, on which all men base their proofs); e.g. that
everything must be either affirmed or denied, and that a thing cannot at

the same time be and not be, and all other such premises:—the question is whether the same science deals with them as with substance, or a different science, and if it is not one science, which of the two must be identified with that which we now seek.—It is not reasonable that these topics should be the object of one science; for why should it be peculiarly appropriate to geometry or to any other science to understand these matters? If then it belongs to every science alike, and cannot belong to all, it is not peculiar to the science which investigates substances, any more than to any other science, to know about these topics.—And, at the same time, in what way can there be a science of the first principles? For we are aware even now what each of them in fact is (at least even other sciences use them as familiar); but if there is a demonstrative science which deals with them, there will have to be an underlying kind, and some of them must be demonstrable attributes and others must be axioms (for it is impossible that there should be demonstration about all of them); for the demonstration must start from certain premises and be about a certain subject and prove certain attributes. Therefore it follows that all attributes that are proved must belong to a single class; for all demonstrative sciences use the axioms.

But if the science of substance and the science which deals with the axioms are different, which of them is by nature more authoritative and prior? The axioms are most universal and are principles of all things. And if it is not the business of the philosopher, to whom else will it belong to inquire what is true and what is untrue about them?

(3) In general, do all substances fall under one science or under more than one? If the latter, to what sort of substance is the present science to be assigned?—On the other hand, it is not reasonable that one science should deal with all. For then there would be one demonstrative science dealing with all attributes. For ever demonstrative science investigates with regard to some subject its essential attributes, starting from the common beliefs. Therefore to investigate the essential attributes of one class of things, starting from one set of beliefs, is the business of one science. For the subject belongs to one science, and the premises belong to one, whether to the same or to another; so that the attributes do so too, whether they are investigated by these sciences or by one compounded out of them.

(5) Further, does our investigation deal with substances alone or also with their attributes? I mean for instance, if the solid is a substance and so are lines and planes, is it the business of the same science to know these and to know the attributes of each of these classes (the attributes about which the mathematical sciences offer proofs), or of a different science? If of the same, the science of substance also must be a demonstrative science, but it is thought that there is no demonstration of the essence of things. And if of another, what will be the science that

investigates the attributes of substance? This is a very difficult question.

(4) Further, must we say that sensible substances alone exist, or that there are others besides these? And are substances of one kind or are there in fact several kinds of substances, as those say who assert the existence both of the Forms and of the intermediates, with which they say the mathematical sciences deal?—The sense in which we say the Forms are both causes and self-dependent substances has been explained in our first remarks about them; while the theory presents difficulties in many ways, the most paradoxical thing of all is the statement that there are certain things besides those in the material universe, and that these are the same as sensible things except that they are eternal while the latter are perishable. For they say there is a man-himself and a horse-itself and health-itself, with no further qualification,—a procedure like that of the people who said there are gods, but in human form. For they were positing nothing but eternal men, nor are the Platonists making the Forms anything other than eternal sensible things.

Further, if we are to posit besides the Forms and the sensibles the intermediates between them, we shall have many difficulties. For clearly on the same principle there will be lines besides the lines-themselves and the sensible lines, and so with each of the other classes of things; so that since astronomy is one of these mathematical sciences there will also be a heaven besides the sensible heaven, and a sun and a moon (and so with the other heavenly bodies) besides the sensible. Yet how are we to believe in these things? It is not reasonable even to suppose such a body immovable, but to suppose it moving is quite impossible.—And similarly with the things of which optics and mathematical harmonics treat; for these also cannot exist apart from the sensible things, for the same reasons. For if there are sensible things and sensations intermediate between Form and individual, evidently there will also be animals intermediate between animals-themselves and the perishable animals.—We might also raise the question, with reference to which kind of existing things we must look for these sciences of intermediates. If geometry is to differ from mensuration only in this, that the latter deals with things that we perceive, and the former with things that are not perceptible, evidently there will also be a science other than medicine, intermediate between medical-science-itself and this individual medical science, and so with each of the other sciences. Yet how is this possible? There would have to be also healthy things besides the perceptible healthy things and the healthy-itself.— And at the same time not even this is true, that mensuration deals with perceptible and perishable magnitudes; for then it would have perished when they perished.

But on the other hand astronomy cannot be dealing with

perceptible magnitudes nor with this heaven above us. For neither are perceptible lines such lines as the geometer speaks of (for no perceptible thing is straight or round in the way in which he defines 'straight' and 'round'; for a hoop touches a straight edge not at a point, but as Protagoras used to say it did, in his refutation of the geometers), nor are the movements and spiral orbits in the heavens like those of which astronomy treats, nor have geometrical points the same nature as the actual stars.—Now there are some who say that these so-called intermediates between the Forms and the perceptible things exist, not apart from the perceptible things, however, but in these; the impossible results of this view would take too long to enumerate, but it is enough to consider even such points as the following:—It is not reasonable that this should be so only in the case of these intermediates, but clearly the Forms also might be in the perceptible things; for both statements are parts of the same theory. Further, it follows from this theory that there are two solids in the same place, and that the intermediates are not immovable, since they are in the moving perceptible things. And in general to what purpose would one suppose them to exist indeed, but to exist in perceptible things? For the same paradoxical results will follow which we have already mentioned; there will be a heaven besides the heaven, only it will be not apart but in the same place; which is still more impossible.

3

(6) Apart from the great difficulty of stating the case truly with regard to these matters, it is very hard to say, with regard to the first principles, whether it is the genera that should be taken as elements and principles, or rather the primary constituents of a thing; e.g. it is the primary parts of which articulate sounds consist that are thought to be elements and principles of articulate sound, not the common genus— articulate sound; and we give the name of 'elements' to those geometrical propositions, the proofs of which are implied in the proofs of the others, either of all or of most. Further, both those who say there are several elements of corporeal things and those who say there is one, say the parts of which bodies are compounded and consist are principles; e.g. Empedocles says fire and water and the rest are the constituent elements of things, but does not describe these as genera of existing things. Besides this, if we want to examine the nature of anything else, we examine the parts of which, e.g. a bed consists and how they are put together, and then we know its nature.

To judge from these arguments, then, the principles of things would not be the genera; but if we know each thing by its definition, and the genera are the principles or starting-points of definitions, the genera must also be the principles of definable things. And if to get the knowledge of the species according to which things are named is to get the knowledge of things, the genera are at least starting-points of the species. And some also of those who say unity or being, or the great and the small, are elements of things, seem to treat them as genera.

But, again, it is not possible to describe the principles in both ways. For the formula of the essence is one; but definition by genera will be different from that which states the constituent parts of a thing.

(7) Besides this, even if the genera are in the highest degree principles, should one regard the first of the genera as principles, or those which are predicated directly of the individuals? This also admits of dispute. For if the universals are always more of the nature of principles, evidently the uppermost of the genera are the principles; for these are predicated of all things. There will, then, be as many principles of things as there are primary genera, so that both being and unity will be principles and substances; for these are most of all predicated of all existing things. But it is not possible that either unity or being should be a single genus of things; for the differentiae of any genus must each of them both have being and be one, but it is not possible for the genus taken apart from its species (any more than for the species of the genus) to be predicated of its proper differentiae; so that if unity or being is a genus, no differentia will either have being or be one. But if unity and being are not genera, neither will they be principles, if the genera are the principles.—Again, the intermediate kinds, in whose nature the differentiae are included, will on this theory be genera, down to the indivisible species; but as it is, some are thought to be genera and others are not thought to be so. Besides this, the differentiae are principles even more than the genera; and if these also are principles, there comes to be practically an infinite number of principles, especially if we suppose the highest genus to be a principle.—But again, if unity is more of the nature of a principle, and the indivisible is one, and everything indivisible is so either in quantity or in species, and that which is so in species is the prior, and genera are divisible into species for man is not the genus of individual men), that which is predicated directly of the individuals will have more unity.— Further, in the case of things in which the distinction of prior and posterior is present, that which is predicable of these things cannot be something apart from them (e.g. if two is the first of numbers, there will not be a Number apart from the kinds of numbers; and similarly there will not be a Figure apart from the kinds of figures; and if the genera of these things do not exist apart from the species, the genera of other things will scarcely do so; for genera of these things are thought to exist if any do). But among the individuals one is not prior and another posterior. Further, where one thing is better and another worse, the better is always prior; so that of these also no genus can exist. From these considerations, then, the species predicated of individuals seem to

be principles rather than the genera. But again, it is not easy to say in what sense these are to be taken as principles. For the principle or cause must exist alongside of the things of which it is the principle, and must be capable of existing in separation from them; but for what reason should we suppose any such thing to exist alongside of the individual, except that it is predicated universally and of all? But if this is the reason, the things that are more universal must be supposed to be more of the nature of principles; so that the highest genera would be the principles.

4

(8) There is a difficulty connected with these, the hardest of all and the most necessary to examine, and of this the discussion now awaits us. If, on the one hand, there is nothing apart from individual things, and the individuals are infinite in number, how then is it possible to get knowledge of the infinite individuals? For all things that we come to know, we come to know in so far as they have some unity and identity, and in so far as some attribute belongs to them universally.

But if this is necessary, and there must be something apart from the individuals, it will be necessary that the genera exist apart from the individuals,—either the lowest or the highest genera; but we found by discussion just now that this is impossible.

Further, if we admit in the fullest sense that something exists apart from the concrete thing, whenever something is predicated of the matter, must there, if there is something apart, be something apart from each set of individuals, or from some and not from others, or from none? (A) If there is nothing apart from individuals, there will be no object of thought, but all things will be objects of sense, and there will not be knowledge of anything, unless we say that sensation is knowledge. Further, nothing will be eternal or unmovable; for all perceptible things perish and are in movement. But if there is nothing eternal, neither can there be a process of coming to be; for there must be something that comes to be, i.e. from which something comes to be, and the ultimate term in this series cannot have come to be, since the series has a limit and since nothing can come to be out of that which is not. Further, if generation and movement exist there must also be a limit; for no movement is infinite, but every movement has an end, and that which is incapable of completing its coming to be cannot be in process of coming to be; and that which has completed its coming to be must he as soon as it has come to be. Further, since the matter exists, because it is ungenerated, it is *a fortiori* reasonable that the substance or essence, that which the matter is at any time coming to be, should exist; for if neither essence nor matter is to be, nothing will be at all, and since this is impossible there must be something besides the concrete thing, viz. the shape or form.

But again (B) if we are to suppose this, it is hard to say in which cases we are to suppose it and in which not. For evidently it is not possible to suppose it in all cases; we could not suppose that there is a house besides the particular houses.—Besides this, will the substance of all the individuals, e.g. of all men, be one? This is paradoxical, for all the things whose substance is one are one. But are the substances many and different? This also is unreasonable.—At the same time, how does the matter become each of the individuals, and how is the concrete thing these two elements?

(9) Again, one might ask the following question also about the first principles. If they are one in kind only, nothing will be numerically one, not even unity-itself and being-itself; and how will knowing exist, if there is not to be something common to a whole set of individuals?

But if there is a common element which is numerically one, and each of the principles is one, and the principles are not as in the case of perceptible things different for different things (e.g. since this particular syllable is the same in kind whenever it occurs, the elements it are also the same in kind; only in kind, for these also, like the syllable, are numerically different in different contexts),—if it is not like this but the principles of things are numerically one, there will be nothing else besides the elements (for there is no difference of meaning between 'numerically one' and 'individual'; for this is just what we mean by the individual—the numerically one, and by the universal we mean that which is predicable of the individuals). Therefore it will be just as if the elements of articulate sound were limited in number; all the language in the world would be confined to the ABC, since there could not be two or more letters of the same kind.

(10) One difficulty which is as great as any has been neglected both by modern philosophers and by their predecessors—whether the principles of perishable and those of imperishable things are the same or different. If they are the same, how are some things perishable and others imperishable, and for what reason? The school of Hesiod and all the theologians thought only of what was plausible to themselves, and had no regard to us. For, asserting the first principles to be gods and born of gods, they say that the beings which did not taste of nectar and ambrosia became mortal; and clearly they are using words which are familiar to themselves, yet what they have said about the very application of these causes is above our comprehension. For if the gods taste of nectar and ambrosia for their pleasure, these are in no wise the causes of their existence; and if they taste them to maintain their existence, how can gods who need food be eternal?—But into the subtleties of the mythologists it is not worth our while to inquire seriously; those, however, who use the language of proof we must cross-examine and ask why, after all, things which consist of the same

elements are, some of them, eternal in nature, while others perish. Since these philosophers mention no cause, and it is unreasonable that things should be as they say, evidently the principles or causes of things cannot be the same. Even the man whom one might suppose to speak most consistently—Empedocles,—even he has made the same mistake; for he maintains that strife is a principle that causes destruction, but even strife would seem no less to produce everything, except the One; for all things excepting God proceed from strife. At least he says:—

> From which all that was and is and will be hereafter—
> Trees, and men and women, took their growth,
> And beasts and birds and water-nourished fish,
> And long-aged gods.

   The implication is evident even apart from these words; for if strife had not been present in things, all things would have been one, according to him; for when they have come together, 'then strife stood outermost.' Hence it also follows on his theory that God most blessed is less wise than all others; for he does not know all the elements; for he has in him no strife, and knowledge is of the like by the like. 'For by earth,' he says,

> we see earth, by water water,
> By ether godlike ether, by fire wasting fire,
> Love by love, and strife by gloomy strife.

But—and this is the point we started from—this at least is evident, that on his theory it follows that strife is as much the cause of existence as of destruction. And similarly love is not specially the cause of existence; for in collecting things into the One it destroys all other things. And at the same time Empedocles mentions no cause of the change itself, except that things are so by nature.

> But when strife at last waxed great in the limbs of the Sphere,
> And sprang to assert its rights as the time was fulfilled
> Which is fixed for them in turn by a mighty oath.

This implies that change was necessary; but he shows no cause of the necessity. But yet so far at least he alone speaks consistently; for he does not make some things perishable and others imperishable, but makes all perishable except the elements. The difficulty we are speaking of now is, why some things are perishable and others are not, if they consist of the same principles.

   Let this suffice as proof of the fact that the principles cannot be the same. But if there are different principles, one difficulty is whether these also will be imperishable or perishable. For if they are perishable, evidently these also must consist of certain elements (for all things that perish, perish by being resolved into the elements of which they consist); so that it follows that prior to the principles there are other principles. But this is impossible, whether the process has a limit or proceeds to infinity. Further, how will perishable things exist, if their principles are to be annulled? But if the principles are imperishable, why will things composed of some imperishable principles be perishable, while those composed of the others are imperishable? This is not probable, but is either impossible or needs much proof. Further, no one has even tried to maintain different principles; they maintain the same principles for all things. But they swallow the difficulty we stated first as if they took it to be something trifling.

(11) The inquiry that is both the hardest of all and the most necessary for knowledge of the truth is whether being and unity are the substances of things, and whether each of them, without being anything else, is being or unity respectively, or we must inquire what being and unity are, with the implication that they have some other underlying nature. For some people think they are of the former, others think they are of the latter character. Plato and the Pythagoreans thought being and unity were nothing else, but this was their nature, their essence being just unity and being. But the natural philosophers take a different line; e.g. Empedocles—as though reducing to something more intelligible—says what unity is; for he would seem to say it is love: at least, this is for all things the cause of their being one. Others say this unity and being, of which things consist and have been made, is fire, and others say it is air. A similar view is expressed by those who make the elements more than one; for these also must say that unity and being are precisely all the things which they say are principles.

(A) If we do not suppose unity and being to be substances, it follows that none of the other universals is a substance; for these are most universal of all, and if there is no unity itself or being-itself, there will scarcely be in any other case anything apart from what are called the individuals. Further, if unity is not a substance, evidently number also will not exist as an entity separate from the individual things; for number is units, and the unit is precisely a certain kind of one.

But (B) if there is a unity-itself and a being itself, unity and being must be their substance; for it is not something else that is predicated universally of the things that are and are one, but just unity and being. But if there is to be a being-itself and a unity-itself, there is much difficulty in seeing how there will be anything else besides these,—I mean, how things will be more than one in number. For what is different from being does not exist, so that it necessarily follows, according to the argument of Parmenides, that all things that are are one and this is being.

There are objections to both views. For whether unity is not a substance or there is a unity-itself, number cannot be a substance. We have already said why this result follows if unity is not a substance; and if it is, the same difficulty arises as arose with regard to being. For whence is there to be another one besides unity-itself? It must be not-one; but all things are either one or many, and of the many each is one.

Further, if unity-itself is indivisible, according to Zeno's postulate it will be nothing. For that which neither when added makes a thing greater nor when subtracted makes it less, he asserts to have no being, evidently assuming that whatever has being is a spatial magnitude. And if it is a magnitude, it is corporeal; for the corporeal has being in every dimension, while the other objects of mathematics, e.g. a plane or a line, added in one way will increase what they are added to, but in another way will not do so, and a point or a unit does so in no way. But, since his theory is of a low order, and an indivisible thing can exist in such a way as to have a defence even against him (for the indivisible when added will make the number, though not the size, greater),—yet how can a magnitude proceed from one such indivisible or from many? It is like saying that the line is made out of points.

But even if one supposes the case to be such that, as some say, number proceeds from unity-itself and something else which is not one, none the less we must inquire why and how the product will be sometimes a number and sometimes a magnitude, if the not-one was inequality and was the same principle in either case. For it is not evident how magnitudes could proceed either from the one and this principle, or from some number and this principle.

5

(14) A question connected with these is whether numbers and bodies and planes and points are substances of a kind, or not. If they are not, it baffles us to say what being is and what the substances of things are. For modifications and movements and relations and dispositions and ratios do not seem to indicate the substance of anything; for all are predicated of a subject, and none is a 'this'. And as to the things which might seem most of all to indicate substance, water and earth and fire and air, of which composite bodies consist, heat and cold and the like are modifications of these, not substances, and the body which is thus modified alone persists as something real and as a substance. But, on the other hand, the body is surely less of a substance than the surface, and the surface than the line, and the line than the unit and the point. For the body is bounded by these; and they are thought to be capable of existing without body, but body incapable of existing without these. This is why, while most of the philosophers and the earlier among them thought that substance and being were identical with body, and that all

other things were modifications of this, so that the first principles of the bodies were the first principles of being, the more recent and those who were held to be wiser thought numbers were the first principles. As we said, then, if these are not substance, there is no substance and no being at all; for the accidents of these it cannot be right to call beings.

But if this is admitted, that lines and points are substance more than bodies, but we do not see to what sort of bodies these could belong (for they cannot be in perceptible bodies), there can be no substance.— Further, these are all evidently divisions of body,—one in breadth, another in depth, another in length.—Besides this, no sort of shape is present in the solid more than any other; so that if the Hermes is not in the stone, neither is the half of the cube in the cube as something determinate; therefore the surface is not in it either; for if any sort of surface were in it, the surface which marks off the half of the cube would be in it too. And the same account applies to the line and to the point and the unit. Therefore, if on the one hand body is in the highest degree substance, and on the other hand these things are so more than body, but these are not even instances of substance, it baffles us to say what being is and what the substance of things is.—For besides what has been said, the questions of generation and instruction confront us with further paradoxes. For if substance, not having existed before, now exists, or having existed before, afterwards does not exist, this change is thought to be accompanied by a process of becoming or perishing; but points and lines and surfaces cannot be in process either of becoming or of perishing, when they at one time exist and at another do not. For when bodies come into contact or are divided, their boundaries simultaneously become one in the one case—when they touch, and two in the other—when they are divided; so that when they have been put together one boundary does not exist but has perished, and when they have been divided the boundaries exist which before did not exist (for it cannot be said that the point, which is indivisible, was divided into two). And if the boundaries come into being and cease to be, from what do they come into being? A similar account may also be given of the 'now' in time; for this also cannot be in process of coming into being or of ceasing to be, but yet seems to be always different, which shows that it is not a substance. And evidently the same is true of points and lines and planes; for the same argument applies, since they are all alike either limits or divisions.

6

In general one might raise the question why after all, besides perceptible things and the intermediates, we have to look for another class of things, i.e. the Forms which we posit. If it is for this reason, because the objects of mathematics, while they differ from the things in this world in some other respect, differ not at all in that there are many of the same kind, so that their first principles cannot be limited in number (just as the elements of all the language in this sensible world are not limited in number, but in kind, unless one takes the elements of this individual syllable or of this individual articulate sound—whose elements will be limited even in number; so is it also in the case of the intermediates; for there also the members of the same kind are infinite in number), so that if there are not—besides perceptible and mathematical objects—others such as some maintain the Forms to be, there will be no substance which is one in number, but only in kind, nor will the first principles of things be determinate in number, but only in kind:—if then this must be so, the Forms also must therefore be held to exist. Even if those who support this view do not express it articulately, still this is what they mean, and they must be maintaining the Forms just because each of the Forms is a substance and none is by accident.

But if we are to suppose both that the Forms exist and that the principles are one in number, not in kind, we have mentioned the impossible results that necessarily follow.

(13) Closely connected with this is the question whether the elements exist potentially or in some other manner. If in some other way, there will be something else prior to the first principles; for the potency is prior to the actual cause, and it is not necessary for everything potential to be actual.—But if the elements exist potentially, it is possible that everything that is should not be. For even that which is not yet is capable of being; for that which is not comes to be, but nothing that is incapable of being comes to be.

(12) We must not only raise these questions about the first principles, but also ask whether they are universal or what we call individuals. If they are universal, they will not be substances; for everything that is common indicates not a 'this' but a 'such', but substance is a 'this'. And if we are to be allowed to lay it down that a common predicate is a 'this' and a single thing, Socrates will be several animals—himself and 'man' and 'animal', if each of these indicates a 'this' and a single thing.

If, then, the principles are universals, these universal. Therefore if there is to be results follow; if they are not universals but of knowledge of the principles there must be the nature of individuals, they will not be other principles prior to them, namely those knowable; for the knowledge of anything is that are universally predicated of them.

Book IV

1

There is a science which investigates being as being and the attributes which belong to this in virtue of its own nature. Now this is not the same as any of the so-called special sciences; for none of these others treats universally of being as being. They cut off a part of being and investigate the attribute of this part; this is what the mathematical sciences for instance do. Now since we are seeking the first principles and the highest causes, clearly there must be some thing to which these belong in virtue of its own nature. If then those who sought the elements of existing things were seeking these same principles, it is necessary that the elements must be elements of being not by accident but just because it is being. Therefore it is of being as being that we also must grasp the first causes.

2

There are many senses in which a thing may be said to 'be', but all that 'is' is related to one central point, one definite kind of thing, and is not said to 'be' by a mere ambiguity. Everything which is healthy is related to health, one thing in the sense that it preserves health, another in the sense that it produces it, another in the sense that it is a symptom of health, another because it is capable of it. And that which is medical is relative to the medical art, one thing being called medical because it possesses it, another because it is naturally adapted to it, another because it is a function of the medical art. And we shall find other words used similarly to these. So, too, there are many senses in which a thing is said to be, but all refer to one starting-point; some things are said to be because they are substances, others because they are affections of substance, others because they are a process towards substance, or destructions or privations or qualities of substance, or productive or generative of substance, or of things which are relative to substance, or negations of one of these thing of substance itself. It is for this reason that we say even of non-being that it is non-being. As, then, there is one science which deals with all healthy things, the same applies in the other cases also. For not only in the case of things which have one common notion does the investigation belong to one science, but also in the case of things which are related to one common nature; for even these in a sense have one common notion. It is clear then that it is the work of one science also to study the things that are, *qua* being.—But everywhere science deals chiefly with that which is primary, and on which the other things depend, and in virtue of which

they get their names. If, then, this is substance, it will be of substances
that the philosopher must grasp the principles and the causes.

Now for each one class of things, as there is one perception, so
there is one science, as for instance grammar, being one science,
investigates all articulate sounds. Hence to investigate all the species of
being *qua* being is the work of a science which is generically one, and
to investigate the several species is the work of the specific parts of the
science.

If, now, being and unity are the same and are one thing in the sense
that they are implied in one another as principle and cause are, not in
the sense that they are explained by the same definition (though it
makes no difference even if we suppose them to be like that—in fact
this would even strengthen our case); for 'one man' and 'man' are the
same thing, and so are 'existent man' and 'man', and the doubling of
the words in 'one man and one existent man' does not express anything
different (it is clear that the two things are not separated either in
coming to be or in ceasing to be); and similarly 'one existent man' adds
nothing to 'existent man', and that it is obvious that the addition in
these cases means the same thing, and unity is nothing apart from
being; and if, further, the substance of each thing is one in no merely
accidental way, and similarly is from its very nature something that
is:—all this being so, there must be exactly as many species of being as
of unity. And to investigate the essence of these is the work of a science
which is generically one—I mean, for instance, the discussion of the
same and the similar and the other concepts of this sort; and nearly all
contraries may be referred to this origin; let us take them as having
been investigated in the 'Selection of Contraries'.

And there are as many parts of philosophy as there are kinds of
substance, so that there must necessarily be among them a first
philosophy and one which follows this. For being falls immediately
into genera; for which reason the sciences too will correspond to these
genera. For the philosopher is like the mathematician, as that word is
used; for mathematics also has parts, and there is a first and a second
science and other successive ones within the sphere of mathematics.

Now since it is the work of one science to investigate opposites,
and plurality is opposed to unity—and it belongs to one science to
investigate the negation and the privation because in both cases we are
really investigating the one thing of which the negation or the privation
is a negation or privation (for we either say simply that that thing is not
present, or that it is not present in some particular class; in the latter
case difference is present over and above what is implied in negation;
for negation means just the absence of the thing in question, while in
privation there is also employed an underlying nature of which the
privation is asserted):—in view of all these facts, the contraries of the
concepts we named above, the other and the dissimilar and the unequal,

and everything else which is derived either from these or from plurality and unity, must fall within the province of the science above named. And contrariety is one of these concepts; for contrariety is a kind of difference, and difference is a kind of otherness. Therefore, since there are many senses in which a thing is said to be one, these terms also will have many senses, but yet it belongs to one science to know them all; for a term belongs to different sciences not if it has different senses, but if it has not one meaning and its definitions cannot be referred to one central meaning. And since all things are referred to that which is primary, as for instance all things which are called one are referred to the primary one, we must say that this holds good also of the same and the other and of contraries in general; so that after distinguishing the various senses of each, we must then explain by reference to what is primary in the case of each of the predicates in question, saying how they are related to it; for some will be called what they are called because they possess it, others because they produce it, and others in other such ways.

It is evident, then, that it belongs to one science to be able to give an account of these concepts as well as of substance (this was one of the questions in our book of problems), and that it is the function of the philosopher to be able to investigate all things. For if it is not the function of the philosopher, who is it who will inquire whether Socrates and Socrates seated are the same thing, or whether one thing has one contrary, or what contrariety is, or how many meanings it has? And similarly with all other such questions. Since, then, these are essential modifications of unity *qua* unity and of being *qua* being, not *qua* numbers or lines or fire, it is clear that it belongs to this science to investigate both the essence of these concepts and their properties. And those who study these properties err not by leaving the sphere of philosophy, but by forgetting that substance, of which they have no correct idea, is prior to these other things. For number *qua* number has peculiar attributes, such as oddness and evenness, commensurability and equality, excess and defect, and these belong to numbers either in themselves or in relation to one another. And similarly the solid and the motionless and that which is in motion and the weightless and that which has weight have other peculiar properties. So too there are certain properties peculiar to being as such, and it is about these that the philosopher has to investigate the truth.—An indication of this may be mentioned:—dialecticians and sophists assume the same guise as the philosopher, for sophistic is Wisdom which exists only in semblance, and dialecticians embrace all things in their dialectic, and being is common to all things; but evidently their dialectic embraces these subjects because these are proper to philosophy.—For sophistic and dialectic turn on the same class of things as philosophy, but this differs from dialectic in the nature of the faculty required and from sophistic in respect of the purpose of the philosophic life. Dialectic is merely critical where philosophy claims to know, and sophistic is what appears to be philosophy but is not.

Again, in the list of contraries one of the two columns is privative, and all contraries are reducible to being and non-being, and to unity and plurality, as for instance rest belongs to unity and movement to plurality. And nearly all thinkers agree that being and substance are composed of contraries; at least all name contraries as their first principles—some name odd and even, some hot and cold, some limit and the unlimited, some love and strife. And all the others as well are evidently reducible to unity and plurality (this reduction we must take for granted), and the principles stated by other thinkers fall entirely under these as their genera. It is obvious then from these considerations too that it belongs to one science to examine being *qua* being. For all things are either contraries or composed of contraries, and unity and plurality are the starting-points of all contraries. And these belong to one science, whether they have or have not one single meaning. Probably the truth is that they have not; yet even if 'one' has several meanings, the other meanings will be related to the primary meaning (and similarly in the case of the contraries), even if being or unity is not a universal and the same in every instance or is not separable from the particular instances (as in fact it probably is not; the unity is in some cases that of common reference, in some cases that of serial succession). And for this reason it does not belong to the geometer to inquire what is contrariety or completeness or unity or being or the same or the other, but only to presuppose these concepts and reason from this starting-point.—Obviously then it is the work of one science to examine being *qua* being, and the attributes which belong to it *qua* being, and the same science will examine not only substances but also their attributes, both those above named and the concepts 'prior' and 'posterior', 'genus' and 'species', 'whole' and 'part', and the others of this sort.

3

We must state whether it belongs to one or to different sciences to inquire into the truths which are in mathematics called axioms, and into substance. Evidently, the inquiry into these also belongs to one science, and that the science of the philosopher; for these truths hold good for everything that is, and not for some special genus apart from others. And all men use them, because they are true of being *qua* being and each genus has being. But men use them just so far as to satisfy their purposes; that is, as far as the genus to which their demonstrations refer extends. Therefore since these truths clearly hold good for all things *qua* being (for this is what is common to them), to him who studies being *qua* being belongs the inquiry into these as well. And for this reason no one who is conducting a special inquiry tries to say anything about their truth or falsity,—neither the geometer nor the arithmetician. Some natural philosophers indeed have done so, and their procedure was intelligible enough; for they thought that they alone were inquiring about the whole of nature and about being. But since there is one kind of thinker who is above even the natural philosopher (for nature is only one particular genus of being), the discussion of these truths also will belong to him whose inquiry is universal and deals with primary substance. Physics also is a kind of Wisdom, but it is not the first kind.—And the attempts of some of those who discuss the terms on which truth should be accepted, are due to a want of training in logic; for they should know these things already when they come to a special study, and not be inquiring into them while they are listening to lectures on it.

Evidently then it belongs to the philosopher, i.e. to him who is studying the nature of all substance, to inquire also into the principles of syllogism. But he who knows best about each genus must be able to state the most certain principles of his subject, so that he whose subject is existing things *qua* existing must be able to state the most certain principles of all things. This is the philosopher, and the most certain principle of all is that regarding which it is impossible to be mistaken; for such a principle must be both the best known (for all men may be mistaken about things which they do not know), and non-hypothetical. For a principle which every one must have who understands anything that is, is not a hypothesis; and that which every one must know who knows anything, he must already have when he comes to a special study. Evidently then such a principle is the most certain of all; which principle this is, let us proceed to say. It is, that the same attribute cannot at the same time belong and not belong to the same subject and in the same respect; we must presuppose, to guard against dialectical objections, any further qualifications which might be added. This, then, is the most certain of all principles, since it answers to the definition given above. For it is impossible for any one to believe the same thing to be and not to be, as some think Heraclitus says. For what a man says, he does not necessarily believe; and if it is impossible that contrary attributes should belong at the same time to the same subject (the usual qualifications must be presupposed in this premiss too), and if an opinion which contradicts another is contrary to it, obviously it is impossible for the same man at the same time to believe the same thing to be and not to be; for if a man were mistaken on this point he would have contrary opinions at the same time. It is for this reason that all who are carrying out a demonstration reduce it to this as an ultimate belief; for this is naturally the starting-point even for all the other axioms.

4

There are some who, as we said, both themselves assert that it is possible for the same thing to be and not to be, and say that people can judge this to be the case. And among others many writers about nature use this language. But we have now posited that it is impossible for anything at the same time to be and not to be, and by this means have shown that this is the most indisputable of all principles.—Some indeed demand that even this shall be demonstrated, but this they do through want of education, for not to know of what things one should demand demonstration, and of what one should not, argues want of education. For it is impossible that there should be demonstration of absolutely everything (there would be an infinite regress, so that there would still be no demonstration); but if there are things of which one should not demand demonstration, these persons could not say what principle they maintain to be more self-evident than the present one.

We can, however, demonstrate negatively even that this view is impossible, if our opponent will only say something; and if he says nothing, it is absurd to seek to give an account of our views to one who cannot give an account of anything, in so far as he cannot do so. For such a man, as such, is from the start no better than a vegetable. Now negative demonstration I distinguish from demonstration proper, because in a demonstration one might be thought to be begging the question, but if another person is responsible for the assumption we shall have negative proof, not demonstration. The starting-point for all such arguments is not the demand that our opponent shall say that something either is or is not (for this one might perhaps take to be a begging of the question), but that he shall say something which is significant both for himself and for another; for this is necessary, if he really is to say anything. For, if he means nothing, such a man will not be capable of reasoning, either with himself or with another. But if any one grants this, demonstration will be possible; for we shall already have something definite. The person responsible for the proof, however, is not he who demonstrates but he who listens; for while disowning reason he listens to reason. And again he who admits this has admitted that something is true apart from demonstration (so that not everything will be 'so and not so').

First then this at least is obviously true, that the word 'be' or 'not be' has a definite meaning, so that not everything will be 'so and not so'.—Again, if 'man' has one meaning, let this be 'two-footed animal'; by having one meaning I understand this:—if 'man' means 'X', then if A is a man 'X' will be what 'being a man' means for him. (It makes no difference even if one were to say a word has several meanings, if only they are limited in number; for to each definition there might be assigned a different word. For instance, we might say that 'man' has not one meaning but several, one of which would have one definition, viz. 'two-footed animal', while there might be also several other definitions if only they were limited in number; for a peculiar name might be assigned to each of the definitions. If, however, they were not limited but one were to say that the word has an infinite number of meanings, obviously reasoning would be impossible; for not to have one meaning is to have no meaning, and if words have no meaning our reasoning with one another, and indeed with ourselves, has been annihilated; for it is impossible to think of anything if we do not think of one thing; but if this is possible, one name might be assigned to this thing.)

Let it be assumed then, as was said at the beginning, that the name has a meaning and has one meaning; it is impossible, then, that 'being a man' should mean precisely 'not being a man', if 'man' not only signifies something about one subject but also has one significance (for we do not identify 'having one significance' with 'signifying something about one subject', since on that assumption even 'musical' and 'white' and 'man' would have had one significance, so that all things would have been one; for they would all have had the same significance).

And it will not be possible to be and not to be the same thing, except in virtue of an ambiguity, just as if one whom we call 'man', others were to call 'not-man'; but the point in question is not this, whether the same thing can at the same time be and not be a man in name, but whether it can in fact.—Now if 'man' and 'not-man' mean nothing different, obviously 'not being a man' will mean nothing different from 'being a man'; so that 'being a man' will be 'not being a man'; for they will be one. For being one means this—being related as 'raiment' and 'dress' are, if their definition is one. And if 'being a man' and 'being a not-man' are to be one, they must mean one thing. But it was shown earlier' that they mean different things.—Therefore, if it is true to say of anything that it is a man, it must be a two-footed animal (for this was what 'man' meant); and if this is necessary, it is impossible that the same thing should not at that time be a two-footed animal; for this is what 'being necessary' means—that it is impossible for the thing not to be. It is, then, impossible that it should be at the same time true to say the same thing is a man and is not a man.

The same account holds good with regard to 'not being a man', for 'being a man' and 'being a not-man' mean different things, since even 'being white' and 'being a man' are different; for the former terms are much more different so that they must *a fortiori* mean different things. And if any one says that 'white' means one and the same thing as 'man', again we shall say the same as what was said before, that it would follow that all things are one, and not only opposites. But if this is impossible, then what we have maintained will follow, if our opponent will only answer our question.

And if, when one asks the question simply, he adds the contradictories, he is not answering the question. For there is nothing to prevent the same thing from being both a man and white and countless other things: but still, if one asks whether it is or is not true to say that this is a man, our opponent must give an answer which means one thing, and not add that 'it is also white and large'. For, besides other reasons, it is impossible to enumerate its accidental attributes, which are infinite in number; let him, then, enumerate either all or none. Similarly, therefore, even if the same thing is a thousand times a man and a not-man, he must not, in answering the question whether this is a man, add that it is also at the same time a not-man, unless he is bound to add also all the other accidents, all that the subject is or is not; and if he does this, he is not observing the rules of argument.

And in general those who say this do away with substance and essence. For they must say that all attributes are accidents, and that there is no such thing as 'being essentially a man' or 'an animal'. For if there is to be any such thing as 'being essentially a man' this will not be 'being a not-man' or 'not being a man' (yet these are negations of it); for there was one thing which it meant, and this was the substance of something. And denoting the substance of a thing means that the essence of the thing is nothing else. But if its being essentially a man is to be the same as either being essentially a not-man or essentially not being a man, then its essence will be something else. Therefore our opponents must say that there cannot be such a definition of anything, but that all attributes are accidental; for this is the distinction between substance and accident—'white' is accidental to man, because though he is white, whiteness is not his essence. But if all statements are accidental, there will be nothing primary about which they are made, if the accidental always implies predication about a subject. The predication, then, must go on *ad infinitum*. But this is impossible; for not even more than two terms can be combined in accidental predication. For (1) an accident is not an accident of an accident, unless it be because both are accidents of the same subject. I mean, for instance, that the white is musical and the latter is white, only because both are accidental to man. But (2) Socrates is musical, not in this sense, that both terms are accidental to something else. Since then some predicates are accidental in this and some in that sense, (a) those which are accidental in the latter sense, in which white is accidental to Socrates, cannot form an infinite series in the upward direction; e.g. Socrates the white has not yet another accident; for no unity can be got out of such a sum. Nor again (b) will 'white' have another term accidental to it, e.g. 'musical'. For this is no more accidental to that than that is to this; and at the same time we have drawn the distinction, that while some predicates are accidental in this sense, others are so in the sense in which 'musical' is accidental to Socrates; and the accident is an accident of an accident not in cases of the latter kind, but only in cases of the other kind, so that not all terms will be accidental. There must, then, even so be something which denotes substance. And if this is so, it has been shown that contradictories cannot be predicated at the same time.

Again, if all contradictory statements are true of the same subject at the same time, evidently all things will be one. For the same thing will be a trireme, a wall, and a man, if of everything it is possible either to affirm or to deny anything (and this premiss must be accepted by those who share the views of Protagoras). For if any one thinks that the man is not a trireme, evidently he is not a trireme; so that he also is a trireme, if, as they say, contradictory statements are both true. And we thus get the doctrine of Anaxagoras, that all things are mixed together; so that nothing really exists. They seem, then, to be speaking of the indeterminate, and, while fancying themselves to be speaking of being, they are speaking about non-being; for it is that which exists potentially and not in complete reality that is indeterminate. But they must predicate of every subject the affirmation or the negation of every attribute. For it is absurd if of each subject its own negation is to be predicable, while the negation of something else which cannot be predicated of it is not to be predicable of it; for instance, if it is true to say of a man that he is not a man, evidently it is also true to say that he is either a trireme or not a trireme. If, then, the affirmative can be predicated, the negative must be predicable too; and if the affirmative is not predicable, the negative, at least, will be more predicable than the negative of the subject itself. If, then, even the latter negative is predicable, the negative of 'trireme' will be also predicable; and, if this is predicable, the affirmative will be so too.

Those, then, who maintain this view are driven to this conclusion, and to the further conclusion that it is not necessary either to assert or to deny. For if it is true that a thing is a man and a not-man, evidently also it will be neither a man nor a not-man. For to the two assertions there answer two negations, and if the former is treated as a single proposition compounded out of two, the latter also is a single proposition opposite to the former.

Again, either the theory is true in all cases, and a thing is both white and not-white, and existent and non-existent, and all other assertions and negations are similarly compatible or the theory is true of some statements and not of others. And if not of all, the exceptions will be contradictories of which admittedly only one is true; but if of all, again either the negation will be true wherever the assertion is, and the assertion true wherever the negation is, or the negation will be true where the assertion is, but the assertion not always true where the negation is. And (a) in the latter case there will be something which fixedly is not, and this will be an indisputable belief; and if non-being is something indisputable and knowable, the opposite assertion will be more knowable. But (b) if it is equally possible also to assert all that it is possible to deny, one must either be saying what is true when one separates the predicates (and says, for instance, that a thing is white, and again that it is not-white), or not. And if (i) it is not true to apply the predicates separately, our opponent is not saying what he professes to say, and also nothing at all exists; but how could non-existent things speak or walk, as he does? Also all things would on this view be one, as has been already said, and man and God and trireme and their contradictories will be the same. For if contradictories can be predicated alike of each subject, one thing will in no wise differ from another; for if it differ, this difference will be something true and peculiar to it. And (ii) if one may with truth apply the predicates separately, the above-mentioned result follows none the less, and, further, it follows that all would then be right and all would be in error, and our opponent himself confesses himself to be in error.—And at the same time our discussion with him is evidently about nothing at all; for he says nothing. For he says neither 'yes' nor 'no', but 'yes and no'; and again he denies both of these and says 'neither yes nor no'; for otherwise there would already be something definite.

Again if when the assertion is true, the negation is false, and when this is true, the affirmation is false, it will not be possible to assert and deny the same thing truly at the same time. But perhaps they might say this was the very question at issue.

Again, is he in error who judges either that the thing is so or that it is not so, and is he right who judges both? If he is right, what can they mean by saying that the nature of existing things is of this kind? And if he is not right, but more right than he who judges in the other way, being will already be of a definite nature, and this will be true, and not at the same time also not true. But if all are alike both wrong and right, one who is in this condition will not be able either to speak or to say anything intelligible; for he says at the same time both 'yes' and 'no.' And if he makes no judgement but 'thinks' and 'does not think', indifferently, what difference will there be between him and a vegetable?—Thus, then, it is in the highest degree evident that neither any one of those who maintain this view nor any one else is really in this position. For why does a man walk to Megara and not stay at home, when he thinks he ought to be walking there? Why does he not walk early some morning into a well or over a precipice, if one happens to be in his way? Why do we observe him guarding against this, evidently because he does not think that falling in is alike good and not good? Evidently, then, he judges one thing to be better and another worse. And if this is so, he must also judge one thing to be a man and another to be not-a-man, one thing to be sweet and another to be not-sweet. For he does not aim at and judge all things alike, when, thinking it desirable to drink water or to see a man, he proceeds to aim at these things; yet he ought, if the same thing were alike a man and not-a-man. But, as was said, there is no one who does not obviously avoid some things and not others. Therefore, as it seems, all men make unqualified judgements, if not about all things, still about what is better and worse. And if this is not knowledge but opinion, they should be all the more anxious about the truth, as a sick man should be more anxious about his health than one who is healthy; for he who has opinions is, in comparison with the man who knows, not in a healthy state as far as the truth is concerned.

Again, however much all things may be 'so and not so', still there is a more and a less in the nature of things; for we should not say that two and three are equally even, nor is he who thinks four things are five equally wrong with him who thinks they are a thousand. If then they are not equally wrong, obviously one is less wrong and therefore more right. If then that which has more of any quality is nearer the norm, there must be some truth to which the more true is nearer. And even if there is not, still there is already something better founded and liker the truth, and we shall have got rid of the unqualified doctrine which would prevent us from determining anything in our thought.

5

From the same opinion proceeds the doctrine of Protagoras, and both doctrines must be alike true or alike untrue. For on the one hand, if all opinions and appearances are true, all statements must be at the same time true and false. For many men hold beliefs in which they conflict with one another, and think those mistaken who have not the same opinions as themselves; so that the same thing must both be and not be. And on the other hand, if this is so, all opinions must be true; for those who are mistaken and those who are right are opposed to one another in their opinions; if, then, reality is such as the view in question supposes, all will be right in their beliefs.

Evidently, then, both doctrines proceed from the same way of thinking. But the same method of discussion must not be used with all opponents; for some need persuasion, and others compulsion. Those who have been driven to this position by difficulties in their thinking can easily be cured of their ignorance; for it is not their expressed argument but their thought that one has to meet. But those who argue for the sake of argument can be cured only by refuting the argument as expressed in speech and in words.

Those who really feel the difficulties have been led to this opinion by observation of the sensible world. (1) They think that contradictories or contraries are true at the same time, because they see contraries coming into existence out of the same thing. If, then, that which is not cannot come to be, the thing must have existed before as both contraries alike, as Anaxagoras says all is mixed in all, and Democritus too; for he says the void and the full exist alike in every part, and yet one of these is being, and the other non-being. To those, then, whose belief rests on these grounds, we shall say that in a sense they speak rightly and in a sense they err. For 'that which is' has two meanings, so that in some sense a thing can come to be out of that which is not, while in some sense it cannot, and the same thing can at the same time be in being and not in being-but not in the same respect. For the same thing can be potentially at the same time two contraries, but it cannot actually. And again we shall ask them to believe that among existing things there is also another kind of substance to which neither movement nor destruction nor generation at all belongs.

And (2) similarly some have inferred from observation of the sensible world the truth of appearances. For they think that the truth should not be determined by the large or small number of those who hold a belief, and that the same thing is thought sweet by some when they taste it, and bitter by others, so that if all were ill or all were mad, and only two or three were well or sane, these would be thought ill and mad, and not the others.

And again, they say that many of the other animals receive impressions contrary to ours; and that even to the senses of each individual, things do not always seem the same. Which, then, of these impressions are true and which are false is not obvious; for the one set is no more true than the other, but both are alike. And this is why Democritus, at any rate, says that either there is no truth or to us at least it is not evident.

And in general it is because these thinkers suppose knowledge to be sensation, and this to be a physical alteration, that they say that what appears to our senses must be true; for it is for these reasons that both Empedocles and Democritus and, one may almost say, all the others have fallen victims to opinions of this sort. For Empedocles says that when men change their condition they change their knowledge;

> For wisdom increases in men according to what is before them.

And elsewhere he says that:—

> So far as their nature changed, so far to them always
> Came changed thoughts into mind.

And Parmenides also expresses himself in the same way:

> For as at each time the much-bent limbs are composed,
> So is the mind of men; for in each and all men
> 'Tis one thing thinks—the substance of their limbs:
> For that of which there is more is thought.

A saying of Anaxagoras to some of his friends is also related,—that things would be for them such as they supposed them to be. And they say that Homer also evidently had this opinion, because he made Hector, when he was unconscious from the blow, lie 'thinking other thoughts',—which implies that even those who are bereft of thought have thoughts, though not the same thoughts. Evidently, then, if both are forms of knowledge, the real things also are at the same time 'both so and not so'. And it is in this direction that the consequences are most difficult. For if those who have seen most of such truth as is possible for us (and these are those who seek and love it most)—if these have such opinions and express these views about the truth, is it not natural that beginners in philosophy should lose heart? For to seek the truth would be to follow flying game.

But the reason why these thinkers held this opinion is that while they were inquiring into the truth of that which is, they thought, 'that which is' was identical with the sensible world; in this, however, there is largely present the nature of the indeterminate—of that which exists in the peculiar sense which we have explained; and therefore, while they speak plausibly, they do not say what is true (for it is fitting to put the matter so rather than as Epicharmus put it against Xenophanes). And again, because they saw that all this world of nature is in movement and that about that which changes no true statement can be made, they said that of course, regarding that which everywhere in every respect is changing, nothing could truly be affirmed. It was this belief that blossomed into the most extreme of the views above mentioned, that of the professed Heracliteans, such as was held by Cratylus, who finally did not think it right to say anything but only moved his finger, and criticized Heraclitus for saying that it is impossible to step twice into the same river; for he thought one could not do it even once.

But we shall say in answer to this argument also that while there is some justification for their thinking that the changing, when it is changing, does not exist, yet it is after all disputable; for that which is losing a quality has something of that which is being lost, and of that which is coming to be, something must already be. And in general if a thing is perishing, will be present something that exists; and if a thing is coming to be, there must be something from which it comes to be and something by which it is generated, and this process cannot go on *ad infinitum*.—But, leaving these arguments, let us insist on this, that it is not the same thing to change in quantity and in quality. Grant that in quantity a thing is not constant; still it is in respect of its form that we know each thing.—And again, it would be fair to criticize those who hold this view for asserting about the whole material universe what they saw only in a minority even of sensible things. For only that region of the sensible world which immediately surrounds us is always in process of destruction and generation; but this is—so to speak—not even a fraction of the whole, so that it would have been juster to acquit this part of the world because of the other part, than to condemn the other because of this.—And again, obviously we shall make to them also the same reply that we made long ago; we must show them and persuade them that there is something whose nature is changeless. Indeed, those who say that things at the same time are and are not, should in consequence say that all things are at rest rather than that they are in movement; for there is nothing into which they can change, since all attributes belong already to all subjects.

Regarding the nature of truth, we must maintain that not everything which appears is true; firstly, because even if sensation—at least of the object peculiar to the sense in question—is not false, still appearance is not the same as sensation.—Again, it is fair to express surprise at our opponents' raising the question whether magnitudes are as great, and colours are of such a nature, as they appear to people at a distance, or as they appear to those close at hand, and whether they are such as they appear to the healthy or to the sick, and whether those things are heavy which appear so to the weak or those which appear so to the strong, and those things true which appear to the sleeping or to the waking. For obviously they do not think these to be open questions; no one, at least, if when he is in Libya he has fancied one night that he is in Athens, starts for the concert hall.—And again with regard to the future, as Plato says, surely the opinion of the physician and that of the ignorant man are not equally weighty, for instance, on the question whether a man will get well or not.—And again, among sensations themselves the sensation of a foreign object and that of the appropriate object, or that of a kindred object and that of the object of the sense in question, are not equally authoritative, but in the case of colour sight, not taste, has the authority, and in the case of flavour taste, not sight; each of which senses never says at the same time of the same object that it simultaneously is 'so and not so'.—But not even at different times does one sense disagree about the quality, but only about that to which the quality belongs. I mean, for instance, that the same wine might seem, if either it or one's body changed, at one time sweet and at another time not sweet; but at least the sweet, such as it is when it exists, has never yet changed, but one is always right about it, and that which is to be sweet is of necessity of such and such a nature. Yet all these views destroy this necessity, leaving nothing to be of necessity, as they leave no essence of anything; for the necessary cannot be in this way and also in that, so that if anything is of necessity, it will not be 'both so and not so'.

And, in general, if only the sensible exists, there would be nothing if animate things were not; for there would be no faculty of sense. Now the view that neither the sensible qualities nor the sensations would exist is doubtless true (for they are affections of the perceiver), but that the substrata which cause the sensation should not exist even apart from sensation is impossible. For sensation is surely not the sensation of itself, but there is something beyond the sensation, which must be prior to the sensation; for that which moves is prior in nature to that which is moved, and if they are correlative terms, this is no less the case.

6

There are, both among those who have these convictions and among those who merely profess these views, some who raise a difficulty by asking, who is to be the judge of the healthy man, and in general who is likely to judge rightly on each class of questions. But such inquiries are like puzzling over the question whether we are now asleep or awake. And all such questions have the same meaning. These people demand that a reason shall be given for everything; for they seek a starting-point, and they seek to get this by demonstration, while it is obvious from their actions that they have no conviction. But their mistake is what we have stated it to be; they seek a reason for things for which no reason can be given; for the starting-point of demonstration is not demonstration.

These, then, might be easily persuaded of this truth, for it is not difficult to grasp; but those who seek merely compulsion in argument seek what is impossible; for they demand to be allowed to contradict themselves—a claim which contradicts itself from the very first.—But if not all things are relative, but some are self-existent, not everything that appears will be true; for that which appears is apparent to some one; so that he who says all things that appear are true, makes all things relative. And, therefore, those who ask for an irresistible argument, and at the same time demand to be called to account for their views, must guard themselves by saying that the truth is not that what appears exists, but that what appears exists for him to whom it appears, and when, and to the sense to which, and under the conditions under which it appears. And if they give an account of their view, but do not give it in this way, they will soon find themselves contradicting themselves. For it is possible that the same thing may appear to be honey to the sight, but not to the taste, and that, since we have two eyes, things may not appear the same to each, if their sight is unlike. For to those who for the reasons named some time ago say that what appears is true, and therefore that all things are alike false and true, for things do not appear either the same to all men or always the same to the same man, but often have contrary appearances at the same time (for touch says there are two objects when we cross our fingers, while sight says there is one)—to these we shall say 'yes, but not to the same sense and in the same part of it and under the same conditions and at the same time', so that what appears will be with these qualifications true. But perhaps for this reason those who argue thus not because they feel a difficulty but for the sake of argument, should say that this is not true, but true for this man. And as has been said before, they must make everything relative—relative to opinion and perception, so that nothing either has come to be or will be without some one's first thinking so. But if things have come to be or will be, evidently not all things will be relative to opinion.—Again, if a thing is one, it is in relation to one thing or to a definite number of things; and if the same thing is both half and equal, it is not to the double that the equal is correlative. If, then, in relation to that which thinks, man and that which is thought are the same, man will not be that which thinks, but only that which is thought. And if each thing is to be relative to that which thinks, that which thinks will be relative to an infinity of specifically different things.

Let this, then, suffice to show (1) that the most indisputable of all beliefs is that contradictory statements are not at the same time true, and (2) what consequences follow from the assertion that they are, and (3) why people do assert this. Now since it is impossible that contradictories should be at the same time true of the same thing, obviously contraries also cannot belong at the same time to the same thing. For of contraries, one is a privation no less than it is a contrary—and a privation of the essential nature; and privation is the denial of a predicate to a determinate genus. If, then, it is impossible to affirm and deny truly at the same time, it is also impossible that contraries should belong to a subject at the same time, unless both belong to it in particular relations, or one in a particular relation and one without qualification.

7

But on the other hand there cannot be an intermediate between contradictories, but of one subject we must either affirm or deny any one predicate. This is clear, in the first place, if we define what the true and the false are. To say of what is that it is not, or of what is not that it is, is false, while to say of what is that it is, and of what is not that it is not, is true; so that he who says of anything that it is, or that it is not, will say either what is true or what is false; but neither what is nor what is not is said to be or not to be.-Again, the intermediate between the contradictories will be so either in the way in which grey is between black and white, or as that which is neither man nor horse is between man and horse. (a) If it were of the latter kind, it could not change into the extremes (for change is from not-good to good, or from good to not-good), but as a matter of fact when there is an intermediate it is always observed to change into the extremes. For there is no change except to opposites and to their intermediates. (b) But if it is really intermediate, in this way too there would have to be a change to white, which was not from not-white; but as it is, this is never seen.—Again, every object of understanding or reason the understanding either affirms or denies—this is obvious from the definition—whenever it says what is true or false. When it connects in one way by assertion or negation, it says what is true, and when it does so in another way, what is false.—Again, there must be an intermediate between all contradictories, if one is not arguing merely for the sake of argument; so that it will be possible for a man to say what is neither true nor untrue, and there will be a middle between that which is and that which is not, so that there will also be a kind of change intermediate between generation and destruction.—Again, in all classes in which the negation of an attribute involves the assertion of its contrary, even in these there will be an intermediate; for instance, in the sphere of numbers there will be number which is neither odd nor not-odd. But this is impossible, as is obvious from the definition.—Again, the process will go on *ad infinitum*, and the number of realities will be not only half as great again, but even greater. For again it will be possible to deny this intermediate with reference both to its assertion and to its negation, and this new term will be some definite thing; for its essence is something different. —Again, when a man, on being asked whether a thing is white, says 'no', he has denied nothing except that it is; and its not being is a negation.

Some people have acquired this opinion as other paradoxical opinions have been acquired; when men cannot refute eristical arguments, they give in to the argument and agree that the conclusion is true. This, then, is why some express this view; others do so because they demand a reason for everything. And the starting-point in dealing with all such people is definition. Now the definition rests on the necessity of their meaning something; for the form of words of which the word is a sign will be its definition.—While the doctrine of Heraclitus, that all things are and are not, seems to make everything true, that of Anaxagoras, that there is an intermediate between the terms of a contradiction, seems to make everything false; for when things are mixed, the mixture is neither good nor not-good, so that one cannot say anything that is true.

8

In view of these distinctions it is obvious that the one-sided theories which some people express about all things cannot be valid—on the one hand the theory that nothing is true (for, say they, there is nothing to prevent every statement from being like the statement 'the diagonal of a square is commensurate with the side'), on the other hand the theory that everything is true. These views are practically the same as that of Heraclitus; for he who says that all things are true and all are false also makes each of these statements separately, so that since they are impossible, the double statement must be impossible too.—Again, there are obviously contradictories which cannot be at the same time true—nor on the other hand can all statements be false; yet this would seem more possible in the light of what has been said.—But against all such views we must postulate, as we said above,' not that something is or is not, but that something has a meaning, so that we must argue from a definition, viz. by assuming what falsity or truth means. If that which it is true to affirm is nothing other than that which it is false to deny, it is impossible that all statements should be false; for one side of the contradiction must be true. Again, if it is necessary with regard to everything either to assert or to deny it, it is impossible that both should be false; for it is one side of the contradiction that is false.—Therefore all such views are also exposed to the often expressed objection, that they destroy themselves. For he who says that everything is true makes even the statement contrary to his own true, and therefore his own not true (for the contrary statement denies that it is true), while he who says everything is false makes himself also false.—And if the former person excepts the contrary statement, saying it alone is not true, while the latter excepts his own as being not false, none the less they are driven to postulate the truth or falsity of an infinite number of statements; for that which says the true statement is true is true, and this process will go on to infinity.

Evidently, again, those who say all things are at rest are not right, nor are those who say all things are in movement. For if all things are at rest, the same statements will always be true and the same always false,—but this obviously changes; for he who makes a statement, himself at one time was not and again will not be. And if all things are in motion, nothing will be true; everything therefore will be false. But it has been shown that this is impossible. Again, it must be that which is that changes; for change is from something to something. But again it is not the case that all things are at rest or in motion sometimes, and nothing for ever; for there is something which always moves the things that are in motion, and the first mover is itself unmoved.

Book V

1

'Beginning' means (1) that part of a thing from which one would start first, e.g. a line or a road has a beginning in either of the contrary directions. (2) That from which each thing would best be originated, e.g. even in learning we must sometimes begin not from the first point and the beginning of the subject, but from the point from which we should learn most easily. (3) That from which, as an immanent part, a thing first comes to be, e.g., as the keel of a ship and the foundation of a house, while in animals some suppose the heart, others the brain, others some other part, to be of this nature. (4) That from which, not as an immanent part, a thing first comes to be, and from which the movement or the change naturally first begins, as a child comes from its father and its mother, and a fight from abusive language. (5) That at whose will that which is moved is moved and that which changes changes, e.g. the magistracies in cities, and oligarchies and monarchies and tyrannies, are called *arhchai*, and so are the arts, and of these especially the architectonic arts. (6) That from which a thing can first be known,-this also is called the beginning of the thing, e.g. the hypotheses are the beginnings of demonstrations. (Causes are spoken of in an equal number of senses; for all causes are beginnings.) It is common, then, to all beginnings to be the first point from which a thing either is or comes to be or is known; but of these some are immanent in the thing and others are outside. Hence the nature of a thing is a beginning, and so is the element of a thing, and thought and will, and essence, and the final cause-for the good and the beautiful are the beginning both of the knowledge and of the movement of many things.

2

'Cause' means (1) that from which, as immanent material, a thing comes into being, e.g. the bronze is the cause of the statue and the silver of the saucer, and so are the classes which include these. (2) The form or pattern, i.e. the definition of the essence, and the classes which include this (e.g. the ratio 2:1 and number in general are causes of the octave), and the parts included in the definition. (3) That from which the change or the resting from change first begins; e.g. the adviser is a cause of the action, and the father a cause of the child, and in general the maker a cause of the thing made and the change-producing of the changing. (4) The end, i.e. that for the sake of which a thing is; e.g. health is the cause of walking. For 'Why does one walk?' we say; 'that one may be healthy'; and in speaking thus we think we have given the cause. The same is true of all the means that intervene before the end, when something else has put the process in motion, as e.g. thinning or purging or drugs or instruments intervene before health is reached; for all these are for the sake of the end, though they differ from one another in that some are instruments and others are actions.

These, then, are practically all the senses in which causes are spoken of, and as they are spoken of in several senses it follows both that there are several causes of the same thing, and in no accidental sense (e.g. both the art of sculpture and the bronze are causes of the statue not in respect of anything else but *qua* statue; not, however, in the same way, but the one as matter and the other as source of the movement), and that things can be causes of one another (e.g. exercise of good condition, and the latter of exercise; not, however, in the same way, but the one as end and the other as source of movement).—Again, the same thing is the cause of contraries; for that which when present causes a particular thing, we sometimes charge, when absent, with the contrary, e.g. we impute the shipwreck to the absence of the steersman, whose presence was the cause of safety; and both-the presence and the privation—are causes as sources of movement.

All the causes now mentioned fall under four senses which are the most obvious. For the letters are the cause of syllables, and the material is the cause of manufactured things, and fire and earth and all such things are the causes of bodies, and the parts are causes of the whole, and the hypotheses are causes of the conclusion, in the sense that they are that out of which these respectively are made; but of these some are cause as the *substratum* (e.g. the parts), others as the essence (the whole, the synthesis, and the form). The semen, the physician, the adviser, and in general the agent, are all sources of change or of rest. The remainder are causes as the end and the good of the other things; for that for the sake of which other things are tends to be the best and the end of the other things; let us take it as making no difference whether we call it good or apparent good.

These, then, are the causes, and this is the number of their kinds, but the varieties of causes are many in number, though when summarized these also are comparatively few. Causes are spoken of in many senses, and even of those which are of the same kind some are causes in a prior and others in a posterior sense, e.g. both 'the physician' and 'the professional man' are causes of health, and both 'the ratio 2:1' and 'number' are causes of the octave, and the classes that include any particular cause are always causes of the particular effect. Again, there are accidental causes and the classes which include these; e.g. while in one sense 'the sculptor' causes the statue, in another sense 'Polyclitus' causes it, because the sculptor happens to be Polyclitus; and the classes that include the accidental cause are also causes, e.g. 'man'—or in general 'animal'—is the cause of the statue, because Polyclitus is a man, and man is an animal. Of accidental causes also some are more remote or nearer than others, as, for instance, if 'the white' and 'the musical' were called causes of the statue, and not only 'Polyclitus' or 'man'. But besides all these varieties of causes, whether proper or accidental, some are called causes as being able to act, others as acting; e.g. the cause of the house's being built is a builder, or a builder who is building.—The same variety of language will be found with regard to the effects of causes; e.g. a thing may be called the cause of this statue or of a statue or in general of an image, and of this bronze or of bronze or of matter in general; and similarly in the case of accidental effects. Again, both accidental and proper causes may be spoken of in combination; e.g. we may say not 'Polyclitus' nor 'the sculptor' but 'Polyclitus the sculptor'. Yet all these are but six in number, while each is spoken of in two ways; for (A) they are causes either as the individual, or as the genus, or as the accidental, or as the genus that includes the accidental, and these either as combined, or as taken simply; and (B) all may be taken as acting or as having a capacity. But they differ inasmuch as the acting causes, i.e. the individuals, exist, or do not exist, simultaneously with the things of which they are causes, e.g. this particular man who is healing, with this particular man who is recovering health, and this particular builder with this particular thing that is being built; but the potential causes are not always in this case; for the house does not perish at the same time as the builder.

3

'Element' means (1) the primary component immanent in a thing, and indivisible in kind into other kinds; e.g. the elements of speech are the parts of which speech consists and into which it is ultimately divided, while they are no longer divided into other forms of speech different in kind from them. If they are divided, their parts are of the same kind, as a part of water is water (while a part of the syllable is not a syllable). Similarly those who speak of the elements of bodies mean the things into which bodies are ultimately divided, while they are no longer divided into other things differing in kind; and whether the things of this sort are one or more, they call these elements. The so-called elements of geometrical proofs, and in general the elements of demonstrations, have a similar character; for the primary demonstrations, each of which is implied in many demonstrations, are called elements of demonstrations; and the primary syllogisms, which have three terms and proceed by means of one middle, are of this nature.

(2) People also transfer the word 'element' from this meaning and apply it to that which, being one and small, is useful for many

purposes; for which reason what is small and simple and indivisible is called an element. Hence come the facts that the most universal things are elements (because each of them being one and simple is present in a plurality of things, either in all or in as many as possible), and that unity and the point are thought by some to be first principles. Now, since the so-called genera are universal and indivisible (for there is no definition of them), some say the genera are elements, and more so than the differentia, because the genus is more universal; for where the differentia is present, the genus accompanies it, but where the genus is present, the differentia is not always so. It is common to all the meanings that the element of each thing is the first component immanent in each.

4

'Nature' means (1) the genesis of growing things—the meaning which would be suggested if one were to pronounce the 'u' in *phusis* long. (2) That immanent part of a growing thing, from which its growth first proceeds. (3) The source from which the primary movement in each natural object is present in it in virtue of its own essence. Those things are said to grow which derive increase from something else by contact and either by organic unity, or by organic adhesion as in the case of embryos. Organic unity differs from contact; for in the latter case there need not be anything besides the contact, but in organic unities there is something identical in both parts, which makes them grow together instead of merely touching, and be one in respect of continuity and quantity, though not of quality.—(4) 'Nature' means the primary material of which any natural object consists or out of which it is made, which is relatively unshaped and cannot be changed from its own potency, as e.g. bronze is said to be the nature of a statue and of bronze utensils, and wood the nature of wooden things; and so in all other cases; for when a product is made out of these materials, the first matter is preserved throughout. For it is in this way that people call the elements of natural objects also their nature, some naming fire, others earth, others air, others water, others something else of the sort, and some naming more than one of these, and others all of them.—(5) 'Nature' means the essence of natural objects, as with those who say the nature is the primary mode of composition, or as Empedocles says:—

> Nothing that is has a nature,
> But only mixing and parting of the mixed,
> And nature is but a name given them by men.

Hence as regards the things that are or come to be by nature, though that from which they naturally come to be or are is already present, we say they have not their nature yet, unless they have their form or shape. That which comprises both of these exists by nature, e.g. the animals and their parts; and not only is the first matter nature (and this in two senses, either the first, counting from the thing, or the first in general; e.g. in the case of works in bronze, bronze is first with reference to them, but in general perhaps water is first, if all things that can be melted are water), but also the form or essence, which is the end of the process of becoming.—(6) By an extension of meaning from this sense of 'nature' every essence in general has come to be called a 'nature', because the nature of a thing is one kind of essence.

From what has been said, then, it is plain that nature in the primary and strict sense is the essence of things which have in themselves, as such, a source of movement; for the matter is called the nature because it is qualified to receive this, and processes of becoming and growing are called nature because they are movements proceeding from this. And nature in this sense is the source of the movement of natural objects, being present in them somehow, either potentially or in complete reality.

5

We call 'necessary' (1) (a) that without which, as a condition, a thing cannot live; e.g. breathing and food are necessary for an animal; for it is incapable of existing without these; (b) the conditions without which good cannot be or come to be, or without which we cannot get rid or be freed of evil; e.g. drinking the medicine is necessary in order that we may be cured of disease, and a man's sailing to Aegina is necessary in order that he may get his money.—(2) The compulsory and compulsion, i.e. that which impedes and tends to hinder, contrary to impulse and purpose. For the compulsory is called necessary (whence the necessary is painful, as Evenus says: 'For every necessary thing is ever irksome'), and compulsion is a form of necessity, as Sophocles says: 'But force necessitates me to this act'. And necessity is held to be something that cannot be persuaded—and rightly, for it is contrary to the movement which accords with purpose and with reasoning.—(3) We say that that which cannot be otherwise is necessarily as it is. And from this sense of 'necessary' all the others are somehow derived; for a thing is said to do or suffer what is necessary in the sense of compulsory, only when it cannot act according to its impulse because of the compelling force,—which implies that necessity is that because of which a thing cannot be otherwise; and similarly as regards the conditions of life and of good; for when in the one case good, in the other life and being, are not possible without certain conditions, these are necessary, and this kind of cause is a sort of necessity. Again, demonstration is a necessary thing because the conclusion cannot be otherwise, if there has been demonstration in the unqualified sense; and the causes of this necessity are the first premisses, i.e. the fact that the propositions from which the syllogism proceeds cannot be otherwise.

Now some things owe their necessity to something other than themselves; others do not, but are themselves the source of necessity in other things. Therefore the necessary in the primary and strict sense is the simple; for this does not admit of more states than one, so that it cannot even be in one state and also in another; for if it did it would already be in more than one. If, then, there are any things that are eternal and unmovable, nothing compulsory or against their nature attaches to them.

6

'One' means (1) that which is one by accident, (2) that which is one by its own nature. (1) Instances of the accidentally one are 'Coriscus and what is musical', and 'musical Coriscus' (for it is the same thing to say 'Coriscus and what is musical', and 'musical Coriscus'), and 'what is musical and what is just', and 'musical Coriscus and just Coriscus'. For all of these are called one by virtue of an accident, 'what is just and what is musical' because they are accidents of one substance, 'what is musical and Coriscus' because the one is an accident of the other; and similarly in a sense 'musical Coriscus' is one with 'Coriscus' because one of the parts of the phrase is an accident of the other, i.e. 'musical' is an accident of Coriscus; and 'musical Coriscus' is one with 'just Coriscus' because one part of each is an accident of one and the same subject. The case is similar if the accident is predicated of a genus or of any universal name, e.g. if one says that man is the same as 'musical man'; for this is either because 'musical' is an accident of man, which is one substance, or because both are accidents of some individual, e.g. Coriscus. Both, however, do not belong to him in the same way, but one presumably as genus and included in his substance, the other as a state or affection of the substance.

The things, then, that are called one in virtue of an accident, are called so in this way. (2) Of things that are called one in virtue of their own nature some (a) are so called because they are continuous, e.g. a bundle is made one by a band, and pieces of wood are made one by glue; and a line, even if it is bent, is called one if it is continuous, as each part of the body is, e.g. the leg or the arm. Of these themselves, the continuous by nature are more one than the continuous by art. A thing is called continuous which has by its own nature one movement and cannot have any other; and the movement is one when it is indivisible, and it is indivisible in respect of time. Those things are continuous by their own nature which are one not merely by contact; for if you put pieces of wood touching one another, you will not say these are one piece of wood or one body or one *continuum* of any other sort. Things, then, that are continuous in any way called one, even if they admit of being bent, and still more those which cannot be bent; e.g. the shin or the thigh is more one than the leg, because the movement of the leg need not be one. And the straight line is more one than the bent; but that which is bent and has an angle we call both one and not one, because its movement may be either simultaneous or not simultaneous; but that of the straight line is always simultaneous, and no part of it which has magnitude rests while another moves, as in the bent line.

(b) (i) Things are called one in another sense because their *substratum* does not differ in kind; it does not differ in the case of things whose kind is indivisible to sense. The *substratum* meant is either the nearest to, or the farthest from, the final state. For, one the one hand, wine is said to be one and water is said to be one, *qua* indivisible in kind; and, on the other hand, all juices, e.g. oil and wine, are said to be one, and so are all things that can be melted, because the ultimate *substratum* of all is the same; for all of these are water or air.

(ii) Those things also are called one whose genus is one though distinguished by opposite differentiae—these too are all called one because the genus which underlies the differentiae is one (e.g. horse, man, and dog form a unity, because all are animals), and indeed in a way similar to that in which the matter is one. These are sometimes called one in this way, but sometimes it is the higher genus that is said to be the same (if they are *infimae species* of their genus)-the genus above the proximate genera; e.g. the isosceles and the equilateral are one and the same figure because both are triangles; but they are not the same triangles.

(c) Two things are called one, when the definition which states the essence of one is indivisible from another definition which shows us the other (though in itself every definition is divisible). Thus even that which has increased or is diminishing is one, because its definition is one, as, in the case of plane figures, is the definition of their form. In general those things the thought of whose essence is indivisible, and cannot separate them either in time or in place or in definition, are most of all one, and of these especially those which are substances. For in general those things that do not admit of division are called one in so far as they do not admit of it; e.g. if two things are indistinguishable *qua* man, they are one kind of man; if *qua* animal, one kind of animal; if *qua* magnitude, one kind of magnitude.—Now most things are called one because they either do or have or suffer or are related to something else that is one, but the things that are primarily called one are those whose substance is one,—and one either in continuity or in form or in definition; for we count as more than one either things that are not continuous, or those whose form is not one, or those whose definition is not one.

While in a sense we call anything one if it is a quantity and continuous, in a sense we do not unless it is a whole, i.e. unless it has unity of form; e.g. if we saw the parts of a shoe put together anyhow we should not call them one all the same (unless because of their continuity); we do this only if they are put together so as to be a shoe and to have already a certain single form. This is why the circle is of all lines most truly one, because it is whole and complete.

(3) The essence of what is one is to be some kind of beginning of number; for the first measure is the beginning, since that by which we first know each class is the first measure of the class; the one, then, is the beginning of the knowable regarding each class. But the one is not the same in all classes. For here it is a quarter-tone, and there it is the vowel or the consonant; and there is another unit of weight and another of movement. But everywhere the one is indivisible either in quantity or in kind. Now that which is indivisible in quantity is called a unit if it is not divisible in any dimension and is without position, a point if it is not divisible in any dimension and has position, a line if it is divisible in one dimension, a plane if in two, a body if divisible in quantity in all—i.e. in three—dimensions. And, reversing the order, that which is divisible in two dimensions is a plane, that which is divisible in one a line, that which is in no way divisible in quantity is a point or a unit,— that which has not position a unit, that which has position a point.

Again, some things are one in number, others in species, others in genus, others by analogy; in number those whose matter is one, in species those whose definition is one, in genus those to which the same figure of predication applies, by analogy those which are related as a third thing is to a fourth. The latter kinds of unity are always found when the former are; e.g. things that are one in number are also one in species, while things that are one in species are not all one in number; but things that are one in species are all one in genus, while things that are so in genus are not all one in species but are all one by analogy; while things that are one by analogy are not all one in genus.

Evidently 'many' will have meanings opposite to those of 'one'; some things are many because they are not continuous, others because their matter—either the proximate matter or the ultimate—is divisible in kind, others because the definitions which state their essence are more than one.

7

Things are said to 'be' (1) in an accidental sense, (2) by their own nature.

(1) In an accidental sense, e.g. we say 'the righteous doer is musical', and 'the man is musical', and 'the musician is a man', just as we say 'the musician builds', because the builder happens to be musical or the musician to be a builder; for here 'one thing is another' means 'one is an accident of another'. So in the cases we have mentioned; for when we say 'the man is musical' and 'the musician is a man', or 'he who is pale is musical' or 'the musician is pale', the last two mean that both attributes are accidents of the same thing; the first that the attribute is an accident of that which is, while 'the musical is a man' means that 'musical' is an accident of a man. (In this sense, too, the not-pale is said to be, because that of which it is an accident is.) Thus when one thing is said in an accidental sense to be another, this is either because both belong to the same thing, and this is, or because that to which the attribute belongs is, or because the subject which has as an attribute that of which it is itself predicated, itself is.

(2) The kinds of essential being are precisely those that are indicated by the figures of predication; for the senses of 'being' are just as many as these figures. Since, then, some predicates indicate what the subject is, others its quality, others quantity, others relation, others activity or passivity, others its 'where', others its 'when', 'being' has a meaning answering to each of these. For there is no difference between 'the man is recovering' and 'the man recovers', nor between 'the man is walking or cutting' and 'the man walks' or 'cuts'; and similarly in all other cases.

(3) Again, 'being' and 'is' mean that a statement is true, 'not being' that it is not true but false,—and this alike in the case of affirmation and of negation; e.g. 'Socrates is musical' means that this is true, or 'Socrates is not-pale' means that this is true; but 'the diagonal of the square is not commensurate with the side' means that it is false to say it is.

(4) Again, 'being' and 'that which is' mean that some of the things we have mentioned 'are' potentially, others in complete reality. For we say both of that which sees potentially and of that which sees actually, that it is 'seeing', and both of that which can actualize its knowledge and of that which is actualizing it, that it knows, and both of that to which rest is already present and of that which can rest, that it rests. And similarly in the case of substances; we say the Hermes is in the stone, and the half of the line is in the line, and we say of that which is not yet ripe that it is corn. When a thing is potential and when it is not yet potential must be explained elsewhere.

8

We call 'substance' (1) the simple bodies, i.e. earth and fire and water and everything of the sort, and in general bodies and the things composed of them, both animals and divine beings, and the parts of these. All these are called substance because they are not predicated of a subject but everything else is predicated of them.—(2) That which, being present in such things as are not predicated of a subject, is the cause of their being, as the soul is of the being of an animal.—(3) The parts which are present in such things, limiting them and marking them as individuals, and by whose destruction the whole is destroyed, as the body is by the destruction of the plane, as some say, and the plane by the destruction of the line; and in general number is thought by some to be of this nature; for if it is destroyed, they say, nothing exists, and it limits all things.—(4) The essence, the formula of which is a definition, is also called the substance of each thing.

It follows, then, that 'substance' has two senses, (A) ultimate *substratum*, which is no longer predicated of anything else, and (B) that which, being a 'this', is also separable and of this nature is the shape or form of each thing.

9

'The same' means (1) that which is the same in an accidental sense, e.g. 'the pale' and 'the musical' are the same because they are accidents of the same thing, and 'a man' and 'musical' because the one is an accident of the other; and 'the musical' is 'a man' because it is an accident of the man. (The complex entity is the same as either of the simple ones and each of these is the same as it; for both 'the man' and 'the musical' are said to be the same as 'the musical man', and this the same as they.) This is why all of these statements are made not universally; for it is not true to say that every man is the same as 'the musical' (for universal attributes belong to things in virtue of their own nature, but accidents do not belong to them in virtue of their own nature); but of the individuals the statements are made without qualification. For 'Socrates' and 'musical Socrates' are thought to be the same; but 'Socrates' is not predicable of more than one subject, and therefore we do not say 'every Socrates' as we say 'every man'.

Some things are said to be the same in this sense, others (2) are the same by their own nature, in as many senses as that which is one by its own nature is so; for both the things whose matter is one either in kind or in number, and those whose essence is one, are said to be the same. Clearly, therefore, sameness is a unity of the being either of more than one thing or of one thing when it is treated as more than one, i.e. when we say a thing is the same as itself; for we treat it as two.

Things are called 'other' if either their kinds or their matters or the definitions of their essence are more than one; and in general 'other' has meanings opposite to those of 'the same'.

'Different' is applied (1) to those things which though other are the same in some respect, only not in number but either in species or in genus or by analogy; (2) to those whose genus is other, and to contraries, and to an things that have their otherness in their essence.

Those things are called 'like' which have the same attributes in every respect, and those which have more attributes the same than different, and those whose quality is one; and that which shares with another thing the greater number or the more important of the attributes (each of them one of two contraries) in respect of which things are capable of altering, is like that other thing. The senses of 'unlike' are opposite to those of 'like'.

10

The term 'opposite' is applied to contradictories, and to contraries, and to relative terms, and to privation and possession, and to the extremes from which and into which generation and dissolution take place; and the attributes that cannot be present at the same time in that which is receptive of both, are said to be opposed,—either themselves of their constituents. Grey and white colour do not belong at the same time to the same thing; hence their constituents are opposed.

The term 'contrary' is applied (1) to those attributes differing in genus which cannot belong at the same time to the same subject, (2) to the most different of the things in the same genus, (3) to the most different of the attributes in the same recipient subject, (4) to the most different of the things that fall under the same faculty, (5) to the things whose difference is greatest either absolutely or in genus or in species. The other things that are called contrary are so called, some because they possess contraries of the above kind, some because they are receptive of such, some because they are productive of or susceptible to such, or are producing or suffering them, or are losses or acquisitions, or possessions or privations, of such. Since 'one' and 'being' have many senses, the other terms which are derived from these, and therefore 'same', 'other', and 'contrary', must correspond, so that they must be different for each category.

The term 'other in species' is applied to things which being of the same genus are not subordinate the one to the other, or which being in the same genus have a difference, or which have a contrariety in their substance; and contraries are other than one another in species (either all contraries or those which are so called in the primary sense), and so are those things whose definitions differ in the *infima species* of the genus (e.g. man and horse are indivisible in genus, but their definitions are different), and those which being in the same substance have a difference. 'The same in species' has the various meanings opposite to these.

11

The words 'prior' and 'posterior' are applied (1) to some things (on the assumption that there is a first, i.e. a beginning, in each class) because they are nearer some beginning determined either absolutely and by nature, or by reference to something or in some place or by certain people; e.g. things are prior in place because they are nearer either to some place determined by nature (e.g. the middle or the last place), or to some chance object; and that which is farther is posterior.—Other things are prior in time; some by being farther from the present, i.e. in the case of past events (for the Trojan war is prior to the Persian, because it is farther from the present), others by being nearer the present, i.e. in the case of future events (for the Nemean games are prior to the Pythian, if we treat the present as beginning and first point, because they are nearer the present).—Other things are prior in movement; for that which is nearer the first mover is prior (e.g. the boy is prior to the man); and the prime mover also is a beginning absolutely.—Others are prior in power; for that which exceeds in power, i.e. the more powerful, is prior; and such is that according to whose will the other—i.e. the posterior—must follow, so that if the prior does not set it in motion the other does not move, and if it sets it in motion it does move; and here will is a beginning.—Others are prior in arrangement; these are the things that are placed at intervals in reference to some one definite thing according to some rule, e.g. in the chorus the second man is prior to the third, and in the lyre the second lowest string is prior to the lowest; for in the one case the leader and in the other the middle string is the beginning.

These, then, are called prior in this sense, but (2) in another sense that which is prior for knowledge is treated as also absolutely prior; of these, the things that are prior in definition do not coincide with those that are prior in relation to perception. For in definition universals are prior, in relation to perception individuals. And in definition also the accident is prior to the whole, e.g. 'musical' to 'musical man', for the definition cannot exist as a whole without the part; yet musicalness cannot exist unless there is some one who is musical.

(3) The attributes of prior things are called prior, e.g. straightness is prior to smoothness; for one is an attribute of a line as such, and the other of a surface.

Some things then are called prior and posterior in this sense, others (4) in respect of nature and substance, i.e. those which can be without other things, while the others cannot be without them,—a distinction which Plato used. (If we consider the various senses of 'being', firstly the subject is prior, so that substance is prior; secondly, according as potency or complete reality is taken into account, different things are prior, for some things are prior in respect of potency, others in respect of complete reality, e.g. in potency the half line is prior to the whole line, and the part to the whole, and the matter to the concrete substance, but in complete reality these are posterior; for it is only when the whole has been dissolved that they will exist in complete reality.) In a sense, therefore, all things that are called prior and posterior are so called with reference to this fourth sense; for some things can exist without others in respect of generation, e.g. the whole without the parts, and others in respect of dissolution, e.g. the part without the whole. And the same is true in all other cases.

12

'Potency' means (1) a source of movement or change, which is in another thing than the thing moved or in the same thing *qua* other; e.g. the art of building is a potency which is not in the thing built, while the art of healing, which is a potency, may be in the man healed, but not in him *qua* healed. 'Potency' then means the source, in general, of change or movement in another thing or in the same thing *qua* other, and also (2) the source of a thing's being moved by another thing or by itself *qua* other. For in virtue of that principle, in virtue of which a patient suffers anything, we call it 'capable' of suffering; and this we do sometimes if it suffers anything at all, sometimes not in respect of everything it suffers, but only if it suffers a change for the better—(3) The capacity of performing this well or according to intention; for sometimes we say of those who merely can walk or speak but not well or not as they intend, that they cannot speak or walk. So too (4) in the case of passivity—(5) The states in virtue of which things are absolutely impassive or unchangeable, or not easily changed for the worse, are called potencies; for things are broken and crushed and bent and in general destroyed not by having a potency but by not having one and by lacking something, and things are impassive with respect to such processes if they are scarcely and slightly affected by them, because of a 'potency' and because they 'can' do something and are in some positive state.

'Potency' having this variety of meanings, so too the 'potent' or 'capable' in one sense will mean that which can begin a movement (or a change in general, for even that which can bring things to rest is a 'potent' thing) in another thing or in itself *qua* other; and in one sense that over which something else has such a potency; and in one sense that which has a potency of changing into something, whether for the worse or for the better (for even that which perishes is thought to be 'capable' of perishing, for it would not have perished if it had not been capable of it; but, as a matter of fact, it has a certain disposition and cause and principle which fits it to suffer this; sometimes it is thought to be of this sort because it has something, sometimes because it is deprived of something; but if privation is in a sense 'having' or 'habit', everything will be capable by having something, so that things are capable both by having a positive habit and principle, and by having the privation of this, if it is possible to have a privation; and if privation is not in a sense 'habit', 'capable' is used in two distinct senses); and a thing is capable in another sense because neither any other thing, nor itself *qua* other, has a potency or principle which can destroy it. Again, all of these are capable either merely because the thing might chance to happen or not to happen, or because it might do so well. This sort of potency is found even in lifeless things, e.g. in instruments; for we say one lyre can speak, and another cannot speak at all, if it has not a good tone.

Incapacity is privation of capacity—i.e. of such a principle as has been described—either in general or in the case of something that would naturally have the capacity, or even at the time when it would naturally already have it; for the senses in which we should call a boy and a man and a eunuch 'incapable of begetting' are distinct.—Again, to either kind of capacity there is an opposite incapacity—both to that which only can produce movement and to that which can produce it well.

Some things, then, are called *adunata* in virtue of this kind of incapacity, while others are so in another sense; i.e. both *dunaton* and *adunaton* are used as follows. The impossible is that of which the contrary is of necessity true, e.g. that the diagonal of a square is commensurate with the side is impossible, because such a statement is a falsity of which the contrary is not only true but also necessary; that it is commensurate, then, is not only false but also of necessity false. The contrary of this, the possible, is found when it is not necessary that the contrary is false, e.g. that a man should be seated is possible; for that he is not seated is not of necessity false. The possible, then, in one sense, as has been said, means that which is not of necessity false; in one, that which is true; in one, that which may be true.—A 'potency' or 'power' in geometry is so called by a change of meaning.—These senses of 'capable' or 'possible' involve no reference to potency. But the senses which involve a reference to potency all refer to the primary kind of potency; and this is a source of change in another thing or in the same thing *qua* other. For other things are called 'capable', some because something else has such a potency over them, some because it has not, some because it has it in a particular way. The same is true of the things that are incapable. Therefore the proper definition of the primary kind of potency will be 'a source of change in another thing or in the same thing *qua* other'.

13

'Quantum' means that which is divisible into two or more constituent parts of which each is by nature a 'one' and a 'this'. A quantum is a plurality if it is numerable, a magnitude if it is a measurable. 'Plurality' means that which is divisible potentially into non-continuous parts, 'magnitude' that which is divisible into continuous parts; of magnitude, that which is continuous in one dimension is length; in two breadth, in three depth. Of these, limited plurality is number, limited length is a line, breadth a surface, depth a solid.

Again, some things are called quanta in virtue of their own nature, others incidentally; e.g. the line is a quantum by its own nature, the musical is one incidentally. Of the things that are quanta by their own nature some are so as substances, e.g. the line is a quantum (for 'a certain kind of quantum' is present in the definition which states what it is), and others are modifications and states of this kind of substance, e.g. much and little, long and short, broad and narrow, deep and shallow, heavy and light, and all other such attributes. And also great and small, and greater and smaller, both in themselves and when taken relatively to each other, are by their own nature attributes of what is quantitative; but these names are transferred to other things also. Of things that are quanta incidentally, some are so called in the sense in which it was said that the musical and the white were quanta, viz. because that to which musicalness and whiteness belong is a quantum, and some are quanta in the way in which movement and time are so; for these also are called quanta of a sort and continuous because the things of which these are attributes are divisible. I mean not that which is moved, but the space through which it is moved; for because that is a quantum movement also is a quantum, and because this is a quantum time is one.

14

'Quality' means (1) the differentia of the essence, e.g. man is an animal of a certain quality because he is two-footed, and the horse is so because it is four-footed; and a circle is a figure of particular quality because it is without angles,—which shows that the essential differentia is a quality.—This, then, is one meaning of quality—the differentia of the essence, but (2) there is another sense in which it applies to the unmovable objects of mathematics, the sense in which the numbers have a certain quality, e.g. the composite numbers which are not in one dimension only, but of which the plane and the solid are copies (these are those which have two or three factors); and in general that which exists in the essence of numbers besides quantity is quality; for the essence of each is what it is once, e.g. that of is not what it is twice or thrice, but what it is once; for 6 is once 6.

(3) All the modifications of substances that move (e.g. heat and cold, whiteness and blackness, heaviness and lightness, and the others of the sort) in virtue of which, when they change, bodies are said to alter. (4) Quality in respect of virtue and vice, and in general, of evil and good.

Quality, then, seems to have practically two meanings, and one of these is the more proper. The primary quality is the differentia of the essence, and of this the quality in numbers is a part; for it is a differentia of essences, but either not of things that move or not of them *qua* moving. Secondly, there are the modifications of things that move, *qua* moving, and the differentiae of movements. Virtue and vice fall among these modifications; for they indicate differentiae of the movement or activity, according to which the things in motion act or are acted on well or badly; for that which can be moved or act in one way is good, and that which can do so in another—the contrary—way is vicious. Good and evil indicate quality especially in living things, and among these especially in those which have purpose.

15

Things are 'relative' (1) as double to half, and treble to a third, and in general that which contains something else many times to that which is contained many times in something else, and that which exceeds to that which is exceeded; (2) as that which can heat to that which can be heated, and that which can cut to that which can be cut, and in general the active to the passive; (3) as the measurable to the measure, and the knowable to knowledge, and the perceptible to perception.

(1) Relative terms of the first kind are numerically related either indefinitely or definitely, to numbers themselves or to 1. E.g. the double is in a definite numerical relation to 1, and that which is 'many times as great' is in a numerical, but not a definite, relation to 1, i.e. not in this or in that numerical relation to it; the relation of that which is half as big again as something else to that something is a definite numerical relation to a number; that which is $(n + 1 / n)$ times something else is in an indefinite relation to that something, as that which is 'many times as great' is in an indefinite relation to 1; the relation of that which exceeds to that which is exceeded is numerically quite indefinite; for number is always commensurate, and 'number' is not predicated of that which is not commensurate, but that which exceeds is, in relation to that which is exceeded, so much and

something more; and this something is indefinite; for it can, indifferently, be either equal or not equal to that which is exceeded.— All these relations, then, are numerically expressed and are determinations of number, and so in another way are the equal and the like and the same. For all refer to unity. Those things are the same whose substance is one; those are like whose quality is one; those are equal whose quantity is one; and 1 is the beginning and measure of number, so that all these relations imply number, though not in the same way.

(2) Things that are active or passive imply an active or a passive potency and the actualizations of the potencies; e.g. that which is capable of heating is related to that which is capable of being heated, because it can heat it, and, again, that which heats is related to that which is heated and that which cuts to that which is cut, in the sense that they actually do these things. But numerical relations are not actualized except in the sense which has been elsewhere stated; actualizations in the sense of movement they have not. Of relations which imply potency some further imply particular periods of time, e.g. that which has made is relative to that which has been made, and that which will make to that which will be made. For it is in this way that a father is called the father of his son; for the one has acted and the other has been acted on in a certain way. Further, some relative terms imply privation of potency, i.e. 'incapable' and terms of this sort, e.g. 'invisible'.

Relative terms which imply number or potency, therefore, are all relative because their very essence includes in its nature a reference to something else, not because something else involves a reference to it; but (3) that which is measurable or knowable or thinkable is called relative because something else involves a reference to it. For 'that which is thinkable' implies that the thought of it is possible, but the thought is not relative to 'that of which it is the thought'; for we should then have said the same thing twice. Similarly sight is the sight of something, not 'of that of which it is the sight' (though of course it is true to say this); in fact it is relative to colour or to something else of the sort. But according to the other way of speaking the same thing would be said twice,—'the sight is of that of which it is.'

Things that are by their own nature called relative are called so sometimes in these senses, sometimes if the classes that include them are of this sort; e.g. medicine is a relative term because its genus, science, is thought to be a relative term. Further, there are the properties in virtue of which the things that have them are called relative, e.g. equality is relative because the equal is, and likeness because the like is. Other things are relative by accident; e.g. a man is relative because he happens to be double of something and double is a relative term; or the white is relative, if the same thing happens to be double and white.

16

What is called 'complete' is (1) that outside which it is not possible to find any, even one, of its parts; e.g. the complete time of each thing is that outside which it is not possible to find any time which is a part proper to it.—(2) That which in respect of excellence and goodness cannot be excelled in its kind; e.g. we have a complete doctor or a complete flute-player, when they lack nothing in respect of the form of their proper excellence. And thus, transferring the word to bad things, we speak of a complete scandal-monger and a complete thief; indeed we even call them good, i.e. a good thief and a good scandal-monger. And excellence is a completion; for each thing is complete and every substance is complete, when in respect of the form of its proper excellence it lacks no part of its natural magnitude.—(3) The things which have attained their end, this being good, are called complete; for things are complete in virtue of having attained their end. Therefore, since the end is something ultimate, we transfer the word to bad things and say a thing has been completely spoilt, and completely destroyed, when it in no wise falls short of destruction and badness, but is at its last point. This is why death, too, is by a figure of speech called the end, because both are last things. But the ultimate purpose is also an end.—Things, then, that are called complete in virtue of their own nature are so called in all these senses, some because in respect of goodness they lack nothing and cannot be excelled and no part proper to them can be found outside them, others in general because they cannot be exceeded in their several classes and no part proper to them is outside them; the others presuppose these first two kinds, and are called complete because they either make or have something of the sort or are adapted to it or in some way or other involve a reference to the things that are called complete in the primary sense.

17

'Limit' means (1) the last point of each thing, i.e. the first point beyond which it is not possible to find any part, and the first point within which every part is; (2) the form, whatever it may be, of a spatial magnitude or of a thing that has magnitude; (3) the end of each thing (and of this nature is that towards which the movement and the action are, not that from which they are—though sometimes it is both, that from which and that to which the movement is, i.e. the final cause); (4) the substance of each thing, and the essence of each; for this is the limit of knowledge; and if of knowledge, of the object also. Evidently, therefore, 'limit' has as many senses as 'beginning', and yet more; for the beginning is a limit, but not every limit is a beginning.

18

'That in virtue of which' has several meanings:—(1) the form or substance of each thing, e.g. that in virtue of which a man is good is the good itself, (2) the proximate subject in which it is the nature of an attribute to be found, e.g. colour in a surface. 'That in virtue of which', then, in the primary sense is the form, and in a secondary sense the matter of each thing and the proximate *substratum* of each.—In general 'that in virtue of which' will found in the same number of senses as 'cause'; for we say indifferently (3) in virtue of what has he come?' or 'for what end has he come?'; and (4) in virtue of what has he inferred wrongly, or inferred?' or 'what is the cause of the inference, or of the wrong inference?'—Further (5) καθό is used in reference to position, e.g. 'at which he stands' or 'along which he walks'; for all such phrases indicate place and position.

Therefore 'in virtue of itself' must likewise have several meanings. The following belong to a thing in virtue of itself:—(1) the essence of each thing, e.g. Callias is in virtue of himself Callias and what it was to be Callias;—(2) whatever is present in the 'what', e.g. Callias is in virtue of himself an animal. For 'animal' is present in his definition; Callias is a particular animal.—(3) Whatever attribute a thing receives in itself directly or in one of its parts; e.g. a surface is white in virtue of itself, and a man is alive in virtue of himself; for the soul, in which life directly resides, is a part of the man.—(4) That which has no cause other than itself; man has more than one cause—animal, two-footed—but yet man is man in virtue of himself.—(5) Whatever attributes belong to a thing alone, and in so far as they belong to it merely by virtue of itself considered apart by itself.

19

'Disposition' means the arrangement of that which has parts, in respect either of place or of potency or of kind; for there must be a certain position, as even the word 'disposition' shows.

20

'Having' means (1) a kind of activity of the haver and of what he has—something like an action or movement. For when one thing makes and one is made, between them there is a making; so too between him who has a garment and the garment which he has there is a having. This sort of having, then, evidently we cannot have; for the process will go on to infinity, if it is to be possible to have the having of what we have.—(2) 'Having' or 'habit' means a disposition according to which that which is disposed is either well or ill disposed, and either in itself or with reference to something else; e.g. health is a 'habit'; for it is such a disposition.—(3) We speak of a 'habit' if there is a portion of such a disposition; and so even the excellence of the parts is a 'habit' of the whole thing.

21

'Affection' means (1) a quality in respect of which a thing can be altered, e.g. white and black, sweet and bitter, heaviness and lightness, and all others of the kind.—(2) The actualization of these-the already accomplished alterations.—(3) Especially, injurious alterations and movements, and, above all painful injuries.—(4) Misfortunes and painful experiences when on a large scale are called affections.

22

We speak of 'privation' (1) if something has not one of the attributes which a thing might naturally have, even if this thing itself would not naturally have it; e.g. a plant is said to be 'deprived' of eyes.—(2) If, though either the thing itself or its genus would naturally have an attribute, it has it not; e.g. a blind man and a mole are in different senses 'deprived' of sight; the latter in contrast with its genus, the former in contrast with his own normal nature.—(3) If, though it would naturally have the attribute, and when it would naturally have it, it has it not; for blindness is a privation, but one is not 'blind' at any and every age, but only if one has not sight at the age at which one would naturally have it. Similarly a thing is called blind if it has not sight in the medium in which, and in respect of the organ in respect of which, and with reference to the object with reference to which, and in the circumstances in which, it would naturally have it.—(4) The violent taking away of anything is called privation.

Indeed there are just as many kinds of privations as there are of words with negative prefixes; for a thing is called unequal because it has not equality though it would naturally have it, and invisible either because it has no colour at all or because it has a poor colour, and apodous either because it has no feet at all or because it has imperfect feet. Again, a privative term may be used because the thing has little of the attribute (and this means having it in a sense imperfectly), e.g. 'kernel-less'; or because it has it not easily or not well (e.g. we call a thing uncuttable not only if it cannot be cut but also if it cannot be cut easily or well); or because it has not the attribute at all; for it is not the one-eyed man but he who is sightless in both eyes that is called blind. This is why not every man is 'good' or 'bad', 'just' or 'unjust', but there is also an intermediate state.

23

To 'have' or 'hold' means many things:—(1) to treat a thing according to one's own nature or according to one's own impulse; so that fever is said to have a man, and tyrants to have their cities, and people to have the clothes they wear.—(2) That in which a thing is present as in something receptive of it is said to have the thing; e.g. the bronze has the form of the statue, and the body has the disease.—(3) As that which contains holds the things contained; for a thing is said to be held by that in which it is as in a container; e.g. we say that the vessel holds the liquid and the city holds men and the ship sailors; and so too that the whole holds the parts.—(4) That which hinders a thing from moving or acting according to its own impulse is said to hold it, as pillars hold the incumbent weights, and as the poets make Atlas hold the heavens, implying that otherwise they would collapse on the earth, as some of the natural philosophers also say. In this way also that which holds things together is said to hold the things it holds together, since they would otherwise separate, each according to its own impulse.

'Being in something' has similar and corresponding meanings to 'holding' or 'having'.

24

'To come from something' means (1) to come from something as from matter, and this in two senses, either in respect of the highest genus or in respect of the lowest species; e.g. in a sense all things that can be melted come from water, but in a sense the statue comes from bronze.—(2) As from the first moving principle; e.g. 'what did the fight come from?' From abusive language, because this was the origin of the fight.—(3) From the compound of matter and shape, as the parts come from the whole, and the verse from the *Iliad*, and the stones from the house; (in every such case the whole is a compound of matter and shape,) for the shape is the end, and only that which attains an end is complete.—(4) As the form from its part, e.g. man from 'two-footed' and syllable from 'letter'; for this is a different sense from that in which the statue comes from bronze; for the composite substance comes from the sensible matter, but the form also comes from the matter of the form.—Some things, then, are said to come from something else in these senses; but (5) others are so described if one of these senses is applicable to a part of that other thing; e.g. the child comes from its father and mother, and plants come from the earth, because they come from a part of those things.—(6) It means coming after a thing in time, e.g. night comes from day and storm from fine weather, because the one comes after the other. Of these things some are so described because they admit of change into one another, as in the cases now mentioned; some merely because they are successive in time, e.g. the voyage took place 'from' the equinox, because it took place after the equinox, and the festival of the Thargelia comes 'from' the Dionysia, because after the Dionysia.

25

'Part' means (1) (a) that into which a quantum can in any way be divided; for that which is taken from a quantum *qua* quantum is always called a part of it, e.g. two is called in a sense a part of three. It means (b), of the parts in the first sense, only those which measure the whole; this is why two, though in one sense it is, in another is not, called a part of three.—(2) The elements into which a kind might be divided apart from the quantity are also called parts of it; for which reason we say the species are parts of the genus.—(3) The elements into which a whole is divided, or of which it consists—the 'whole' meaning either the form or that which has the form; e.g. of the bronze sphere or of the bronze cube both the bronze—i.e. the matter in which the form is-and the characteristic angle are parts.—(4) The elements in the definition which explains a thing are also parts of the whole; this is why the genus is called a part of the species, though in another sense the species is part of the genus.

26

'A whole' means (1) that from which is absent none of the parts of which it is said to be naturally a whole, and (2) that which so contains the things it contains that they form a unity; and this in two senses—either as being each severally one single thing, or as making up the unity between them. For (a) that which is true of a whole class and is said to hold good as a whole (which implies that it is a kind whole) is true of a whole in the sense that it contains many things by being predicated of each, and by all of them, e.g. man, horse, god, being severally one single thing, because all are living things. But (b) the continuous and limited is a whole, when it is a unity consisting of several parts, especially if they are present only potentially, but, failing this, even if they are present actually. Of these things themselves, those which are so by nature are wholes in a higher degree than those which are so by art, as we said in the case of unity also, wholeness being in fact a sort of oneness.

Again (3) of quanta that have a beginning and a middle and an end, those to which the position does not make a difference are called totals, and those to which it does, wholes. Those which admit of both descriptions are both wholes and totals. These are the things whose nature remains the same after transposition, but whose form does not, e.g. wax or a coat; they are called both wholes and totals; for they have both characteristics. Water and all liquids and number are called totals, but 'the whole number' or 'the whole water' one does not speak of, except by an extension of meaning. To things, to which *qua* one the term 'total' is applied, the term 'all' is applied when they are treated as separate; 'this total number,' 'all these units.'

27

It is not any chance quantitative thing that can be said to be 'mutilated'; it must be a whole as well as divisible. For not only is two not 'mutilated' if one of the two ones is taken away (for the part removed by mutilation is never equal to the remainder), but in general no number is thus mutilated; for it is also necessary that the essence remain; if a cup is mutilated, it must still be a cup; but the number is no longer the same. Further, even if things consist of unlike parts, not even these things can all be said to be mutilated, for in a sense a number has unlike parts (e.g. two and three) as well as like; but in general of the things to which their position makes no difference, e.g. water or fire, none can be mutilated; to be mutilated, things must be such as in virtue of their essence have a certain position. Again, they must be continuous; for a musical scale consists of unlike parts and has position, but cannot become mutilated. Besides, not even the things that are wholes are mutilated by the privation of any part. For the parts removed must be neither those which determine the essence nor any chance parts, irrespective of their position; e.g. a cup is not mutilated if it is bored through, but only if the handle or a projecting part is removed, and a man is mutilated not if the flesh or the spleen is removed, but if an extremity is, and that not every extremity but one which when completely removed cannot grow again. Therefore baldness is not a mutilation.

28

The term 'race' or 'genus' is used (1) if generation of things which have the same form is continuous, e.g. 'while the race of men lasts' means 'while the generation of them goes on continuously'.—(2) It is used with reference to that which first brought things into existence; for it is thus that some are called Hellenes by race and others Ionians, because the former proceed from Hellen and the latter from Ion as their first begetter. And the word is used in reference to the begetter more than to the matter, though people also get a race-name from the female, e.g. 'the descendants of Pyrrha'.—(3) There is genus in the sense in which 'plane' is the genus of plane figures and solid' of solids; for each of the figures is in the one case a plane of such and such a kind, and in the other a solid of such and such a kind; and this is what underlies the differentiae. Again (4) in definitions the first constituent element, which is included in the 'what', is the genus, whose differentiae the qualities are said to be.—'Genus' then is used in all these ways, (1) in reference to continuous generation of the same kind, (2) in reference to the first mover which is of the same kind as the things it moves, (3) as matter; for that to which the differentia or quality belongs is the *substratum*, which we call matter.

Those things are said to be 'other in genus' whose proximate *substratum* is different, and which are not analysed the one into the other nor both into the same thing (e.g. form and matter are different in genus); and things which belong to different categories of being (for some of the things that are said to 'be' signify essence, others a quality, others the other categories we have before distinguished); these also are not analysed either into one another or into some one thing.

29

'The false' means (1) that which is false as a thing, and that (a) because it is not put together or cannot be put together, e.g. 'that the diagonal of a square is commensurate with the side' or 'that you are sitting'; for one of these is false always, and the other sometimes; it is in these two senses that they are non-existent. (b) There are things which exist, but whose nature it is to appear either not to be such as they are or to be things that do not exist, e.g. a sketch or a dream; for these are something, but are not the things the appearance of which they produce in us. We call things false in this way, then,—either because they themselves do not exist, or because the appearance which results from them is that of something that does not exist.

(2) A false account is the account of non-existent objects, in so far as it is false. Hence every account is false when applied to something other than that of which it is true; e.g. the account of a circle is false when applied to a triangle. In a sense there is one account of each thing, i.e. the account of its essence, but in a sense there are many, since the thing itself and the thing itself with an attribute are in a sense the same, e.g. Socrates and musical Socrates (a false account is not the account of anything, except in a qualified sense). Hence Antisthenes was too simple-minded when he claimed that nothing could be described except by the account proper to it,—one predicate to one subject; from which the conclusion used to be drawn that there could be no contradiction, and almost that there could be no error. But it is possible to describe each thing not only by the account of itself, but also by that of something else. This may be done altogether falsely indeed, but there is

also a way in which it may be done truly; e.g. eight may be described as a double number by the use of the definition of two.

These things, then, are called false in these senses, but (3) a false man is one who is ready at and fond of such accounts, not for any other reason but for their own sake, and one who is good at impressing such accounts on other people, just as we say things are which produce a false appearance. This is why the proof in the *Hippias* that the same man is false and true is misleading. For it assumes that he is false who can deceive (i.e. the man who knows and is wise); and further that he who is willingly bad is better. This is a false result of induction—for a man who limps willingly is better than one who does so unwillingly—by 'limping' Plato means 'mimicking a limp', for if the man were lame willingly, he would presumably be worse in this case as in the corresponding case of moral character.

30

'Accident' means (1) that which attaches to something and can be truly asserted, but neither of necessity nor usually, e.g. if some one in digging a hole for a plant has found treasure. This—the finding of treasure—is for the man who dug the hole an accident; for neither does the one come of necessity from the other or after the other, nor, if a man plants, does he usually find treasure. And a musical man might be pale; but since this does not happen of necessity nor usually, we call it an accident. Therefore since there are attributes and they attach to subjects, and some of them attach to these only in a particular place and at a particular time, whatever attaches to a subject, but not because it was this subject, or the time this time, or the place this place, will be an accident. Therefore, too, there is no definite cause for an accident, but a chance cause, i.e. an indefinite one. Going to Aegina was an accident for a man, if he went not in order to get there, but because he was carried out of his way by a storm or captured by pirates. The accident has happened or exists,-not in virtue of the subject's nature, however, but of something else; for the storm was the cause of his coming to a place for which he was not sailing, and this was Aegina.

'Accident' has also (2) another meaning, i.e. all that attaches to each thing in virtue of itself but is not in its essence, as having its angles equal to two right angles attaches to the triangle. And accidents of this sort may be eternal, but no accident of the other sort is. This is explained elsewhere.

Book VI

1

We are seeking the principles and the causes of the things that are, and obviously of them *qua* being. For, while there is a cause of health and of good condition, and the objects of mathematics have first principles and elements and causes, and in general every science which is ratiocinative or at all involves reasoning deals with causes and principles, more or less precise, all these sciences mark off some particular being—some genus, and inquire into this, but not into being simply nor *qua* being, nor do they offer any discussion of the essence of the things of which they treat; but starting from the essence—some making it plain to the senses, others assuming it as a hypothesis—they then demonstrate, more or less cogently, the essential attributes of the genus with which they deal. It is obvious, therefore, that such an induction yields no demonstration of substance or of the essence, but some other way of exhibiting it. And similarly the sciences omit the question whether the genus with which they deal exists or does not exist, because it belongs to the same kind of thinking to show what it is and that it is.

And since natural science, like other sciences, is in fact about one class of being, i.e. to that sort of substance which has the principle of its movement and rest present in itself, evidently it is neither practical nor productive. For in the case of things made the principle is in the maker—it is either reason or art or some faculty, while in the case of things done it is in the doer—viz. will, for that which is done and that which is willed are the same. Therefore, if all thought is either practical or productive or theoretical, physics must be a theoretical science, but it will theorize about such being as admits of being moved, and about substance-as-defined for the most part only as not separable from matter. Now, we must not fail to notice the mode of being of the essence and of its definition, for, without this, inquiry is but idle. Of things defined, i.e. of 'whats', some are like 'snub', and some like 'concave'. And these differ because 'snub' is bound up with matter (for what is snub is a concave nose), while concavity is independent of perceptible matter. If then all natural things are a analogous to the snub in their nature;—e.g. nose, eye, face, flesh, bone, and, in general, animal; leaf, root, bark, and, in general, plant (for none of these can be defined without reference to movement—they always have matter), it is clear how we must seek and define the 'what' in the case of natural objects, and also that it belongs to the student of nature to study even soul in a certain sense, i.e. so much of it as is not independent of matter.

That physics, then, is a theoretical science, is plain from these considerations. Mathematics also, however, is theoretical; but whether its objects are immovable and separable from matter, is not at present clear; still, it is clear that some mathematical theorems consider them *qua* immovable and *qua* separable from matter. But if there is something which is eternal and immovable and separable, clearly the knowledge of it belongs to a theoretical science,—not, however, to physics (for physics deals with certain movable things) nor to mathematics, but to a science prior to both. For physics deals with things which exist separately but are not immovable, and some parts of mathematics deal with things which are immovable but presumably do not exist separately, but as embodied in matter; while the first science deals with things which both exist separately and are immovable. Now all causes must be eternal, but especially these; for they are the causes that operate on so much of the divine as appears to us. There must, then, be three theoretical philosophies, mathematics, physics, and what we may call theology, since it is obvious that if the divine is present anywhere, it is present in things of this sort. And the highest science must deal with the highest genus. Thus, while the theoretical sciences are more to be desired than the other sciences, this is more to be desired than the other theoretical sciences. For one might raise the question whether first philosophy is universal, or deals with one genus, i.e. some one kind of being; for not even the mathematical sciences are all alike in this respect,—geometry and astronomy deal with a certain particular kind of thing, while universal mathematics applies alike to all. We answer that if there is no substance other than those which are formed by nature, natural science will be the first science; but if there is an immovable substance, the science of this must be prior and must be first philosophy, and universal in this way, because it is first. And it will belong to this to consider being *qua* being—both what it is and the attributes which belong to it *qua* being.

2

But since the unqualified term 'being' has several meanings, of which one was seen' to be the accidental, and another the true ('non-being' being the false), while besides these there are the figures of predication (e.g. the 'what', quality, quantity, place, time, and any similar meanings which 'being' may have), and again besides all these there is that which 'is' potentially or actually:—since 'being' has many meanings, we must say regarding the accidental, that there can be no scientific treatment of it. This is confirmed by the fact that no science— practical, productive, or theoretical—troubles itself about it. For on the one hand he who produces a house does not produce all the attributes that come into being along with the house; for these are innumerable; the house that has been made may quite well be pleasant for some people, hurtful for some, and useful to others, and different—to put it shortly—from all things that are; and the science of building does not aim at producing any of these attributes. And in the same way the geometer does not consider the attributes which attach thus to figures, nor whether 'triangle' is different from 'triangle whose angles are equal to two right angles'.—And this happens naturally enough; for the accidental is practically a mere name. And so Plato was in a sense not wrong in ranking sophistic as dealing with that which is not. For the arguments of the sophists deal, we may say, above all with the accidental; e.g. the question whether 'musical' and 'lettered' are different or the same, and whether 'musical Coriscus' and 'Coriscus' are the same, and whether 'everything which is, but is not eternal, has come to be', with the paradoxical conclusion that if one who was musical has come to be lettered, he must also have been lettered and have come to be musical, and all the other arguments of this sort; the accidental is obviously akin to non-being. And this is clear also from arguments such as the following: things which are in another sense come into being and pass out of being by a process, but things which are accidentally do not. But still we must, as far as we can, say further, regarding the accidental, what its nature is and from what cause it proceeds; for it will perhaps at the same time become clear why there is no science of it.

Since, among things which are, some are always in the same state and are of necessity (not necessity in the sense of compulsion but that which we assert of things because they cannot be otherwise), and some are not of necessity nor always, but for the most part, this is the principle and this the cause of the existence of the accidental; for that which is neither always nor for the most part, we call accidental. For instance, if in the dog-days there is wintry and cold weather, we say this is an accident, but not if there is sultry heat, because the latter is always or for the most part so, but not the former. And it is an accident that a man is pale (for this is neither always nor for the most part so), but it is not by accident that he is an animal. And that the builder produces health is an accident, because it is the nature not of the builder but of the doctor to do this,—but the builder happened to be a doctor. Again, a confectioner, aiming at giving pleasure, may make something wholesome, but not in virtue of the confectioner's art; and therefore we say 'it was an accident', and while there is a sense in which he makes it, in the unqualified sense he does not. For to other things answer faculties productive of them, but to accidental results there corresponds no determinate art nor faculty; for of things which are or come to be by accident, the cause also is accidental. Therefore, since not all things either are or come to be of necessity and always, but, the majority of things are for the most part, the accidental must exist; for instance a pale man is not always nor for the most part musical, but since this sometimes happens, it must be accidental (if not, everything will be of necessity). The matter, therefore, which is capable of being otherwise than as it usually is, must be the cause of the accidental. And we must take as our starting-point the question whether there is nothing that is neither always nor for the most part. Surely this is impossible. There is, then, besides these something which is fortuitous and accidental. But while the usual exists, can nothing be said to be always, or are there eternal things? This must be considered later,' but that there is no science of the accidental is obvious; for all science is either of that which is always or of that which is for the most part. (For how else is one to learn or to teach another? The thing must be determined as occurring either always or for the most part, e.g. that honey-water is useful for a patient in a fever is true for the most part.) But that which is contrary to the usual law science will be unable to state, i.e. when the thing does not happen, e.g. 'on the day of new moon'; for even that which happens on the day of new moon happens then either always or for the most part; but the accidental is contrary to such laws. We have stated, then, what the accidental is, and from what cause it arises, and that there is no science which deals with it.

3

That there are principles and causes which are generable and destructible without ever being in course of being generated or destroyed, is obvious. For otherwise all things will be of necessity, since that which is being generated or destroyed must have a cause which is not accidentally its cause. Will A exist or not? It will if B happens; and if not, not. And B will exist if C happens. And thus if time is constantly subtracted from a limited extent of time, one will obviously come to the present. This man, then, will die by violence, if he goes out; and he will do this if he gets thirsty; and he will get thirsty if something else happens; and thus we shall come to that which is now present, or to some past event. For instance, he will go out if he gets thirsty; and he will get thirsty if he is eating pungent food; and this is either the case or not; so that he will of necessity die, or of necessity not die. And similarly if one jumps over to past events, the same account will hold good; for this—I mean the past condition—is already present in something. Everything, therefore, that will be, will be of necessity; e.g. it is necessary that he who lives shall one day die; for already some condition has come into existence, e.g. the presence of contraries in the same body. But whether he is to die by disease or by violence is not yet determined, but depends on the happening of something else. Clearly then the process goes back to a certain starting-point, but this no longer points to something further. This then will be the starting-point for the fortuitous, and will have nothing else as cause of its coming to be. But to what sort of starting-point and what sort of cause we thus refer the fortuitous—whether to matter or to the purpose or to the motive power, must be carefully considered.

4

Let us dismiss accidental being; for we have sufficiently determined its nature. But since that which is in the sense of being true, or is not in the sense of being false, depends on combination and separation, and truth and falsity together depend on the allocation of a pair of contradictory judgements (for the true judgement affirms where the subject and predicate really are combined, and denies where they are separated, while the false judgement has the opposite of this allocation; it is another question, how it happens that we think things together or apart; by 'together' and 'apart' I mean thinking them so that there is no succession in the thoughts but they become a unity); for falsity and truth are not in things—it is not as if the good were true, and the bad were in itself false—but in thought; while with regard to simple concepts and 'whats' falsity and truth do not exist even in thought:— this being so, we must consider later what has to be discussed with regard to that which is or is not in this sense. But since the combination and the separation are in thought and not in the things, and that which is in this sense is a different sort of 'being' from the things that are in the full sense (for the thought attaches or removes either the subject's 'what' or its having a certain quality or quantity or something else), that which is accidentally and that which is in the sense of being true must be dismissed. For the cause of the former is indeterminate, and that of the latter is some affection of the thought, and both are related to the remaining genus of being, and do not indicate the existence of any separate class of being. Therefore let these be dismissed, and let us consider the causes and the principles of being itself, *qua* being. (It was clear in our discussion of the various meanings of terms, that 'being' has several meanings.)

Book VII

1

There are several senses in which a thing may be said to 'be', as we pointed out previously in our book on the various senses of words;' for in one sense the 'being' meant is 'what a thing is' or a 'this', and in another sense it means a quality or quantity or one of the other things that are predicated as these are. While 'being' has all these senses, obviously that which 'is' primarily is the 'what', which indicates the substance of the thing. For when we say of what quality a thing is, we say that it is good or bad, not that it is three cubits long or that it is a man; but when we say what it is, we do not say 'white' or 'hot' or 'three cubits long', but 'a man' or 'a god'. And all other things are said to be because they are, some of them, quantities of that which is in this primary sense, others qualities of it, others affections of it, and others some other determination of it. And so one might even raise the question whether the words 'to walk', 'to be healthy', 'to sit' imply that each of these things is existent, and similarly in any other case of this sort; for none of them is either self-subsistent or capable of being separated from substance, but rather, if anything, it is that which walks or sits or is healthy that is an existent thing. Now these are seen to be more real because there is something definite which underlies them (i.e. the substance or individual), which is implied in such a predicate; for we never use the word 'good' or 'sitting' without implying this. Clearly then it is in virtue of this category that each of the others also is. Therefore that which is primarily, i.e. not in a qualified sense but without qualification, must be substance.

Now there are several senses in which a thing is said to be first; yet substance is first in every sense—(1) in definition, (2) in order of knowledge, (3) in time. For (3) of the other categories none can exist independently, but only substance. And (1) in definition also this is first; for in the definition of each term the definition of its substance must be present. And (2) we think we know each thing most fully, when we know what it is, e.g. what man is or what fire is, rather than when we know its quality, its quantity, or its place; since we know each of these predicates also, only when we know what the quantity or the quality is.

And indeed the question which was raised of old and is raised now and always, and is always the subject of doubt, viz. what being is, is just the question, what is substance? For it is this that some assert to be one, others more than one, and that some assert to be limited in number, others unlimited. And so we also must consider chiefly and primarily and almost exclusively what that is which is in this sense.

2

Substance is thought to belong most obviously to bodies; and so we say that not only animals and plants and their parts are substances, but also natural bodies such as fire and water and earth and everything of the sort, and all things that are either parts of these or composed of these (either of parts or of the whole bodies), e.g. the physical universe and its parts, stars and moon and sun. But whether these alone are substances, or there are also others, or only some of these, or others as well, or none of these but only some other things, are substances, must be considered. Some think the limits of body, i.e. surface, line, point, and unit, are substances, and more so than body or the solid.

Further, some do not think there is anything substantial besides sensible things, but others think there are eternal substances which are more in number and more real; e.g. Plato posited two kinds of substance—the Forms and objects of mathematics—as well as a third kind, viz. the substance of sensible bodies. And Speusippus made still more kinds of substance, beginning with the One, and assuming principles for each kind of substance, one for numbers, another for spatial magnitudes, and then another for the soul; and by going on in this way he multiplies the kinds of substance. And some say Forms and numbers have the same nature, and the other things come after them— lines and planes—until we come to the substance of the material universe and to sensible bodies.

Regarding these matters, then, we must inquire which of the common statements are right and which are not right, and what substances there are, and whether there are or are not any besides sensible substances, and how sensible substances exist, and whether there is a substance capable of separate existence (and if so why and how) or no such substance, apart from sensible substances; and we must first sketch the nature of substance.

3

The word 'substance' is applied, if not in more senses, still at least to four main objects; for both the essence and the universal and the genus, are thought to be the substance of each thing, and fourthly the *substratum*. Now the *substratum* is that of which everything else is predicated, while it is itself not predicated of anything else. And so we must first determine the nature of this; for that which underlies a thing primarily is thought to be in the truest sense its substance. And in one sense matter is said to be of the nature of *substratum*, in another, shape, and in a third, the compound of these. (By the matter I mean, for instance, the bronze, by the shape the pattern of its form, and by the compound of these the statue, the concrete whole.) Therefore if the form is prior to the matter and more real, it will be prior also to the compound of both, for the same reason.

We have now outlined the nature of substance, showing that it is that which is not predicated of a stratum, but of which all else is predicated. But we must not merely state the matter thus; for this is not enough. The statement itself is obscure, and further, on this view, matter becomes substance. For if this is not substance, it baffles us to say what else is. When all else is stripped off evidently nothing but matter remains. For while the rest are affections, products, and potencies of bodies, length, breadth, and depth are quantities and not substances (for a quantity is not a substance), but the substance is rather that to which these belong primarily. But when length and breadth and depth are taken away we see nothing left unless there is something that is bounded by these; so that to those who consider the question thus matter alone must seem to be substance. By matter I mean that which in itself is neither a particular thing nor of a certain quantity nor assigned to any other of the categories by which being is determined. For there is something of which each of these is predicated, whose being is different from that of each of the predicates (for the predicates other than substance are predicated of substance, while substance is predicated of matter). Therefore the ultimate *substratum* is of itself neither a particular thing nor of a particular quantity nor otherwise positively characterized; nor yet is it the negations of these, for negations also will belong to it only by accident.

If we adopt this point of view, then, it follows that matter is substance. But this is impossible; for both separability and 'thisness' are thought to belong chiefly to substance. And so form and the compound of form and matter would be thought to be substance, rather than matter. The substance compounded of both, i.e. of matter and shape, may be dismissed; for it is posterior and its nature is obvious. And matter also is in a sense manifest. But we must inquire into the third kind of substance; for this is the most perplexing.

Some of the sensible substances are generally admitted to be substances, so that we must look first among these. For it is an advantage to advance to that which is more knowable. For learning proceeds for all in this way-through that which is less knowable by nature to that which is more knowable; and just as in conduct our task is to start from what is good for each and make what is without qualification good good for each, so it is our task to start from what is more knowable to oneself and make what is knowable by nature knowable to oneself. Now what is knowable and primary for particular sets of people is often knowable to a very small extent, and has little or nothing of reality. But yet one must start from that which is barely knowable but knowable to oneself, and try to know what is knowable without qualification, passing, as has been said, by way of those very things which one does know.

4

Since at the start we distinguished the various marks by which we determine substance, and one of these was thought to be the essence, we must investigate this. And first let us make some linguistic remarks about it. The essence of each thing is what it is said to be *propter se*. For being you is not being musical, since you are not by your very nature musical. What, then, you are by your very nature is your essence.

Nor yet is the whole of this the essence of a thing; not that which is *propter se* as white is to a surface, because being a surface is not identical with being white. But again the combination of both—'being a white surface'—is not the essence of surface, because 'surface' itself is added. The formula, therefore, in which the term itself is not present but its meaning is expressed, this is the formula of the essence of each thing. Therefore if to be a white surface is to be a smooth surface, to be white and to be smooth are one and the same.

But since there are also compounds answering to the other categories (for there is a *substratum* for each category, e.g. for quality, quantity, time, place, and motion), we must inquire whether there is a formula of the essence of each of them, i.e. whether to these compounds also there belongs an essence, e.g. 'white man'. Let the compound be denoted by 'cloak'. What is the essence of cloak? But, it may be said, this also is not a *propter se* expression. We reply that there are just two ways in which a predicate may fail to be true of a subject *propter se*, and one of these results from the addition, and the other from the omission, of a determinant. One kind of predicate is not *propter se* because the term that is being defined is combined with another determinant, e.g. if in defining the essence of white one were to state the formula of white man; the other because in the subject another determinant is combined with that which is expressed in the formula, e.g. if 'cloak' meant 'white man', and one were to define cloak as white; white man is white indeed, but its essence is not to be white.

But is being-a-cloak an essence at all? Probably not. For the essence is precisely what something is; but when an attribute is asserted of a subject other than itself, the complex is not precisely what some 'this' is, e.g. white man is not precisely what some 'this' is, since thisness belongs only to substances. Therefore there is an essence only of those things whose formula is a definition. But we have a definition not where we have a word and a formula identical in meaning (for in that case all formulae or sets of words would be definitions; for there will be some name for any set of words whatever, so that even the *Iliad* will be a definition), but where there is a formula of something primary; and primary things are those which do not imply the predication of one element in them of another element. Nothing, then, which is not a species of a genus will have an essence—only species will have it, for these are thought to imply not merely that the subject participates in the attribute and has it as an affection, or has it by accident; but for ever thing else as well, if it has a name, there be a formula of its meaning—viz. that this attribute belongs to this subject; or instead of a simple formula we shall be able to give a more accurate one; but there will be no definition nor essence.

Or has 'definition', like 'what a thing is', several meanings? 'What a thing is' in one sense means substance and the 'this', in another one or other of the predicates, quantity, quality, and the like. For as 'is' belongs to all things, not however in the same sense, but to one sort of thing primarily and to others in a secondary way, so too 'what a thing is' belongs in the simple sense to substance, but in a limited sense to the other categories. For even of a quality we might ask what it is, so that quality also is a 'what a thing is',—not in the simple sense, however, but just as, in the case of that which is not, some say, emphasizing the linguistic form, that that is which is not is—not is simply, but is non-existent; so too with quality.

We must no doubt inquire how we should express ourselves on each point, but certainly not more than how the facts actually stand. And so now also, since it is evident what language we use, essence will belong, just as 'what a thing is' does, primarily and in the simple sense to substance, and in a secondary way to the other categories also,—not essence in the simple sense, but the essence of a quality or of a quantity. For it must be either by an equivocation that we say these are, or by adding to and taking from the meaning of 'are' (in the way in which that which is not known may be said to be known),—the truth being that we use the word neither ambiguously nor in the same sense, but just as we apply the word 'medical' by virtue of a reference to one and the same thing, not meaning one and the same thing, nor yet speaking ambiguously; for a patient and an operation and an instrument are called medical neither by an ambiguity nor with a single meaning, but with reference to a common end. But it does not matter at all in which of the two ways one likes to describe the facts; this is evident, that definition and essence in the primary and simple sense belong to substances. Still they belong to other things as well, only not in the primary sense. For if we suppose this it does not follow that there is a definition of every word which means the same as any formula; it must mean the same as a particular kind of formula; and this condition is satisfied if it is a formula of something which is one, not by continuity like the *Iliad* or the things that are one by being bound together, but in one of the main senses of 'one', which answer to the senses of 'is'; now 'that which is' in one sense denotes a 'this', in another a quantity, in another a quality. And so there can be a formula or definition even of white man, but not in the sense in which there is a definition either of white or of a substance.

5

It is a difficult question, if one denies that a formula with an added determinant is a definition, whether any of the terms that are not simple but coupled will be definable. For we must explain them by adding a determinant. E.g. there is the nose, and concavity, and snubness, which is compounded out of the two by the presence of the one in the other, and it is not by accident that the nose has the attribute either of concavity or of snubness, but in virtue of its nature; nor do they attach to it as whiteness does to Callias, or to man (because Callias, who happens to be a man, is white), but as 'male' attaches to animal and 'equal' to quantity, and as all so-called 'attributes *propter se*' attach to their subjects. And such attributes are those in which is involved either the formula or the name of the subject of the particular attribute, and which cannot be explained without this; e.g. white can be explained apart from man, but not female apart from animal. Therefore there is either no essence and definition of any of these things, or if there is, it is in another sense, as we have said.

But there is also a second difficulty about them. For if snub nose and concave nose are the same thing, snub and concave will be the thing; but if snub and concave are not the same (because it is impossible to speak of snubness apart from the thing of which it is an attribute *propter se*, for snubness is concavity-in-a-nose), either it is impossible to say 'snub nose' or the same thing will have been said twice, concave-nose nose; for snub nose will be concave-nose nose. And so it is absurd that such things should have an essence; if they have, there will be an infinite regress; for in snub-nose nose yet another 'nose' will be involved.

Clearly, then, only substance is definable. For if the other categories also are definable, it must be by addition of a determinant, e.g. the qualitative is defined thus, and so is the odd, for it cannot be defined apart from number; nor can female be defined apart from animal. (When I say 'by addition' I mean the expressions in which it turns out that we are saying the same thing twice, as in these instances.) And if this is true, coupled terms also, like 'odd number', will not be definable (but this escapes our notice because our formulae are not accurate.). But if these also are definable, either it is in some other way or, as we definition and essence must be said to have more than one sense. Therefore in one sense nothing will have a definition and nothing will have an essence, except substances, but in another sense other things will have them. Clearly, then, definition is the formula of the essence, and essence belongs to substances either alone or chiefly and primarily and in the unqualified sense.

6

We must inquire whether each thing and its essence are the same or different. This is of some use for the inquiry concerning substance; for each thing is thought to be not different from its substance, and the essence is said to be the substance of each thing.

Now in the case of accidental unities the two would be generally thought to be different, e.g. white man would be thought to be different from the essence of white man. For if they are the same, the essence of man and that of white man are also the same; for a man and a white man are the same thing, as people say, so that the essence of white man and that of man would be also the same. But perhaps it does not follow that the essence of accidental unities should be the same as that of the simple terms. For the extreme terms are not in the same way identical with the middle term. But perhaps this might be thought to follow, that the extreme terms, the accidents, should turn out to be the same, e.g. the essence of white and that of musical; but this is not actually thought to be the case.

But in the case of so-called self-subsistent things, is a thing necessarily the same as its essence? E.g. if there are some substances which have no other substances nor entities prior to them—substances such as some assert the Ideas to be?—If the essence of good is to be different from good-itself, and the essence of animal from animal-itself, and the essence of being from being-itself, there will, firstly, be other substances and entities and Ideas besides those which are asserted, and, secondly, these others will be prior substances, if essence is substance. And if the posterior substances and the prior are severed from each other, (a) there will be no knowledge of the former, and (b) the latter will have no being. (By 'severed' I mean, if the good-itself has not the essence of good, and the latter has not the property of being good.) For (a) there is knowledge of each thing only when we know its essence. And (b) the case is the same for other things as for the good; so that if the essence of good is not good, neither is the essence of reality real, nor the essence of unity one. And all essences alike exist or none of them does; so that if the essence of reality is not real, neither is any of the others. Again, that to which the essence of good does not belong is not good.—The good, then, must be one with the essence of good, and the beautiful with the essence of beauty, and so with all things which do not depend on something else but are self-subsistent and primary. For it is enough if they are this, even if they are not Forms; or rather, perhaps, even if they are Forms. (At the same time it is clear that if there are Ideas such as some people say there are, it will not be *substratum* that is substance; for these must be substances, but not predicable of a *substratum*; for if they were they would exist only by being participated in.)

Each thing itself, then, and its essence are one and the same in no merely accidental way, as is evident both from the preceding arguments and because to know each thing, at least, is just to know its essence, so that even by the exhibition of instances it becomes clear that both must be one.

(But of an accidental term, e.g. 'the musical' or 'the white', since it has two meanings, it is not true to say that it itself is identical with its essence; for both that to which the accidental quality belongs, and the accidental quality, are white, so that in a sense the accident and its essence are the same, and in a sense they are not; for the essence of white is not the same as the man or the white man, but it is the same as the attribute white.)

The absurdity of the separation would appear also if one were to assign a name to each of the essences; for there would be yet another essence besides the original one, e.g. to the essence of horse there will belong a second essence. Yet why should not some things be their essences from the start, since essence is substance? But indeed not only are a thing and its essence one, but the formula of them is also the same, as is clear even from what has been said; for it is not by accident that the essence of one, and the one, are one. Further, if they are to be different, the process will go on to infinity; for we shall have (1) the essence of one, and (2) the one, so that to terms of the former kind the same argument will be applicable.

Clearly, then, each primary and self-subsistent thing is one and the same as its essence. The sophistical objections to this position, and the question whether Socrates and to be Socrates are the same thing, are obviously answered by the same solution; for there is no difference either in the standpoint from which the question would be asked, or in that from which one could answer it successfully. We have explained, then, in what sense each thing is the same as its essence and in what sense it is not.

7

Of things that come to be, some come to be by nature, some by art, some spontaneously. Now everything that comes to be comes to be by the agency of something and from something and comes to be something. And the something which I say it comes to be may be found in any category; it may come to be either a 'this' or of some size or of some quality or somewhere.

Now natural comings to be are the comings to be of those things which come to be by nature; and that out of which they come to be is what we call matter; and that by which they come to be is something which exists naturally; and the something which they come to be is a man or a plant or one of the things of this kind, which we say are substances if anything is—all things produced either by nature or by art have matter; for each of them is capable both of being and of not being, and this capacity is the matter in each—and, in general, both that from which they are produced is nature, and the type according to which they are produced is nature (for that which is produced, e.g. a plant or an animal, has a nature), and so is that by which they are produced—the so-called 'formal' nature, which is specifically the same (though this is in another individual); for man begets man.

Thus, then, are natural products produced; all other productions are called 'makings'. And all makings proceed either from art or from a faculty or from thought. Some of them happen also spontaneously or by luck just as natural products sometimes do; for there also the same things sometimes are produced without seed as well as from seed. Concerning these cases, then, we must inquire later, but from art proceed the things of which the form is in the soul of the artist. (By form I mean the essence of each thing and its primary substance.) For even contraries have in a sense the same form; for the substance of a privation is the opposite substance, e.g. health is the substance of disease (for disease is the absence of health); and health is the formula in the soul or the knowledge of it. The healthy subject is produced as the result of the following train of thought:—since this is health, if the subject is to be healthy this must first be present, e.g. a uniform state of body, and if this is to be present, there must be heat; and the physician goes on thinking thus until he reduces the matter to a final something which he himself can produce. Then the process from this point onward, i.e. the process towards health, is called a 'making'. Therefore it follows that in a sense health comes from health and house from house, that with matter from that without matter; for the medical art and the building art are the form of health and of the house, and when I speak of substance without matter I mean the essence.

Of the productions or processes one part is called thinking and the other making,—that which proceeds from the starting-point and the form is thinking, and that which proceeds from the final step of the thinking is making. And each of the other, intermediate, things is produced in the same way. I mean, for instance, if the subject is to be healthy his bodily state must be made uniform. What then does being made uniform imply? This or that. And this depends on his being made warm. What does this imply? Something else. And this something is present potentially; and what is present potentially is already in the physician's power.

The active principle then and the starting point for the process of becoming healthy is, if it happens by art, the form in the soul, and if spontaneously, it is that, whatever it is, which starts the making, for the man who makes by art, as in healing the starting-point is perhaps the production of warmth (and this the physician produces by rubbing). Warmth in the body, then, is either a part of health or is followed (either directly or through several intermediate steps) by something similar which is a part of health; and this, viz. that which produces the part of health, is the limiting-point—and so too with a house (the stones are the limiting-point here) and in all other cases. Therefore, as the saying goes, it is impossible that anything should be produced if there were nothing existing before. Obviously then some part of the result will pre-exist of necessity; for the matter is a part; for this is present in the process and it is this that becomes something. But is the matter an element even in the formula? We certainly describe in both ways what brazen circles are; we describe both the matter by saying it is brass, and the form by saying that it is such and such a figure; and figure is the proximate genus in which it is placed. The brazen circle, then, has its matter in its formula.

As for that out of which as matter they are produced, some things are said, when they have been produced, to be not that but 'thaten'; e.g. the statue is not gold but golden. And a healthy man is not said to be that from which he has come. The reason is that though a thing comes both from its privation and from its *substratum*, which we call its matter (e.g. what becomes healthy is both a man and an invalid), it is said to come rather from its privation (e.g. it is from an invalid rather than from a man that a healthy subject is produced). And so the healthy subject is not said to he an invalid, but to be a man, and the man is said to be healthy. But as for the things whose privation is obscure and nameless, e.g. in brass the privation of a particular shape or in bricks and timber the privation of arrangement as a house, the thing is thought to be produced from these materials, as in the former case the healthy man is produced from an invalid. And so, as there also a thing is not said to be that from which it comes, here the statue is not said to be wood but is said by a verbal change to be wooden, not brass but brazen, not gold but golden, and the house is said to be not bricks but bricken (though we should not say without qualification, if we looked at the matter carefully, even that a statue is produced from wood or a house from bricks, because coming to be implies change in that from which a thing comes to be, and not permanence). It is for this reason, then, that we use this way of speaking.

8

Since anything which is produced is produced by something (and this I call the starting-point of the production), and from something (and let this be taken to be not the privation but the matter; for the meaning we attach to this has already been explained), and since something is produced (and this is either a sphere or a circle or whatever else it may chance to be), just as we do not make the *substratum* (the brass), so we do not make the sphere, except incidentally, because the brazen sphere is a sphere and we make the former. For to make a 'this' is to make a 'this' out of the *substratum* in the full sense of the word. (I mean that to make the brass round is not to make the round or the sphere, but something else, i.e. to produce this form in something different from itself. For if we make the form, we must make it out of something else; for this was assumed. E.g. we make a brazen sphere; and that in the sense that out of this, which is brass, we make this other, which is a sphere.) If, then, we also make the *substratum* itself, clearly we shall make it in the same way, and the processes of making will regress to infinity. Obviously then the form also, or whatever we ought to call the shape present in the sensible thing, is not produced, nor is there any production of it, nor is the essence produced; for this is that which is made to be in something else either by art or by nature or by some faculty. But that there is a brazen sphere, this we make. For we make it out of brass and the sphere; we bring the form into this particular matter, and the result is a brazen sphere. But if the essence of sphere in general is to be produced, something must be produced out of something. For the product will always have to be divisible, and one part must be this and another that; I mean the one must be matter and the other form. If, then, a sphere is 'the figure whose circumference is at all points equidistant from the centre', part of this will be the medium in which the thing made will be, and part will be in that medium, and the whole will be the thing produced, which corresponds to the brazen sphere. It is obvious, then, from what has been said, that that which is spoken of as form or substance is not produced, but the concrete thing which gets its name from this is produced, and that in everything which is generated matter is present, and one part of the thing is matter and the other form.

Is there, then, a sphere apart from the individual spheres or a house apart from the bricks? Rather we may say that no 'this' would ever have been coming to be, if this had been so, but that the 'form' means the 'such', and is not a 'this'—a definite thing; but the artist makes, or the father begets, a 'such' out of a 'this'; and when it has been begotten, it is a 'this such'. And the whole 'this', Callias or Socrates, is analogous to 'this brazen sphere', but man and animal to 'brazen sphere' in general. Obviously, then, the cause which consists of the Forms (taken in the sense in which some maintain the existence of the Forms, i.e. if they are something apart from the individuals) is useless, at least with regard to comings-to-be and to substances; and the Forms need not, for this reason at least, be self-subsistent substances. In some cases indeed it is even obvious that the begetter is of the same kind as the begotten (not, however, the same nor one in number, but in form), i.e. in the case of natural products (for man begets man), unless something happens contrary to nature, e.g. the production of a mule by a horse. (And even these cases are similar; for that which would be found to be common to horse and ass, the genus next above them, has not received a name, but it would doubtless be both in fact something like a mule.) Obviously, therefore, it is quite unnecessary to set up a Form as a pattern (for we should have looked for Forms in these cases if in any; for these are substances if anything is so); the begetter is adequate to the making of the product and to the causing of the form in the matter. And when we have the whole, such and such a form in this flesh and in these bones, this is Callias or Socrates; and they are different in virtue of their matter (for that is different), but the same in form; for their form is indivisible.

9

The question might be raised, why some things are produced spontaneously as well as by art, e.g. health, while others are not, e.g. a house. The reason is that in some cases the matter which governs the production in the making and producing of any work of art, and in which a part of the product is present,—some matter is such as to be set in motion by itself and some is not of this nature, and of the former kind some can move itself in the particular way required, while other matter is incapable of this; for many things can be set in motion by themselves but not in some particular way, e.g. that of dancing. The things, then, whose matter is of this sort, e.g. stones, cannot be moved in the particular way required, except by something else, but in another way they can move themselves—and so it is with fire. Therefore some things will not exist apart from some one who has the art of making them, while others will; for motion will be started by these things which have not the art but can themselves be moved by other things which have not the art or with a motion starting from a part of the product.

And it is clear also from what has been said that in a sense every product of art is produced from a thing which shares its name (as natural products are produced), or from a part of itself which shares its name (e.g. the house is produced from a house, *qua* produced by reason; for the art of building is the form of the house), or from something which contains a art of it,—if we exclude things produced by accident; for the cause of the thing's producing the product directly *per se* is a part of the product. The heat in the movement caused heat in the body, and this is either health, or a part of health, or is followed by a part of health or by health itself. And so it is said to cause health, because it causes that to which health attaches as a consequence.

Therefore, as in syllogisms, substance is the starting-point of everything. It is from 'what a thing is' that syllogisms start; and from it also we now find processes of production to start.

Things which are formed by nature are in the same case as these products of art. For the seed is productive in the same way as the things that work by art; for it has the form potentially, and that from which the seed comes has in a sense the same name as the offspring—only in a sense, for we must not expect parent and offspring always to have exactly the same name, as in the production of 'human being' from 'human' for a 'woman' also can be produced by a 'man'—unless the offspring be an imperfect form; which is the reason why the parent of a mule is not a mule. The natural things which (like the artificial objects previously considered) can be produced spontaneously are those whose matter can be moved even by itself in the way in which the seed usually moves it; those things which have not such matter cannot be produced except from the parent animals themselves.

But not only regarding substance does our argument prove that its form does not come to be, but the argument applies to all the primary classes alike, i.e. quantity, quality, and the other categories. For as the brazen sphere comes to be, but not the sphere nor the brass, and so too in the case of brass itself, if it comes to be, it is its concrete unity that comes to be (for the matter and the form must always exist before), so is it both in the case of substance and in that of quality and quantity and the other categories likewise; for the quality does not come to be, but the wood of that quality, and the quantity does not come to be, but the wood or the animal of that size. But we may learn from these instances a peculiarity of substance, that there must exist beforehand in complete reality another substance which produces it, e.g. an animal if an animal is produced; but it is not necessary that a quality or quantity should pre-exist otherwise than potentially.

10

Since a definition is a formula, and every formula has parts, and as the formula is to the thing, so is the part of the formula to the part of the thing, the question is already being asked whether the formula of the parts must be present in the formula of the whole or not. For in some cases the formulae of the parts are seen to be present, and in some not. The formula of the circle does not include that of the segments, but that of the syllable includes that of the letters; yet the circle is divided into segments as the syllable is into letters.—And further if the parts are prior to the whole, and the acute angle is a part of the right angle and the finger a part of the animal, the acute angle will be prior to the right angle and finger to the man. But the latter are thought to be prior; for in formula the parts are explained by reference to them, and in respect also of the power of existing apart from each other the wholes are prior to the parts.

Perhaps we should rather say that 'part' is used in several senses. One of these is 'that which measures another thing in respect of quantity'. But let this sense be set aside; let us inquire about the parts of which substance consists. If then matter is one thing, form another, the compound of these a third, and both the matter and the form and the compound are substance even the matter is in a sense called part of a thing, while in a sense it is not, but only the elements of which the formula of the form consists. E.g. of concavity flesh (for this is the matter in which it is produced) is not a part, but of snubness it is a part;

and the bronze is a part of the concrete statue, but not of the statue when this is spoken of in the sense of the form. (For the form, or the thing as having form, should be said to be the thing, but the material element by itself must never be said to be so.) And so the formula of the circle does not include that of the segments, but the formula of the syllable includes that of the letters; for the letters are parts of the formula of the form, and not matter, but the segments are parts in the sense of matter on which the form supervenes; yet they are nearer the form than the bronze is when roundness is produced in bronze. But in a sense not even every kind of letter will be present in the formula of the syllable, e.g. particular waxen letters or the letters as movements in the air; for in these also we have already something that is part of the syllable only in the sense that it is its perceptible matter. For even if the line when divided passes away into its halves, or the man into bones and muscles and flesh, it does not follow that they are composed of these as parts of their essence, but rather as matter; and these are parts of the concrete thing, but not also of the form, i.e. of that to which the formula refers; wherefore also they are not present in the formulae. In one kind of formula, then, the formula of such parts will be present, but in another it must not be present, where the formula does not refer to the concrete object. For it is for this reason that some things have as their constituent principles parts into which they pass away, while some have not. Those things which are the form and the matter taken together, e.g. the snub, or the bronze circle, pass away into these materials, and the matter is a part of them; but those things which do not involve matter but are without matter, and whose formulae are formulae of the form only, do not pass away,—either not at all or at any rate not in this way. Therefore these materials are principles and parts of the concrete things, while of the form they are neither parts nor principles. And therefore the clay statue is resolved into clay and the ball into bronze and Callias into flesh and bones, and again the circle into its segments; for there is a sense of 'circle' in which involves matter. For 'circle' is used ambiguously, meaning both the circle, unqualified, and the individual circle, because there is no name peculiar to the individuals.

The truth has indeed now been stated, but still let us state it yet more clearly, taking up the question again. The parts of the formula, into which the formula is divided, are prior to it, either all or some of them. The formula of the right angle, however, does not include the formula of the acute, but the formula of the acute includes that of the right angle; for he who defines the acute uses the right angle; for the acute is 'less than a right angle'. The circle and the semicircle also are in a like relation; for the semicircle is defined by the circle; and so is the finger by the whole body, for a finger is 'such and such a part of a man'. Therefore the parts which are of the nature of matter, and into which as its matter a thing is divided, are posterior; but those which are of the nature of parts of the formula, and of the substance according to its formula, are prior, either all or some of them. And since the soul of animals (for this is the substance of a living being) is their substance according to the formula, i.e. the form and the essence of a body of a certain kind (at least we shall define each part, if we define it well, not without reference to its function, and this cannot belong to it without perception), so that the parts of soul are prior, either all or some of them, to the concrete 'animal', and so too with each individual animal; and the body and parts are posterior to this, the essential substance, and it is not the substance but the concrete thing that is divided into these parts as its matter:—this being so, to the concrete thing these are in a sense prior, but in a sense they are not. For they cannot even exist if severed from the whole; for it is not a finger in any and every state that is the finger of a living thing, but a dead finger is a finger only in name. Some parts are neither prior nor posterior to the whole, i.e. those which are dominant and in which the formula, i.e. the essential substance, is immediately present, e.g. perhaps the heart or the brain; for it does not matter in the least which of the two has this quality. But man and horse and terms which are thus applied to individuals, but universally, are not substance but something composed of this particular formula and this particular matter treated as universal; and as regards the individual, Socrates already includes in him ultimate individual matter; and similarly in all other cases. 'A part' may be a part either of the form (i.e. of the essence), or of the compound of the form and the matter, or of the matter itself. But only the parts of the form are parts of the formula, and the formula is of the universal; for 'being a circle' is the same as the circle, and 'being a soul' the same as the soul. But when we come to the concrete thing, e.g. this circle, i.e. one of the individual circles, whether perceptible or intelligible (I mean by intelligible circles the mathematical, and by perceptible circles those of bronze and of wood),—of these there is no definition, but they are known by the aid of intuitive thinking or of perception; and when they pass out of this complete realization it is not clear whether they exist or not; but they are always stated and recognized by means of the universal formula. But matter is unknowable in itself. And some matter is perceptible and some intelligible, perceptible matter being for instance bronze and wood and all matter that is changeable, and intelligible matter being that which is present in perceptible things not *qua* perceptible, i.e. the objects of mathematics.

We have stated, then, how matters stand with regard to whole and part, and their priority and posteriority. But when any one asks whether the right angle and the circle and the animal are prior, or the things into which they are divided and of which they consist, i.e. the parts, we must meet the inquiry by saying that the question cannot be answered simply. For if even bare soul is the animal or the living thing, or the soul of each individual is the individual itself, and 'being a circle' is the circle, and 'being a right angle' and the essence of the right angle is the right angle, then the whole in one sense must be called posterior to the art in one sense, i.e. to the parts included in the formula and to the parts of the individual right angle (for both the material right angle which is made of bronze, and that which is formed by individual lines, are posterior to their parts); while the immaterial right angle is posterior to the parts included in the formula, but prior to those included in the particular instance, and the question must not be answered simply. If, however, the soul is something different and is not identical with the animal, even so some parts must, as we have maintained, be called prior and others must not.

11

Another question is naturally raised, viz. what sort of parts belong to the form and what sort not to the form, but to the concrete thing. Yet if this is not plain it is not possible to define any thing; for definition is of the universal and of the form. If then it is not evident what sort of parts are of the nature of matter and what sort are not, neither will the formula of the thing be evident. In the case of things which are found to occur in specifically different materials, as a circle may exist in bronze or stone or wood, it seems plain that these, the bronze or the stone, are no part of the essence of the circle, since it is found apart from them. Of things which are not seen to exist apart, there is no reason why the same may not be true, just as if all circles that had ever been seen were of bronze; for none the less the bronze would be no part of the form; but it is hard to eliminate it in thought. E.g. the form of man is always found in flesh and bones and parts of this kind; are these then also parts of the form and the formula? No, they are matter; but because man is not found also in other matters we are unable to perform the abstraction.

Since this is thought to be possible, but it is not clear when it is the case, some people already raise the question even in the case of the circle and the triangle, thinking that it is not right to define these by reference to lines and to the continuous, but that all these are to the circle or the triangle as flesh and bones are to man, and bronze or stone to the statue; and they reduce all things to numbers, and they say the formula of 'line' is that of 'two'. And of those who assert the Ideas some make 'two' the line-itself, and others make it the Form of the line; for in some cases they say the Form and that of which it is the Form are the same, e.g. 'two' and the Form of two; but in the case of 'line' they say this is no longer so.

It follows then that there is one Form for many things whose form is evidently different (a conclusion which confronted the Pythagoreans also); and it is possible to make one thing the Form-itself of all, and to hold that the others are not Forms; but thus all things will be one.

We have pointed out, then, that the question of definitions contains some difficulty, and why this is so. And so to reduce all things thus to Forms and to eliminate the matter is useless labour; for some things surely are a particular form in a particular matter, or particular things in a particular state. And the comparison which Socrates the younger used to make in the case of 'animal' is not sound; for it leads away from the truth, and makes one suppose that man can possibly exist without his parts, as the circle can without the bronze. But the case is not similar; for an animal is something perceptible, and it is not possible to define it without reference to movement—nor, therefore, without reference to the parts' being in a certain state. For it is not a hand in any and every state that is a part of man, but only when it can fulfil its work, and therefore only when it is alive; if it is not alive it is not a part.

Regarding the objects of mathematics, why are the formulae of the parts not parts of the formulae of the wholes; e.g. why are not the semicircles included in the formula of the circle? It cannot be said, 'because these parts are perceptible things'; for they are not. But perhaps this makes no difference; for even some things which are not perceptible must have matter; indeed there is some matter in everything which is not an essence and a bare form but a 'this'. The semicircles, then, will not be parts of the universal circle, but will be parts of the individual circles, as has been said before; for while one kind of matter is perceptible, there is another which is intelligible.

It is clear also that the soul is the primary substance and the body is matter, and man or animal is the compound of both taken universally; and 'Socrates' or 'Coriscus', if even the soul of Socrates may be called Socrates, has two meanings (for some mean by such a term the soul, and others mean the concrete thing), but if 'Socrates' or 'Coriscus' means simply this particular soul and this particular body, the individual is analogous to the universal in its composition.

Whether there is, apart from the matter of such substances, another kind of matter, and one should look for some substance other than these, e.g. numbers or something of the sort, must be considered later. For it is for the sake of this that we are trying to determine the nature of perceptible substances as well, since in a sense the inquiry about perceptible substances is the work of physics, i.e. of second philosophy; for the physicist must come to know not only about the matter, but also about the substance expressed in the formula, and even more than about the other. And in the case of definitions, how the elements in the formula are parts of the definition, and why the definition is one formula (for clearly the thing is one, but in virtue of what is the thing one, although it has parts?),—this must be considered later.

What the essence is and in what sense it is independent, has been stated universally in a way which is true of every case, and also why the formula of the essence of some things contains the parts of the thing defined, while that of others does not. And we have stated that in the formula of the substance the material parts will not be present (for they are not even parts of the substance in that sense, but of the concrete substance; but of this there is in a sense a formula, and in a sense there is not; for there is no formula of it with its matter, for this is indefinite, but there is a formula of it with reference to its primary substance—e.g. in the case of man the formula of the soul—, for the substance is the indwelling form, from which and the matter the so-called concrete substance is derived; e.g. concavity is a form of this sort, for from this and the nose arise 'snub nose' and 'snubness'); but in the concrete substance, e.g. a snub nose or Callias, the matter also will be present. And we have stated that the essence and the thing itself are in some cases the same; i.e. in the case of primary substances, e.g. curvature and the essence of curvature if this is primary. (By a 'primary' substance I mean one which does not imply the presence of something in something else, i.e. in something that underlies it which acts as matter.) But things which are of the nature of matter, or of wholes that include matter, are not the same as their essences, nor are accidental unities like that of 'Socrates' and 'musical'; for these are the same only by accident.

12

Now let us treat first of definition, in so far as we have not treated of it in the Analytics; for the problem stated in them is useful for our inquiries concerning substance. I mean this problem:—wherein can consist the unity of that, the formula of which we call a definition, as for instance, in the case of man, 'two-footed animal'; for let this be the formula of man. Why, then, is this one, and not many, viz. 'animal' and 'two-footed'? For in the case of 'man' and 'pale' there is a plurality when one term does not belong to the other, but a unity when it does belong and the subject, man, has a certain attribute; for then a unity is produced and we have 'the pale man'. In the present case, on the other hand, one does not share in the other; the genus is not thought to share in its differentiae (for then the same thing would share in contraries; for the differentiae by which the genus is divided are contrary). And even if the genus does share in them, the same argument applies, since the differentiae present in man are many, e.g. endowed with feet, two-footed, featherless. Why are these one and not many? Not because they are present in one thing; for on this principle a unity can be made out of all the attributes of a thing. But surely all the attributes in the definition must be one; for the definition is a single formula and a formula of substance, so that it must be a formula of some one thing; for substance means a 'one' and a 'this', as we maintain.

We must first inquire about definitions reached by the method of divisions. There is nothing in the definition except the first-named and the differentiae. The other genera are the first genus and along with this the differentiae that are taken with it, e.g. the first may be 'animal', the next 'animal which is two-footed', and again 'animal which is two-footed and featherless', and similarly if the definition includes more terms. And in general it makes no difference whether it includes many or few terms,—nor, therefore, whether it includes few or simply two; and of the two the one is differentia and the other genus; e.g. in 'two-footed animal' 'animal' is genus, and the other is differentia.

If then the genus absolutely does not exist apart from the species-of-a-genus, or if it exists but exists as matter (for the voice is genus and matter, but its differentiae make the species, i.e. the letters, out of it), clearly the definition is the formula which comprises the differentiae.

But it is also necessary that the division be by the differentia of the differentia; e.g. 'endowed with feet' is a differentia of 'animal'; again the differentia of 'animal endowed with feet' must be of it *qua* endowed with feet. Therefore we must not say, if we are to speak rightly, that of that which is endowed with feet one part has feathers and one is featherless (if we do this we do it through incapacity); we must divide it only into cloven-footed and not cloven; for these are differentiae in the foot; cloven-footedness is a form of footedness. And the process wants always to go on so till it reaches the species that contain no differences. And then there will be as many kinds of foot as there are differentiae, and the kinds of animals endowed with feet will be equal in number to the differentiae. If then this is so, clearly the last differentia will be the substance of the thing and its definition, since it is not right to state the same things more than once in our definitions; for it is superfluous. And this does happen; for when we say 'animal endowed with feet and two-footed' we have said nothing other than 'animal having feet, having two feet'; and if we divide this by the proper division, we shall be saying the same thing more than once—as many times as there are differentiae.

If then a differentia of a differentia be taken at each step, one differentia—the last—will be the form and the substance; but if we divide according to accidental qualities, e.g. if we were to divide that which is endowed with feet into the white and the black, there will be as many differentiae as there are cuts. Therefore it is plain that the definition is the formula which contains the differentiae, or, according to the right method, the last of these. This would be evident, if we were to change the order of such definitions, e.g. of that of man, saying 'animal which is two-footed and endowed with feet'; for 'endowed with feet' is superfluous when 'two-footed' has been said. But there is no order in the substance; for how are we to think the one element posterior and the other prior? Regarding the definitions, then, which are reached by the method of divisions, let this suffice as our first attempt at stating their nature.

13

Let us return to the subject of our inquiry, which is substance. As the *substratum* and the essence and the compound of these are called substance, so also is the universal. About two of these we have spoken; both about the essence and about the *substratum*, of which we have said that it underlies in two senses, either being a 'this'—which is the way in which an animal underlies its attributes—or as the matter underlies the complete reality. The universal also is thought by some to be in the fullest sense a cause, and a principle; therefore let us attack the discussion of this point also. For it seems impossible that any universal term should be the name of a substance. For firstly the substance of each thing is that which is peculiar to it, which does not belong to anything else; but the universal is common, since that is called universal which is such as to belong to more than one thing. Of which individual then will this be the substance? Either of all or of none; but it cannot be the substance of all. And if it is to be the substance of one, this one will be the others also; for things whose substance is one and whose essence is one are themselves also one.

Further, substance means that which is not predicable of a subject, but the universal is predicable of some subject always.

But perhaps the universal, while it cannot be substance in the way in which the essence is so, can be present in this; e.g. 'animal' can be present in 'man' and 'horse'. Then clearly it is a formula of the essence. And it makes no difference even if it is not a formula of everything that is in the substance; for none the less the universal will be the substance of something, as 'man' is the substance of the individual man in whom it is present, so that the same result will follow once more; for the universal, e.g. 'animal', will be the substance of that in which it is present as something peculiar to it. And further it is impossible and absurd that the 'this', i.e. the substance, if it consists of parts, should not consist of substances nor of what is a 'this', but of quality; for that which is not substance, i.e. the quality, will then be prior to substance and to the 'this'. Which is impossible; for neither in formula nor in time nor in coming to be can the modifications be prior to the substance; for then they will also be separable from it. Further, Socrates will contain a substance present in a substance, so that this will be the substance of two things. And in general it follows, if man and such things are substance, that none of the elements in their formulae is the substance of anything, nor does it exist apart from the species or in anything else;

I mean, for instance, that no 'animal' exists apart from the particular kinds of animal, nor does any other of the elements present in formulae exist apart.

If, then, we view the matter from these standpoints, it is plain that no universal attribute is a substance, and this is plain also from the fact that no common predicate indicates a 'this', but rather a 'such'. If not, many difficulties follow and especially the 'third man'.

The conclusion is evident also from the following consideration. A substance cannot consist of substances present in it in complete reality; for things that are thus in complete reality two are never in complete reality one, though if they are potentially two, they can be one (e.g. the double line consists of two halves—potentially; for the complete realization of the halves divides them from one another); therefore if the substance is one, it will not consist of substances present in it and present in this way, which Democritus describes rightly; he says one thing cannot be made out of two nor two out of one; for he identifies substances with his indivisible magnitudes. It is clear therefore that the same will hold good of number, if number is a synthesis of units, as is said by some; for two is either not one, or there is no unit present in it in complete reality. But our result involves a difficulty. If no substance can consist of universals because a universal indicates a 'such', not a 'this', and if no substance can be composed of substances existing in complete reality, every substance would be incomposite, so that there would not even be a formula of any substance. But it is thought by all and was stated long ago that it is either only, or primarily, substance that can defined; yet now it seems that not even substance can. There cannot, then, be a definition of anything; or in a sense there can be, and in a sense there cannot. And what we are saying will be plainer from what follows.

14

It is clear also from these very facts what consequence confronts those who say the Ideas are substances capable of separate existence, and at the same time make the Form consist of the genus and the differentiae. For if the Forms exist and 'animal' is present in 'man' and 'horse', it is either one and the same in number, or different. (In formula it is clearly one; for he who states the formula will go through the formula in either case.) If then there is a 'man-in-himself' who is a 'this' and exists apart, the parts also of which he consists, e.g. 'animal' and 'two-footed', must indicate 'thises', and be capable of separate existence, and substances; therefore 'animal', as well as 'man', must be of this sort.

Now (1) if the 'animal' in 'the horse' and in 'man' is one and the same, as you are with yourself, (a) how will the one in things that exist apart be one, and how will this 'animal' escape being divided even from itself?

Further, (b) if it is to share in 'two-footed' and 'many-footed', an impossible conclusion follows; for contrary attributes will belong at the same time to it although it is one and a 'this'. If it is not to share in them, what is the relation implied when one says the animal is two-footed or possessed of feet? But perhaps the two things are 'put together' and are 'in contact', or are 'mixed'. Yet all these expressions are absurd.

But (2) suppose the Form to be different in each species. Then there will be practically an infinite number of things whose substance is animal'; for it is not by accident that 'man' has 'animal' for one of its elements. Further, many things will be 'animal-itself'. For (i) the 'animal' in each species will be the substance of the species; for it is after nothing else that the species is called; if it were, that other would be an element in 'man', i.e. would be the genus of man. And further, (ii) all the elements of which 'man' is composed will be Ideas. None of them, then, will be the Idea of one thing and the substance of another; this is impossible. The 'animal', then, present in each species of animals will be animal-itself. Further, from what is this 'animal' in each species derived, and how will it be derived from animal-itself? Or how can this 'animal', whose essence is simply animality, exist apart from animal-itself?

Further, (3) in the case of sensible things both these consequences and others still more absurd follow. If, then, these consequences are impossible, clearly there are not Forms of sensible things in the sense in which some maintain their existence.

15

Since substance is of two kinds, the concrete thing and the formula (I mean that one kind of substance is the formula taken with the matter, while another kind is the formula in its generality), substances in the former sense are capable of destruction (for they are capable also of generation), but there is no destruction of the formula in the sense that it is ever in course of being destroyed (for there is no generation of it either; the being of house is not generated, but only the being of this house), but without generation and destruction formulae are and are not; for it has been shown that no one begets nor makes these. For this reason, also, there is neither definition of nor demonstration about sensible individual substances, because they have matter whose nature is such that they are capable both of being and of not being; for which reason all the individual instances of them are destructible. If then demonstration is of necessary truths and definition is a scientific process, and if, just as knowledge cannot be sometimes knowledge and sometimes ignorance, but the state which varies thus is opinion, so too demonstration and definition cannot vary thus, but it is opinion that deals with that which can be otherwise than as it is, clearly there can neither be definition of nor demonstration about sensible individuals. For perishing things are obscure to those who have the relevant knowledge, when they have passed from our perception; and though the formulae remain in the soul unchanged, there will no longer be either definition or demonstration. And so when one of the definition-mongers defines any individual, he must recognize that his definition may always be overthrown; for it is not possible to define such things.

Nor is it possible to define any Idea. For the Idea is, as its supporters say, an individual, and can exist apart; and the formula must consist of words; and he who defines must not invent a word (for it would be unknown), but the established words are common to all the members of a class; these then must apply to something besides the thing defined; e.g. if one were defining you, he would say 'an animal which is lean' or 'pale', or something else which will apply also to some one other than you. If any one were to say that perhaps all the attributes taken apart may belong to many subjects, but together they belong only to this one, we must reply first that they belong also to both the elements; e.g. 'two-footed animal' belongs to animal and to the two-footed. (And in the case of eternal entities this is even necessary, since the elements are prior to and parts of the compound; nay more, they can also exist apart, if 'man' can exist apart. For either neither or both can. If, then, neither can, the genus will not exist apart from the various species; but if it does, the differentia will also.) Secondly, we must reply that 'animal' and 'two-footed' are prior in being to 'two-footed animal'; and things which are prior to others are not destroyed when the others are.

Again, if the Ideas consist of Ideas (as they must, since elements are simpler than the compound), it will be further necessary that the elements also of which the Idea consists, e.g. 'animal' and 'two-footed', should be predicated of many subjects. If not, how will they come to be known? For there will then be an Idea which cannot be predicated of more subjects than one. But this is not thought possible— every Idea is thought to be capable of being shared.

As has been said, then, the impossibility of defining individuals escapes notice in the case of eternal things, especially those which are unique, like the sun or the moon. For people err not only by adding attributes whose removal the sun would survive, e.g. 'going round the earth' or 'night-hidden' (for from their view it follows that if it stands still or is visible, it will no longer be the sun; but it is strange if this is so; for 'the sun' means a certain substance); but also by the mention of attributes which can belong to another subject; e.g. if another thing with the stated attributes comes into existence, clearly it will be a sun; the formula therefore is general. But the sun was supposed to be an individual, like Cleon or Socrates. After all, why does not one of the supporters of the Ideas produce a definition of an Idea? It would become clear, if they tried, that what has now been said is true.

16

Evidently even of the things that are thought to be substances, most are only potencies,—both the parts of animals (for none of them exists separately; and when they are separated, then too they exist, all of them, merely as matter) and earth and fire and air; for none of them is a unity, but as it were a mere heap, till they are worked up and some unity is made out of them. One might most readily suppose the parts of living things and the parts of the soul nearly related to them to turn out to be both, i.e. existent in complete reality as well as in potency, because they have sources of movement in something in their joints; for which reason some animals live when divided. Yet all the parts must exist only potentially, when they are one and continuous by nature,—not by force or by growing into one, for such a phenomenon is an abnormality.

Since the term 'unity' is used like the term 'being', and the substance of that which is one is one, and things whose substance is numerically one are numerically one, evidently neither unity nor being can be the substance of things, just as being an element or a principle cannot be the substance, but we ask what, then, the principle is, that we may reduce the thing to something more knowable. Now of these concepts 'being' and 'unity' are more substantial than 'principle' or 'element' or 'cause', but not even the former are substance, since in general nothing that is common is substance; for substance does not belong to anything but to itself and to that which has it, of which it is the substance. Further, that which is one cannot be in many places at the same time, but that which is common is present in many places at the same time; so that clearly no universal exists apart from its individuals.

But those who say the Forms exist, in one respect are right, in giving the Forms separate existence, if they are substances; but in another respect they are not right, because they say the one over many is a Form. The reason for their doing this is that they cannot declare what are the substances of this sort, the imperishable substances which exist apart from the individual and sensible substances. They make them, then, the same in kind as the perishable things (for this kind of substance we know)—'man-himself' and 'horse-itself', adding to the sensible things the word 'itself'. Yet even if we had not seen the stars, none the less, I suppose, would they have been eternal substances apart from those which we knew; so that now also if we do not know what non-sensible substances there are, yet it is doubtless necessary that there should he some.—Clearly, then, no universal term is the name of a substance, and no substance is composed of substances.

17

Let us state what, i.e. what kind of thing, substance should be said to be, taking once more another starting-point; for perhaps from this we shall get a clear view also of that substance which exists apart from sensible substances. Since, then, substance is a principle and a cause, let us pursue it from this starting-point. The 'why' is always sought in this form—'why does one thing attach to some other?' For to inquire why the musical man is a musical man, is either to inquire—as we have said why the man is musical, or it is something else. Now 'why a thing is itself' is a meaningless inquiry (for (to give meaning to the question 'why') the fact or the existence of the thing must already be evident— e.g. that the moon is eclipsed—but the fact that a thing is itself is the single reason and the single cause to be given in answer to all such questions as why the man is man, or the musician musical', unless one were to answer 'because each thing is inseparable from itself, and its being one just meant this'; this, however, is common to all things and is a short and easy way with the question). But we can inquire why man is an animal of such and such a nature. This, then, is plain, that we are not inquiring why he who is a man is a man. We are inquiring, then, why something is predicable of something (that it is predicable must be clear; for if not, the inquiry is an inquiry into nothing). E.g. why does it thunder? This is the same as 'why is sound produced in the clouds?' Thus the inquiry is about the predication of one thing of another. And why are these things, i.e. bricks and stones, a house? Plainly we are seeking the cause. And this is the essence (to speak abstractly), which in some cases is the end, e.g. perhaps in the case of a house or a bed, and in some cases is the first mover; for this also is a cause. But while the efficient cause is sought in the case of genesis and destruction, the final cause is sought in the case of being also.

The object of the inquiry is most easily overlooked where one term is not expressly predicated of another (e.g. when we inquire 'what man is'), because we do not distinguish and do not say definitely that certain elements make up a certain whole. But we must articulate our meaning before we begin to inquire; if not, the inquiry is on the border-line between being a search for something and a search for nothing. Since we must have the existence of the thing as something given, clearly the question is why the matter is some definite thing; e.g. why are these materials a house? Because that which was the essence of a house is present. And why is this individual thing, or this body having this form, a man? Therefore what we seek is the cause, i.e. the form, by reason of which the matter is some definite thing; and this is the substance of the thing. Evidently, then, in the case of simple terms no inquiry nor teaching is possible; our attitude towards such things is other than that of inquiry.

Since that which is compounded out of something so that the whole is one, not like a heap but like a syllable—now the syllable is not its elements, ba is not the same as b and a, nor is flesh fire and earth (for when these are separated the wholes, i.e. the flesh and the syllable, no longer exist, but the elements of the syllable exist, and so do fire and earth); the syllable, then, is something-not only its elements (the vowel and the consonant) but also something else, and the flesh is not only fire and earth or the hot and the cold, but also something else:—if, then, that something must itself be either an element or composed of elements, (1) if it is an element the same argument will again apply; for flesh will consist of this and fire and earth and something still further, so that the process will go on to infinity. But (2) if it is a compound, clearly it will be a compound not of one but of more than one (or else that one will be the thing itself), so that again in this case we can use the same argument as in the case of flesh or of the syllable. But it would seem that this 'other' is something, and not an element, and that it is the cause which makes this thing flesh and that a syllable. And similarly in all other cases. And this is the substance of each thing (for this is the primary cause of its being); and since, while some things are not substances, as many as are substances are formed in accordance with a nature of their own and by a process of nature, their substance would seem to be this kind of 'nature', which is not an element but a principle. An element, on the other hand, is that into which a thing is divided and which is present in it as matter; e.g. a and b are the elements of the syllable.

Book VIII

1

We must reckon up the results arising from what has been said, and compute the sum of them, and put the finishing touch to our inquiry. We have said that the causes, principles, and elements of substances are the object of our search. And some substances are recognized by every one, but some have been advocated by particular schools. Those generally recognized are the natural substances, i.e. fire, earth, water, air, &c., the simple bodies; second plants and their parts, and animals and the parts of animals; and finally the physical universe and its parts; while some particular schools say that Forms and the objects of mathematics are substances. But there are arguments which lead to the conclusion that there are other substances, the essence and the *substratum*. Again, in another way the genus seems more substantial than the various species, and the universal than the particulars. And with the universal and the genus the Ideas are connected; it is in virtue of the same argument that they are thought to be substances. And since the essence is substance, and the definition is a formula of the essence, for this reason we have discussed definition and essential predication. Since the definition is a formula, and a formula has parts, we had to consider also with respect to the notion of 'part', what are parts of the substance and what are not, and whether the parts of the substance are also parts of the definition. Further, too, neither the universal nor the genus is a substance; we must inquire later into the Ideas and the objects of mathematics; for some say these are substances as well as the sensible substances.

But now let us resume the discussion of the generally recognized substances. These are the sensible substances, and sensible substances all have matter. The *substratum* is substance, and this is in one sense the matter (and by matter I mean that which, not being a 'this' actually, is potentially a 'this'), and in another sense the formula or shape (that which being a 'this' can be separately formulated), and thirdly the complex of these two, which alone is generated and destroyed, and is, without qualification, capable of separate existence; for of substances completely expressible in a formula some are separable and some are separable and some are not.

But clearly matter also is substance; for in all the opposite changes that occur there is something which underlies the changes, e.g. in respect of place that which is now here and again elsewhere, and in respect of increase that which is now of one size and again less or greater, and in respect of alteration that which is now healthy and again diseased; and similarly in respect of substance there is something that is now being generated and again being destroyed, and now underlies the process as a 'this' and again underlies it in respect of a privation of positive character. And in this change the others are involved. But in either one or two of the others this is not involved; for it is not necessary if a thing has matter for change of place that it should also have matter for generation and destruction.

The difference between becoming in the full sense and becoming in a qualified sense has been stated in our physical works.

2

Since the substance which exists as underlying and as matter is generally recognized, and this that which exists potentially, it remains for us to say what is the substance, in the sense of actuality, of sensible things. Democritus seems to think there are three kinds of difference between things; the underlying body, the matter, is one and the same, but they differ either in rhythm, i.e. shape, or in turning, i.e. position, or in inter-contact, i.e. order. But evidently there are many differences; for instance, some things are characterized by the mode of composition of their matter, e.g. the things formed by blending, such as honey-water; and others by being bound together, e.g. bundle; and others by being glued together, e.g. a book; and others by being nailed together, e.g. a casket; and others in more than one of these ways; and others by position, e.g. threshold and lintel (for these differ by being placed in a certain way); and others by time, e.g. dinner and breakfast; and others by place, e.g. the winds; and others by the affections proper to sensible things, e.g. hardness and softness, density and rarity, dryness and wetness; and some things by some of these qualities, others by them all, and in general some by excess and some by defect. Clearly, then, the word 'is' has just as many meanings; a thing is a threshold because it lies in such and such a position, and its being means its lying in that position, while being ice means having been solidified in such and such a way. And the being of some things will be defined by all these qualities, because some parts of them are mixed, others are blended, others are bound together, others are solidified, and others use the other differentiae; e.g. the hand or the foot requires such complex definition. We must grasp, then, the kinds of differentiae (for these will be the principles of the being of things), e.g. the things characterized by the more and the less, or by the dense and the rare, and by other such qualities; for all these are forms of excess and defect. And anything that is characterized by shape or by smoothness and roughness is characterized by the straight and the curved. And for other things their being will mean their being mixed, and their not being will mean the opposite.

It is clear, then, from these facts that, since its substance is the cause of each thing's being, we must seek in these differentiae what is the cause of the being of each of these things. Now none of these differentiae is substance, even when coupled with matter, yet it is what is analogous to substance in each case; and as in substances that which is predicated of the matter is the actuality itself, in all other definitions also it is what most resembles full actuality. E.g. if we had to define a threshold, we should say 'wood or stone in such and such a position', and a house we should define as 'bricks and timbers in such and such a position',(or a purpose may exist as well in some cases), and if we had to define ice we should say 'water frozen or solidified in such and such a way', and harmony is 'such and such a blending of high and low'; and similarly in all other cases.

Obviously, then, the actuality or the formula is different when the matter is different; for in some cases it is the composition, in others the mixing, and in others some other of the attributes we have named. And so, of the people who go in for defining, those who define a house as stones, bricks, and timbers are speaking of the potential house, for these are the matter; but those who propose 'a receptacle to shelter chattels and living beings', or something of the sort, speak of the actuality. Those who combine both of these speak of the third kind of substance, which is composed of matter and form (for the formula that gives the differentiae seems to be an account of the form or actuality, while that which gives the components is rather an account of the matter); and the same is true of the kind of definitions which Archytas used to accept; they are accounts of the combined form and matter. E.g. what is still weather? Absence of motion in a large expanse of air; air is the matter, and absence of motion is the actuality and substance. What is a calm? Smoothness of sea; the material *substratum* is the sea, and the actuality or shape is smoothness. It is obvious then, from what has been said, what sensible substance is and how it exists—one kind of it as matter, another as form or actuality, while the third kind is that which is composed of these two.

3

We must not fail to notice that sometimes it is not clear whether a name means the composite substance, or the actuality or form, e.g. whether 'house' is a sign for the composite thing, 'a covering consisting of bricks and stones laid thus and thus', or for the actuality or form, 'a covering', and whether a line is 'twoness in length' or 'twoness', and whether an animal is soul in a body' or 'a soul'; for soul is the substance or actuality of some body. 'Animal' might even be applied to both, not as something definable by one formula, but as related to a single thing. But this question, while important for another purpose, is of no importance for the inquiry into sensible substance; for the essence certainly attaches to the form and the actuality. For 'soul' and 'to be soul' are the same, but 'to be man' and 'man' are not the same, unless even the bare soul is to be called man; and thus on one interpretation the thing is the same as its essence, and on another it is not.

If we examine we find that the syllable does not consist of the letters + juxtaposition, nor is the house bricks + juxtaposition. And this is right; for the juxtaposition or mixing does not consist of those things of which it is the juxtaposition or mixing. And the same is true in all other cases; e.g. if the threshold is characterized by its position, the position is not constituted by the threshold, but rather the latter is constituted by the former. Nor is man animal + biped, but there must be something besides these, if these are matter,—something which is neither an element in the whole nor a compound, but is the substance; but this people eliminate, and state only the matter. If, then, this is the cause of the thing's being, and if the cause of its being is its substance, they will not be stating the substance itself.

(This, then, must either be eternal or it must be destructible without being ever in course of being destroyed, and must have come to be without ever being in course of coming to be. But it has been proved and explained elsewhere that no one makes or begets the form, but it is the individual that is made, i.e. the complex of form and matter that is generated. Whether the substances of destructible things can exist apart, is not yet at all clear; except that obviously this is impossible in some cases—in the case of things which cannot exist apart from the individual instances, e.g. house or utensil. Perhaps, indeed, neither these things themselves, nor any of the other things which are not formed by nature, are substances at all; for one might say that the nature in natural objects is the only substance to be found in destructible things.)

Therefore the difficulty which used to be raised by the school of Antisthenes and other such uneducated people has a certain timeliness. They said that the 'what' cannot be defined (for the definition so called is a 'long rigmarole') but of what sort a thing, e.g. silver, is, they thought it possible actually to explain, not saying what it is, but that it is like tin. Therefore one kind of substance can be defined and formulated, i.e. the composite kind, whether it be perceptible or intelligible; but the primary parts of which this consists cannot be defined, since a definitory formula predicates something of something, and one part of the definition must play the part of matter and the other that of form.

It is also obvious that, if substances are in a sense numbers, they are so in this sense and not, as some say, as numbers of units. For a definition is a sort of number; for (1) it is divisible, and into indivisible parts (for definitory formulae are not infinite), and number also is of this nature. And (2) as, when one of the parts of which a number consists has been taken from or added to the number, it is no longer the same number, but a different one, even if it is the very smallest part that has been taken away or added, so the definition and the essence will no longer remain when anything has been taken away or added. And (3) the number must be something in virtue of which it is one, and this these thinkers cannot state, what makes it one, if it is one (for either it is not one but a sort of heap, or if it is, we ought to say what it is that makes one out of many); and the definition is one, but similarly they cannot say what makes it one. And this is a natural result; for the same reason is applicable, and substance is one in the sense which we have explained, and not, as some say, by being a sort of unit or point; each is a complete reality and a definite nature. And (4) as number does not admit of the more and the less, neither does substance, in the sense of form, but if any substance does, it is only the substance which involves matter. Let this, then, suffice for an account of the generation and destruction of so-called substances—in what sense it is possible and in what sense impossible—and of the reduction of things to number.

4

Regarding material substance we must not forget that even if all things come from the same first cause or have the same things for their first causes, and if the same matter serves as starting-point for their generation, yet there is a matter proper to each, e.g. for phlegm the sweet or the fat, and for bile the bitter, or something else; though perhaps these come from the same original matter. And there come to be several matters for the same thing, when the one matter is matter for the other; e.g. phlegm comes from the fat and from the sweet, if the fat comes from the sweet; and it comes from bile by analysis of the bile into its ultimate matter. For one thing comes from another in two senses, either because it will be found at a later stage, or because it is produced if the other is analysed into its original constituents. When the matter is one, different things may be produced owing to difference in the moving cause; e.g. from wood may be made both a chest and a bed. But some different things must have their matter different; e.g. a saw could not be made of wood, nor is this in the power of the moving cause; for it could not make a saw of wool or of wood. But if, as a matter of fact, the same thing can be made of different material, clearly the art, i.e. the moving principle, is the same; for if both the matter and the moving cause were different, the product would be so too.

When one inquires into the cause of something, one should, since 'causes' are spoken of in several senses, state all the possible causes. what is the material cause of man? Shall we say 'the menstrual fluid'? What is moving cause? Shall we say 'the seed'? The formal cause? His essence. The final cause? His end. But perhaps the latter two are the same.—It is the proximate causes we must state. What is the material cause? We must name not fire or earth, but the matter peculiar to the thing.

Regarding the substances that are natural and generable, if the causes are really these and of this number and we have to learn the causes, we must inquire thus, if we are to inquire rightly. But in the case of natural but eternal substances another account must be given. For perhaps some have no matter, or not matter of this sort but only such as can be moved in respect of place. Nor does matter belong to those things which exist by nature but are not substances; their *substratum* is the substance. E.g. what is the cause of eclipse? What is its matter? There is none; the moon is that which suffers eclipse. What is the moving cause which extinguished the light? The earth. The final cause perhaps does not exist. The formal principle is the definitory formula, but this is obscure if it does not include the cause. E.g. what is eclipse? Deprivation of light. But if we add 'by the earth's coming in between', this is the formula which includes the cause. In the case of sleep it is not clear what it is that proximately has this affection. Shall we say that it is the animal? Yes, but the animal in virtue of what, i.e. what is the proximate subject? The heart or some other part. Next, by what is it produced? Next, what is the affection—that of the proximate subject, not of the whole animal? Shall we say that it is immobility of such and such a kind? Yes, but to what process in the proximate subject is this due?

5

Since some things are and are not, without coming to be and ceasing to be, e.g. points, if they can be said to be, and in general forms (for it is not 'white' comes to be, but the wood comes to be white, if everything that comes to be comes from something and comes to be something), not all contraries can come from one another, but it is in different senses that a pale man comes from a dark man, and pale comes from dark. Nor has everything matter, but only those things which come to be and change into one another. Those things which, without ever being in course of changing, are or are not, have no matter.

There is difficulty in the question how the matter of each thing is related to its contrary states. E.g. if the body is potentially healthy, and disease is contrary to health, is it potentially both healthy and diseased? And is water potentially wine and vinegar? We answer that it is the matter of one in virtue of its positive state and its form, and of the other in virtue of the privation of its positive state and the corruption of it contrary to its nature. It is also hard to say why wine is not said to be the matter of vinegar nor potentially vinegar (though vinegar is produced from it), and why a living man is not said to be potentially dead. In fact they are not, but the corruptions in question are accidental, and it is the matter of the animal that is itself in virtue of its corruption the potency and matter of a corpse, and it is water that is the matter of vinegar. For the corpse comes from the animal, and vinegar from wine, as night from day. And all the things which change thus into one another must go back to their matter; e.g. if from a corpse is produced an animal, the corpse first goes back to its matter, and only then becomes an animal; and vinegar first goes back to water, and only then becomes wine.

6

To return to the difficulty which has been stated with respect both to definitions and to numbers, what is the cause of their unity? In the case of all things which have several parts and in which the totality is not, as it were, a mere heap, but the whole is something beside the parts, there is a cause; for even in bodies contact is the cause of unity in some cases, and in others viscosity or some other such quality. And a definition is a set of words which is one not by being connected together, like the *Iliad*, but by dealing with one object.—What then, is it that makes man one; why is he one and not many, e.g. animal + biped, especially if there are, as some say, an animal-itself and a biped-itself? Why are not those Forms themselves the man, so that men would exist by participation not in man, nor in-one Form, but in two, animal and biped, and in general man would be not one but more than one thing, animal and biped?

Clearly, then, if people proceed thus in their usual manner of definition and speech, they cannot explain and solve the difficulty. But if, as we say, one element is matter and another is form, and one is potentially and the other actually, the question will no longer be thought a difficulty. For this difficulty is the same as would arise if 'round bronze' were the definition of 'cloak'; for this word would be a sign of the definitory formula, so that the question is, what is the cause of the unity of 'round' and 'bronze'? The difficulty disappears, because the one is matter, the other form. What, then, causes this—that which was potentially to be actually—except, in the case of things which are generated, the agent? For there is no other cause of the potential sphere's becoming actually a sphere, but this was the essence of either. Of matter some is intelligible, some perceptible, and in a formula there is always an element of matter as well as one of actuality; e.g. the circle is 'a plane figure'. But of the things which have no matter, either intelligible or perceptible, each is by its nature essentially a kind of unity, as it is essentially a kind of being—individual substance, quality, or quantity (and so neither 'existent' nor 'one' is present in their definitions), and the essence of each of them is by its very nature a kind of unity as it is a kind of being—and so none of these has any reason outside itself, for being one, nor for being a kind of being; for each is by its nature a kind of being and a kind of unity, not as being in the genus 'being' or 'one' nor in the sense that being and unity can exist apart from particulars.

Owing to the difficulty about unity some speak of 'participation', and raise the question, what is the cause of participation and what is it to participate; and others speak of 'communion', as Lycophron says knowledge is a communion of knowing with the soul; and others say life is a 'composition' or 'connexion' of soul with body. Yet the same account applies to all cases; for being healthy, too, will on this showing be either a 'communion' or a 'connexion' or a 'composition' of soul and health, and the fact that the bronze is a triangle will be a 'composition' of bronze and triangle, and the fact that a thing is white will be a 'composition' of surface and whiteness. The reason is that people look for a unifying formula, and a difference, between potency and complete reality. But, as has been said, the proximate matter and the form are one and the same thing, the one potentially, and the other actually. Therefore it is like asking what in general is the cause of unity and of a thing's being one; for each thing is a unity, and the potential and the actual are somehow one. Therefore there is no other cause here unless there is something which caused the movement from potency into actuality. And all things which have no matter are without qualification essentially unities.

Book IX

1

We have treated of that which is primarily and to which all the other categories of being are referred—i.e. of substance. For it is in virtue of the concept of substance that the others also are said to be— quantity and quality and the like; for all will be found to involve the concept of substance, as we said in the first part of our work. And since 'being' is in one way divided into individual thing, quality, and quantity, and is in another way distinguished in respect of potency and complete reality, and of function, let us now add a discussion of potency and complete reality. And first let us explain potency in the strictest sense, which is, however, not the most useful for our present purpose. For potency and actuality extend beyond the cases that involve a reference to motion. But when we have spoken of this first kind, we shall in our discussions of actuality' explain the other kinds of potency as well.

We have pointed out elsewhere that 'potency' and the word 'can' have several senses. Of these we may neglect all the potencies that are so called by an equivocation. For some are called so by analogy, as in geometry we say one thing is or is not a 'power' of another by virtue of the presence or absence of some relation between them. But all potencies that conform to the same type are originative sources of some kind, and are called potencies in reference to one primary kind of potency, which is an originative source of change in another thing or in the thing itself *qua* other. For one kind is a potency of being acted on, i.e. the originative source, in the very thing acted on, of its being passively changed by another thing or by itself *qua* other; and another kind is a state of insusceptibility to change for the worse and to destruction by another thing or by the thing itself *qua* other by virtue of an originative source of change. In all these definitions is implied the formula if potency in the primary sense.—And again these so-called potencies are potencies either of merely acting or being acted on, or of acting or being acted on well, so that even in the formulae of the latter the formulae of the prior kinds of potency are somehow implied.

Obviously, then, in a sense the potency of acting and of being acted on is one (for a thing may be 'capable' either because it can itself be acted on or because something else can be acted on by it), but in a sense the potencies are different. For the one is in the thing acted on; it is because it contains a certain originative source, and because even the matter is an originative source, that the thing acted on is acted on, and one thing by one, another by another; for that which is oily can be burnt, and that which yields in a particular way can be crushed; and similarly in all other cases. But the other potency is in the agent, e.g. heat and the art of building are present, one in that which can produce heat and the other in the man who can build. And so, in so far as a thing is an organic unity, it cannot be acted on by itself; for it is one and not two different things. And 'impotence' and 'impotent' stand for the privation which is contrary to potency of this sort, so that every potency belongs to the same subject and refers to the same process as a corresponding impotence. Privation has several senses; for it means (1) that which has not a certain quality and (2) that which might naturally have it but has not it, either (a) in general or (b) when it might naturally have it, and either (a) in some particular way, e.g. when it has not it completely, or (b) when it has not it at all. And in certain cases if things which naturally have a quality lose it by violence, we say they have suffered privation.

2

Since some such originative sources are present in soulless things, and others in things possessed of soul, and in soul, and in the rational part of the soul, clearly some potencies will, be non-rational and some will be non-rational and some will be accompanied by a rational formula. This is why all arts, i.e. all productive forms of knowledge, are potencies; they are originative sources of change in another thing or in the artist himself considered as other.

And each of those which are accompanied by a rational formula is alike capable of contrary effects, but one non-rational power produces one effect; e.g. the hot is capable only of heating, but the medical art can produce both disease and health. The reason is that science is a rational formula, and the same rational formula explains a thing and its privation, only not in the same way; and in a sense it applies to both, but in a sense it applies rather to the positive fact. Therefore such sciences must deal with contraries, but with one in virtue of their own nature and with the other not in virtue of their nature; for the rational formula applies to one object in virtue of that object's nature, and to the other, in a sense, accidentally. For it is by denial and removal that it exhibits the contrary; for the contrary is the primary privation, and this is the removal of the positive term. Now since contraries do not occur in the same thing, but science is a potency which depends on the possession of a rational formula, and the soul possesses an originative source of movement; therefore, while the wholesome produces only health and the calorific only heat and the frigorific only cold, the scientific man produces both the contrary effects. For the rational formula is one which applies to both, though not in the same way, and it is in a soul which possesses an originative source of movement; so that the soul will start both processes from the same originative source, having linked them up with the same thing. And so the things whose potency is according to a rational formula act contrariwise to the things whose potency is non-rational; for the products of the former are included under one originative source, the rational formula.

It is obvious also that the potency of merely doing a thing or having it done to one is implied in that of doing it or having it done well, but the latter is not always implied in the former: for he who does a thing well must also do it, but he who does it merely need not also do it well.

3

There are some who say, as the Megaric school does, that a thing 'can' act only when it is acting, and when it is not acting it 'cannot' act, e.g. that he who is not building cannot build, but only he who is building, when he is building; and so in all other cases. It is not hard to see the absurdities that attend this view.

For it is clear that on this view a man will not be a builder unless he is building (for to be a builder is to be able to build), and so with the other arts. If, then, it is impossible to have such arts if one has not at some time learnt and acquired them, and it is then impossible not to have them if one has not sometime lost them (either by forgetfulness or by some accident or by time; for it cannot be by the destruction of the object, for that lasts for ever), a man will not have the art when he has ceased to use it, and yet he may immediately build again; how then will he have got the art? And similarly with regard to lifeless things; nothing will be either cold or hot or sweet or perceptible at all if people are not perceiving it; so that the upholders of this view will have to maintain the doctrine of Protagoras. But, indeed, nothing will even have perception if it is not perceiving, i.e. exercising its perception. If, then, that is blind which has not sight though it would naturally have it, when it would naturally have it and when it still exists, the same people will be blind many times in the day—and deaf too.

Again, if that which is deprived of potency is incapable, that which is not happening will be incapable of happening; but he who says of that which is incapable of happening either that it is or that it will be will say what is untrue; for this is what incapacity meant. Therefore these views do away with both movement and becoming. For that which stands will always stand, and that which sits will always sit, since if it is sitting it will not get up; for that which, as we are told, cannot get up will be incapable of getting up. But we cannot say this, so that evidently potency and actuality are different (but these views make potency and actuality the same, and so it is no small thing they are seeking to annihilate), so that it is possible that a thing may be capable of being and not he, and capable of not being and yet he, and similarly with the other kinds of predicate; it may be capable of walking and yet not walk, or capable of not walking and yet walk. And a thing is capable of doing something if there will be nothing impossible in its having the actuality of that of which it is said to have the capacity. I mean, for instance, if a thing is capable of sitting and it is open to it to sit, there will be nothing impossible in its actually sitting; and similarly if it is capable of being moved or moving, or of standing or making to stand, or of being or coming to be, or of not being or not coming to be.

The word 'actuality', which we connect with 'complete reality', has, in the main, been extended from movements to other things; for actuality in the strict sense is thought to be identical with movement. And so people do not assign movement to non-existent things, though they do assign some other predicates. E.g. they say that non-existent things are objects of thought and desire, but not that they are moved; and this because, while *ex hypothesi* they do not actually exist, they would have to exist actually if they were moved. For of non-existent things some exist potentially; but they do not exist, because they do not exist in complete reality.

4

If what we have described is identical with the capable or convertible with it, evidently it cannot be true to say 'this is capable of being but will not be', which would imply that the things incapable of being would on this showing vanish. Suppose, for instance, that a man—one who did not take account of that which is incapable of being—were to say that the diagonal of the square is capable of being measured but will not be measured, because a thing may well be capable of being or coming to be, and yet not be or be about to be. But from the premisses this necessarily follows, that if we actually supposed that which is not, but is capable of being, to be or to have come to be, there will be nothing impossible in this; but the result will be impossible, for the measuring of the diagonal is impossible. For the false and the impossible are not the same; that you are standing now is false, but that you should be standing is not impossible.

At the same time it is clear that if, when A is real, B must be real, then, when A is possible, B also must be possible. For if B need not be possible, there is nothing to prevent its not being possible. Now let A be supposed possible. Then, when A was possible, we agreed that nothing impossible followed if A were supposed to be real; and then B must of course be real. But we supposed B to be impossible. Let it be impossible then. If, then, B is impossible, A also must be so. But the first was supposed impossible; therefore the second also is impossible. If, then, A is possible, B also will be possible, if they were so related that if A, is real, B must be real. If, then, A and B being thus related, B is not possible on this condition, and B will not be related as was supposed. And if when A is possible, B must be possible, then if A is real, B also must be real. For to say that B must be possible, if A is possible, means this, that if A is real both at the time when and in the way in which it was supposed capable of being real, B also must then and in that way be real.

5

As all potencies are either innate, like the senses, or come by practice, like the power of playing the flute, or by learning, like artistic power, those which come by practice or by rational formula we must acquire by previous exercise but this is not necessary with those which are not of this nature and which imply passivity.

Since that which is 'capable' is capable of something and at some time in some way (with all the other qualifications which must be present in the definition), and since some things can produce change according to a rational formula and their potencies involve such a formula, while other things are non-rational and their potencies are non-rational, and the former potencies must be in a living thing, while the latter can be both in the living and in the lifeless; as regards potencies of the latter kind, when the agent and the patient meet in the way appropriate to the potency in question, the one must act and the other be acted on, but with the former kind of potency this is not necessary. For the non-rational potencies are all productive of one effect each, but the rational produce contrary effects, so that if they produced their effects necessarily they would produce contrary effects at the same time; but this is impossible. There must, then, be something else that decides; I mean by this, desire or will. For whichever of two things the animal desires decisively, it will do, when it is present, and meets the passive object, in the way appropriate to the potency in question. Therefore everything which has a rational potency, when it desires that for which it has a potency and in the circumstances in which it has the potency, must do this. And it has the potency in question when the passive object is present and is in a certain state; if not it will not be able to act. (To add the qualification 'if nothing external prevents it' is not further necessary; for it has the potency on the terms on which this is a potency of acting, and it is this not in all circumstances but on certain conditions, among which will be the exclusion of external hindrances; for these are barred by some of the positive qualifications.) And so even if one has a rational wish, or an appetite, to do two things or contrary things at the same time, one will not do them; for it is not on these terms that one has the potency for them, nor is it a potency of doing both at the same time, since one will do the things which it is a potency of doing, on the terms on which one has the potency.

6

Since we have treated of the kind of potency which is related to movement, let us discuss actuality—what, and what kind of thing, actuality is. For in the course of our analysis it will also become clear, with regard to the potential, that we not only ascribe potency to that whose nature it is to move something else, or to be moved by something else, either without qualification or in some particular way, but also use the word in another sense, which is the reason of the inquiry in the course of which we have discussed these previous senses also. Actuality, then, is the existence of a thing not in the way which we express by 'potentially'; we say that potentially, for instance, a statue of Hermes is in the block of wood and the half-line is in the whole, because it might be separated out, and we call even the man who is not studying a man of science, if he is capable of studying; the thing that stands in contrast to each of these exists actually. Our meaning can be seen in the particular cases by induction, and we must not seek a definition of everything but be content to grasp the analogy, that it is as that which is building is to that which is capable of building, and the waking to the sleeping, and that which is seeing to that which has its eyes shut but has sight, and that which has been shaped out of the matter to the matter, and that which has been wrought up to the unwrought. Let actuality be defined by one member of this antithesis, and the potential by the other. But all things are not said in the same sense to exist actually, but only by analogy—as A is in B or to B, C is in D or to D; for some are as movement to potency, and the others as substance to some sort of matter.

But also the infinite and the void and all similar things are said to exist potentially and actually in a different sense from that which applies to many other things, e.g. to that which sees or walks or is seen. For of the latter class these predicates can at some time be also truly asserted without qualification; for the seen is so called sometimes because it is being seen, sometimes because it is capable of being seen. But the infinite does not exist potentially in the sense that it will ever actually have separate existence; it exists potentially only for knowledge. For the fact that the process of dividing never comes to an end ensures that this activity exists potentially, but not that the infinite exists separately.

Since of the actions which have a limit none is an end but all are relative to the end, e.g. the removing of fat, or fat-removal, and the bodily parts themselves when one is making them thin are in movement in this way (i.e. without being already that at which the movement aims), this is not an action or at least not a complete one (for it is not an end); but that movement in which the end is present is an action. E.g. at the same time we are seeing and have seen, are understanding and have understood, are thinking and have thought (while it is not true that at the same time we are learning and have learnt, or are being cured and have been cured). At the same time we are living well and have lived well, and are happy and have been happy. If not, the process would have had sometime to cease, as the process of making thin ceases: but, as things are, it does not cease; we are living and have lived. Of these processes, then, we must call the one set movements, and the other actualities. For every movement is incomplete—making thin, learning, walking, building; these are movements, and incomplete at that. For it is not true that at the same time a thing is walking and has walked, or is building and has built, or is coming to be and has come to be, or is being moved and has been moved, but what is being moved is different from what has been moved, and what is moving from what has moved. But it is the same thing that at the same time has seen and is seeing, seeing, or is thinking and has thought. The latter sort of process, then, I call an actuality, and the former a movement.

7

What, and what kind of thing, the actual is, may be taken as explained by these and similar considerations. But we must distinguish when a thing exists potentially and when it does not; for it is not at any and every time. E.g. is earth potentially a man? No—but rather when it has already become seed, and perhaps not even then. It is just as it is with being healed; not everything can be healed by the medical art or by luck, but there is a certain kind of thing which is capable of it, and only this is potentially healthy. And (1) the delimiting mark of that which as a result of thought comes to exist in complete reality from having existed potentially is that if the agent has willed it it comes to pass if nothing external hinders, while the condition on the other side— viz. in that which is healed—is that nothing in it hinders the result. It is on similar terms that we have what is potentially a house; if nothing in the thing acted on—i.e. in the matter—prevents it from becoming a house, and if there is nothing which must be added or taken away or changed, this is potentially a house; and the same is true of all other things the source of whose becoming is external. And (2) in the cases in which the source of the becoming is in the very thing which comes to be, a thing is potentially all those things which it will be of itself if nothing external hinders it. E.g. the seed is not yet potentially a man; for it must be deposited in something other than itself and undergo a change. But when through its own motive principle it has already got such and such attributes, in this state it is already potentially a man; while in the former state it needs another motive principle, just as earth is not yet potentially a statue (for it must first change in order to become brass.)

It seems that when we call a thing not something else but 'thaten'—e.g. a casket is not 'wood' but 'wooden', and wood is not 'earth' but 'earthen', and again earth will illustrate our point if it is similarly not something else but 'thaten'—that other thing is always potentially (in the full sense of that word) the thing which comes after it in this series. E.g. a casket is not 'earthen' nor 'earth', but 'wooden'; for this is potentially a casket and this is the matter of a casket, wood in general of a casket in general, and this particular wood of this particular casket. And if there is a first thing, which is no longer, in reference to something else, called 'thaten', this is prime matter; e.g. if earth is 'airy' and air is not 'fire' but 'fiery', fire is prime matter, which is not a 'this'. For the subject or *substratum* is differentiated by being a 'this' or not being one; i.e. the *substratum* of modifications is, e.g. a man, i.e. a body and a soul, while the modification is 'musical' or 'pale'. (The subject is called, when music comes to be present in it, not 'music' but 'musical', and the man is not 'paleness' but 'pale', and not 'ambulation' or 'movement' but 'walking' or 'moving',—which is akin to the 'thaten'.) Wherever this is so, then, the ultimate subject is a substance; but when this is not so but the predicate is a form and a 'this', the ultimate subject is matter and material substance. And it is only right that 'thaten' should be used with reference both to the matter and to the accidents; for both are indeterminates.

We have stated, then, when a thing is to be said to exist potentially and when it is not.

8

From our discussion of the various senses of 'prior', it is clear that actuality is prior to potency. And I mean by potency not only that definite kind which is said to be a principle of change in another thing or in the thing itself regarded as other, but in general every principle of movement or of rest. For nature also is in the same genus as potency; for it is a principle of movement—not, however, in something else but in the thing itself *qua* itself. To all such potency, then, actuality is prior both in formula and in substantiality; and in time it is prior in one sense, and in another not.

(1) Clearly it is prior in formula; for that which is in the primary sense potential is potential because it is possible for it to become active; e.g. I mean by 'capable of building' that which can build, and by 'capable of seeing' that which can see, and by 'visible' that which can be seen. And the same account applies to all other cases, so that the formula and the knowledge of the one must precede the knowledge of the other.

(2) In time it is prior in this sense: the actual which is identical in species though not in number with a potentially existing thing is to it. I mean that to this particular man who now exists actually and to the corn and to the seeing subject the matter and the seed and that which is capable of seeing, which are potentially a man and corn and seeing, but not yet actually so, are prior in time; but prior in time to these are other actually existing things, from which they were produced. For from the potentially existing the actually existing is always produced by an actually existing thing, e.g. man from man, musician by musician; there is always a first mover, and the mover already exists actually. We have said in our account of substance that everything that is produced is something produced from something and by something, and that the same in species as it.

This is why it is thought impossible to be a builder if one has built nothing or a harper if one has never played the harp; for he who learns to play the harp learns to play it by playing it, and all other learners do similarly. And thence arose the sophistical quibble, that one who does not possess a science will be doing that which is the object of the science; for he who is learning it does not possess it. But since, of that which is coming to be, some part must have come to be, and, of that which, in general, is changing, some part must have changed (this is shown in the treatise on movement), he who is learning must, it would seem, possess some part of the science. But here too, then, it is clear that actuality is in this sense also, viz. in order of generation and of time, prior to potency.

But (3) it is also prior in substantiality; firstly, (a) because the things that are posterior in becoming are prior in form and in substantiality (e.g. man is prior to boy and human being to seed; for the one already has its form, and the other has not), and because everything that comes to be moves towards a principle, i.e. an end (for that for the sake of which a thing is, is its principle, and the becoming is for the sake of the end), and the actuality is the end, and it is for the sake of this that the potency is acquired. For animals do not see in order that they may have sight, but they have sight that they may see. And similarly men have the art of building that they may build, and theoretical science that they may theorize; but they do not theorize that they may have theoretical science, except those who are learning by practice; and these do not theorize except in a limited sense, or because they have no need to theorize. Further, matter exists in a potential state, just because it may come to its form; and when it exists actually, then it is in its form. And the same holds good in all cases, even those in which the end is a movement. And so, as teachers think they have achieved their end when they have exhibited the pupil at work, nature does likewise. For if this is not the case, we shall have Pauson's Hermes over again, since it will be hard to say about the knowledge, as about the figure in the picture, whether it is within or without. For the action is the end, and the actuality is the action. And so even the word 'actuality' is derived from 'action', and points to the complete reality.

And while in some cases the exercise is the ultimate thing (e.g. in sight the ultimate thing is seeing, and no other product besides this results from sight), but from some things a product follows (e.g. from the art of building there results a house as well as the act of building), yet none the less the act is in the former case the end and in the latter more of an end than the potency is. For the act of building is realized in the thing that is being built, and comes to be, and is, at the same time as the house.

Where, then, the result is something apart from the exercise, the actuality is in the thing that is being made, e.g. the act of building is in the thing that is being built and that of weaving in the thing that is being woven, and similarly in all other cases, and in general the movement is in the thing that is being moved; but where there is no product apart from the actuality, the actuality is present in the agents, e.g. the act of seeing is in the seeing subject and that of theorizing in the theorizing subject and the life is in the soul (and therefore well-being also; for it is a certain kind of life).

Obviously, therefore, the substance or form is actuality. According to this argument, then, it is obvious that actuality is prior in substantial being to potency; and as we have said, one actuality always precedes another in time right back to the actuality of the eternal prime mover.

But (b) actuality is prior in a stricter sense also; for eternal things are prior in substance to perishable things, and no eternal thing exists potentially. The reason is this. Every potency is at one and the same time a potency of the opposite; for, while that which is not capable of being present in a subject cannot be present, everything that is capable of being may possibly not be actual. That, then, which is capable of being may either be or not be; the same thing, then, is capable both of being and of not being. And that which is capable of not being may possibly not be; and that which may possibly not be is perishable, either in the full sense, or in the precise sense in which it is said that it possibly may not be, i.e. in respect either of place or of quantity or quality; 'in the full sense' means 'in respect of substance'. Nothing, then, which is in the full sense imperishable is in the full sense potentially existent (though there is nothing to prevent its being so in some respect, e.g. potentially of a certain quality or in a certain place); all imperishable things, then, exist actually. Nor can anything which is of necessity exist potentially; yet these things are primary; for if these did not exist, nothing would exist. Nor does eternal movement, if there be such, exist potentially; and, if there is an eternal mobile, it is not in motion in virtue of a potentiality, except in respect of 'whence' and 'whither' (there is nothing to prevent its having matter which makes it capable of movement in various directions). And so the sun and the stars and the whole heaven are ever active, and there is no fear that they may sometime stand still, as the natural philosophers fear they may. Nor do they tire in this activity; for movement is not for them, as it is for perishable things, connected with the potentiality for opposites, so that the continuity of the movement should be laborious; for it is that kind of substance which is matter and potency, not actuality, that causes this.

Imperishable things are imitated by those that are involved in change, e.g. earth and fire. For these also are ever active; for they have their movement of themselves and in themselves. But the other potencies, according to our previous discussion, are all potencies for opposites; for that which can move another in this way can also move it not in this way, i.e. if it acts according to a rational formula; and the same non-rational potencies will produce opposite results by their presence or absence.

If, then, there are any entities or substances such as the dialecticians say the Ideas are, there must be something much more scientific than science-itself and something more mobile than movement-itself; for these will be more of the nature of actualities, while science-itself and movement-itself are potencies for these.

Obviously, then, actuality is prior both to potency and to every principle of change.

9

That the actuality is also better and more valuable than the good potency is evident from the following argument. Everything of which we say that it can do something, is alike capable of contraries, e.g. that of which we say that it can be well is the same as that which can be ill, and has both potencies at once; for the same potency is a potency of health and illness, of rest and motion, of building and throwing down, of being built and being thrown down. The capacity for contraries, then, is present at the same time; but contraries cannot be present at the same time, and the actualities also cannot be present at the same time, e.g. health and illness. Therefore, while the good must be one of them, the capacity is both alike, or neither; the actuality, then, is better. Also in the case of bad things the end or actuality must be worse than the potency; for that which 'can' is both contraries alike. Clearly, then, the bad does not exist apart from bad things; for the bad is in its nature posterior to the potency. And therefore we may also say that in the things which are from the beginning, i.e. in eternal things, there is nothing bad, nothing defective, nothing perverted (for perversion is something bad).

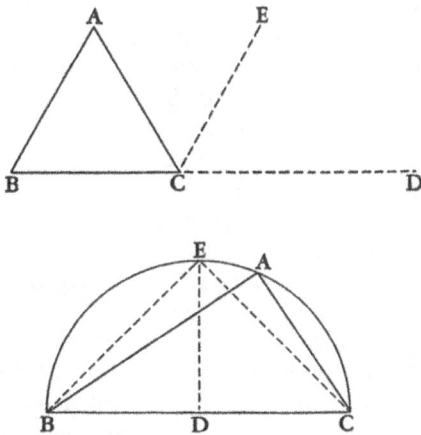

It is an activity also that geometrical constructions are discovered; for we find them by dividing. If the figures had been already divided, the constructions would have been obvious; but as it is they are present only potentially. Why are the angles of the triangle equal to two right angles? Because the angles about one point are equal to two right angles. If, then, the line parallel to the side had been already drawn upwards, the reason would have been evident to any one as soon as he saw the figure. Why is the angle in a semicircle in all cases a right angle? If three lines are equal—the two which form the base, and the perpendicular from the centre—the conclusion is evident at a glance to one who knows the former proposition. Obviously, therefore, the potentially existing constructions are discovered by being brought to actuality; the reason is that the geometer's thinking is an actuality; so that the potency proceeds from an actuality; and therefore it is by making constructions that people come to know them (though the single actuality is later in generation than the corresponding potency). (See diagram.)

10

The terms 'being' and 'non-being' are employed firstly with reference to the categories, and secondly with reference to the potency or actuality of these or their non-potency or non-actuality, and thirdly in the sense of true and false. This depends, on the side of the objects, on their being combined or separated, so that he who thinks the separated to be separated and the combined to be combined has the truth, while he whose thought is in a state contrary to that of the objects is in error. This being so, when is what is called truth or falsity present, and when is it not? We must consider what we mean by these terms. It is not because we think truly that you are pale, that you are pale, but because you are pale we who say this have the truth. If, then, some things are always combined and cannot be separated, and others are always separated and cannot be combined, while others are capable either of combination or of separation, 'being' is being combined and one, and 'not being' is being not combined but more than one. Regarding contingent facts, then, the same opinion or the same statement comes to be false and true, and it is possible for it to be at one time correct and at another erroneous; but regarding things that cannot be otherwise opinions are not at one time true and at another false, but the same opinions are always true or always false.

But with regard to incomposites, what is being or not being, and truth or falsity? A thing of this sort is not composite, so as to 'be' when it is compounded, and not to 'be' if it is separated, like 'that the wood is white' or 'that the diagonal is incommensurable'; nor will truth and falsity be still present in the same way as in the previous cases. In fact, as truth is not the same in these cases, so also being is not the same; but (a) truth or falsity is as follows—contact and assertion are truth (assertion not being the same as affirmation), and ignorance is non-contact. For it is not possible to be in error regarding the question what a thing is, save in an accidental sense; and the same holds good regarding non-composite substances (for it is not possible to be in error about them). And they all exist actually, not potentially; for otherwise they would have come to be and ceased to be; but, as it is, being itself does not come to be (nor cease to be); for if it had done so it would have had to come out of something. About the things, then, which are essences and actualities, it is not possible to be in error, but only to know them or not to know them. But we do inquire what they are, viz. whether they are of such and such a nature or not.

(b) As regards the 'being' that answers to truth and the 'non-being' that answers to falsity, in one case there is truth if the subject and the attribute are really combined, and falsity if they are not combined; in the other case, if the object is existent it exists in a particular way, and if it does not exist in this way does not exist at all. And truth means knowing these objects, and falsity does not exist, nor error, but only ignorance—and not an ignorance which is like blindness; for blindness is akin to a total absence of the faculty of thinking.

It is evident also that about unchangeable things there can be no error in respect of time, if we assume them to be unchangeable. E.g. if we suppose that the triangle does not change, we shall not suppose that at one time its angles are equal to two right angles while at another time they are not (for that would imply change). It is possible, however, to suppose that one member of such a class has a certain attribute and another has not; e.g. while we may suppose that no even number is prime, we may suppose that some are and some are not. But regarding a numerically single number not even this form of error is possible; for we cannot in this case suppose that one instance has an attribute and another has not, but whether our judgement be true or false, it is implied that the fact is eternal.

Book X

1

We have said previously, in our distinction of the various meanings of words, that 'one' has several meanings; the things that are directly and of their own nature and not accidentally called one may be summarized under four heads, though the word is used in more senses. (1) There is the continuous, either in general, or especially that which is continuous by nature and not by contact nor by being together; and of these, that has more unity and is prior, whose movement is more indivisible and simpler. (2) That which is a whole and has a certain shape and form is one in a still higher degree; and especially if a thing is of this sort by nature, and not by force like the things which are unified by glue or nails or by being tied together, i.e. if it has in itself the cause of its continuity. A thing is of this sort because its movement is one and indivisible in place and time; so that evidently if a thing has by nature a principle of movement that is of the first kind (i.e. local movement) and the first in that kind (i.e. circular movement), this is in the primary sense one extended thing. Some things, then, are one in this way, *qua* continuous or whole, and the other things that are one are those whose definition is one. Of this sort are the things the thought of which is one, i.e. those the thought of which is indivisible; and it is indivisible if the thing is indivisible in kind or in number. (3) In number, then, the individual is indivisible, and (4) in kind, that which in intelligibility and in knowledge is indivisible, so that that which causes substances to be one must be one in the primary sense. 'One', then, has all these meanings—the naturally continuous and the whole, and the individual and the universal. And all these are one because in some cases the movement, in others the thought or the definition is indivisible.

But it must be observed that the questions, what sort of things are said to be one, and what it is to be one and what is the definition of it, should not be assumed to be the same. 'One' has all these meanings, and each of the things to which one of these kinds of unity belongs will be one; but 'to be one' will sometimes mean being one of these things, and sometimes being something else which is even nearer to the meaning of the word 'one' while these other things approximate to its application. This is also true of 'element' or 'cause', if one had both to specify the things of which it is predicable and to render the definition of the word. For in a sense fire is an element (and doubtless also 'the indefinite' or something else of the sort is by its own nature the element), but in a sense it is not; for it is not the same thing to be fire and to be an element, but while as a particular thing with a nature of its own fire is an element, the name 'element' means that it has this attribute, that there is something which is made of it as a primary constituent. And so with 'cause' and 'one' and all such terms. For this reason, too, 'to be one' means 'to be indivisible, being essentially one means a "this" and capable of being isolated either in place, or in form or thought'; or perhaps 'to be whole and indivisible'; but it means especially 'to be the first measure of a kind', and most strictly of quantity; for it is from this that it has been extended to the other categories. For measure is that by which quantity is known; and quantity *qua* quantity is known either by a 'one' or by a number, and all number is known by a 'one'. Therefore all quantity *qua* quantity is known by the one, and that by which quantities are primarily known is the one itself; and so the one is the starting-point of number *qua* number. And hence in the other classes too 'measure' means that by which each is first known, and the measure of each is a unit—in length, in breadth, in depth, in weight, in speed. (The words 'weight' and 'speed' are common to both contraries; for each of them has two meanings—'weight' means both that which has any amount of gravity and that which has an excess of gravity, and 'speed' both that which has any amount of movement and that which has an excess of movement; for even the slow has a certain speed and the comparatively light a certain weight.)

In all these, then, the measure and starting-point is something one and indivisible, since even in lines we treat as indivisible the line a foot long. For everywhere we seek as the measure something one and indivisible; and this is that which is simple either in quality or in quantity. Now where it is thought impossible to take away or to add, there the measure is exact (hence that of number is most exact; for we posit the unit as indivisible in every respect); but in all other cases we imitate this sort of measure. For in the case of a furlong or a talent or of anything comparatively large any addition or subtraction might more easily escape our notice than in the case of something smaller; so that the first thing from which, as far as our perception goes, nothing can be subtracted, all men make the measure, whether of liquids or of solids, whether of weight or of size; and they think they know the quantity when they know it by means of this measure. And indeed they know movement too by the simple movement and the quickest; for this occupies least time. And so in astronomy a 'one' of this sort is the starting-point and measure (for they assume the movement of the heavens to be uniform and the quickest, and judge the others by reference to it), and in music the quarter-tone (because it is the least interval), and in speech the letter. And all these are ones in this sense—not that 'one' is something predicable in the same sense of all of these, but in the sense we have mentioned.

But the measure is not always one in number—sometimes there are several; e.g. the quarter-tones (not to the ear, but as determined by the ratios) are two, and the articulate sounds by which we measure are more than one, and the diagonal of the square and its side are measured by two quantities, and all spatial magnitudes reveal similar varieties of unit. Thus, then, the one is the measure of all things, because we come to know the elements in the substance by dividing the things either in respect of quantity or in respect of kind. And the one is indivisible just because the first of each class of things is indivisible. But it is not in the same way that every 'one' is indivisible e.g. a foot and a unit; the latter is indivisible in every respect, while the former must be placed among things which are undivided to perception, as has been said already—only to perception, for doubtless every continuous thing is divisible.

The measure is always homogeneous with the thing measured; the measure of spatial magnitudes is a spatial magnitude, and in particular that of length is a length, that of breadth a breadth, that of articulate sound an articulate sound, that of weight a weight, that of units a unit. (For we must state the matter so, and not say that the measure of numbers is a number; we ought indeed to say this if we were to use the corresponding form of words, but the claim does not really correspond—it is as if one claimed that the measure of units is units and not a unit; number is a plurality of units.)

Knowledge, also, and perception, we call the measure of things for the same reason, because we come to know something by them—while as a matter of fact they are measured rather than measure other things. But it is with us as if some one else measured us and we came to know how big we are by seeing that he applied the cubit-measure to such and such a fraction of us. But Protagoras says 'man is the measure of all things', as if he had said 'the man who knows' or 'the man who perceives'; and these because they have respectively knowledge and perception, which we say are the measures of objects. Such thinkers are saying nothing, then, while they appear to be saying something remarkable.

Evidently, then, unity in the strictest sense, if we define it according to the meaning of the word, is a measure, and most properly of quantity, and secondly of quality. And some things will be one if they are indivisible in quantity, and others if they are indivisible in quality; and so that which is one is indivisible, either absolutely or *qua* one.

2

With regard to the substance and nature of the one we must ask in which of two ways it exists. This is the very question that we reviewed in our discussion of problems, viz. what the one is and how we must conceive of it, whether we must take the one itself as being a substance (as both the Pythagoreans say in earlier and Plato in later times), or there is, rather, an underlying nature and the one should be described more intelligibly and more in the manner of the physical philosophers, of whom one says the one is love, another says it is air, and another the indefinite.

If, then, no universal can be a substance, as has been said our discussion of substance and being, and if being itself cannot be a substance in the sense of a one apart from the many (for it is common to the many), but is only a predicate, clearly unity also cannot be a substance; for being and unity are the most universal of all predicates. Therefore, on the one hand, genera are not certain entities and substances separable from other things; and on the other hand the one cannot be a genus, for the same reasons for which being and substance cannot be genera.

Further, the position must be similar in all the kinds of unity. Now 'unity' has just as many meanings as 'being'; so that since in the sphere of qualities the one is something definite—some particular kind of thing—and similarly in the sphere of quantities, clearly we must in every category ask what the one is, as we must ask what the existent is, since it is not enough to say that its nature is just to be one or existent. But in colours the one is a colour, e.g. white, and then the other colours are observed to be produced out of this and black, and black is the privation of white, as darkness of light. Therefore if all existent things were colours, existent things would have been a number, indeed, but of what? Clearly of colours; and the 'one' would have been a particular 'one', i.e. white. And similarly if all existing things were tunes, they would have been a number, but a number of quarter-tones, and their essence would not have been number; and the one would have been something whose substance was not to be one but to be the quarter-tone. And similarly if all existent things had been articulate sounds, they would have been a number of letters, and the one would have been a vowel. And if all existent things were rectilinear figures, they would have been a number of figures, and the one would have been the triangle. And the same argument applies to all other classes. Since, therefore, while there are numbers and a one both in affections and in qualities and in quantities and in movement, in all cases the number is a number of particular things and the one is one something, and its substance is not just to be one, the same must be true of substances also; for it is true of all cases alike.

That the one, then, in every class is a definite thing, and in no case is its nature just this, unity, is evident; but as in colours the one-itself which we must seek is one colour, so too in substance the one-itself is one substance. That in a sense unity means the same as being is clear from the facts that its meanings correspond to the categories one to one, and it is not comprised within any category (e.g. it is comprised neither in 'what a thing is' nor in quality, but is related to them just as being is); that in 'one man' nothing more is predicated than in 'man' (just as being is nothing apart from substance or quality or quantity); and that to be one is just to be a particular thing.

3

The one and the many are opposed in several ways, of which one is the opposition of the one and plurality as indivisible and divisible; for that which is either divided or divisible is called a plurality, and that which is indivisible or not divided is called one. Now since opposition is of four kinds, and one of these two terms is privative in meaning, they must be contraries, and neither contradictory nor correlative in meaning. And the one derives its name and its explanation from its contrary, the indivisible from the divisible, because plurality and the divisible is more perceptible than the indivisible, so that in definition plurality is prior to the indivisible, because of the conditions of perception.

To the one belong, as we indicated graphically in our distinction of the contraries, the same and the like and the equal, and to plurality belong the other and the unlike and the unequal. 'The same' has several meanings; (1) we sometimes mean 'the same numerically'; again, (2) we call a thing the same if it is one both in definition and in number, e.g. you are one with yourself both in form and in matter; and again, (3) if the definition of its primary essence is one; e.g. equal straight lines are the same, and so are equal and equal-angled quadrilaterals; there are many such, but in these equality constitutes unity.

Things are like if, not being absolutely the same, nor without difference in respect of their concrete substance, they are the same in form; e.g. the larger square is like the smaller, and unequal straight lines are like; they are like, but not absolutely the same. Other things are like, if, having the same form, and being things in which difference of degree is possible, they have no difference of degree. Other things, if they have a quality that is in form one and same—e.g. whiteness—in a greater or less degree, are called like because their form is one. Other things are called like if the qualities they have in common are more numerous than those in which they differ—either the qualities in general or the prominent qualities; e.g. tin is like silver, *qua* white, and gold is like fire, *qua* yellow and red.

Evidently, then, 'other' and 'unlike' also have several meanings. And the other in one sense is the opposite of the same (so that everything is either the same as or other than everything else). In another sense things are other unless both their matter and their definition are one (so that you are other than your neighbour). The other in the third sense is exemplified in the objects of mathematics. 'Other or the same' can therefore be predicated of everything with regard to everything else—but only if the things are one and existent, for 'other' is not the contradictory of 'the same'; which is why it is not predicated of non-existent things (while 'not the same' is so predicated). It is predicated of all existing things; for everything that is existent and one is by its very nature either one or not one with anything else.

The other, then, and the same are thus opposed. But difference is not the same as otherness. For the other and that which it is other than need not be other in some definite respect (for everything that is existent is either other or the same), but that which is different is different from some particular thing in some particular respect, so that there must be something identical whereby they differ. And this identical thing is genus or species; for everything that differs differs either in genus or in species, in genus if the things have not their matter in common and are not generated out of each other (i.e. if they belong to different figures of predication), and in species if they have the same genus ('genus' meaning that identical thing which is essentially predicated of both the different things).

Contraries are different, and contrariety is a kind of difference. That we are right in this supposition is shown by induction. For all of these too are seen to be different; they are not merely other, but some are other in genus, and others are in the same line of predication, and therefore in the same genus, and the same in genus. We have distinguished elsewhere what sort of things are the same or other in genus.

4

Since things which differ may differ from one another more or less, there is also a greatest difference, and this I call contrariety. That contrariety is the greatest difference is made clear by induction. For things which differ in genus have no way to one another, but are too far distant and are not comparable; and for things that differ in species the extremes from which generation takes place are the contraries, and the distance between extremes—and therefore that between the contraries—is the greatest.

But surely that which is greatest in each class is complete. For that is greatest which cannot be exceeded, and that is complete beyond which nothing can be found. For the complete difference marks the end of a series (just as the other things which are called complete are so called because they have attained an end), and beyond the end there is nothing; for in everything it is the extreme and includes all else, and therefore there is nothing beyond the end, and the complete needs nothing further. From this, then, it is clear that contrariety is complete difference; and as contraries are so called in several senses, their modes of completeness will answer to the various modes of contrariety which attach to the contraries.

This being so, it is clear that one thing have more than one contrary (for neither can there be anything more extreme than the extreme, nor can there be more than two extremes for the one interval), and, to put the matter generally, this is clear if contrariety is a difference, and if difference, and therefore also the complete difference, must be between two things.

And the other commonly accepted definitions of contraries are also necessarily true. For not only is (1) the complete difference the greatest difference (for we can get no difference beyond it of things differing either in genus or in species; for it has been shown that there is no 'difference' between anything and the things outside its genus, and among the things which differ in species the complete difference is the greatest); but also (2) the things in the same genus which differ most are contrary (for the complete difference is the greatest difference between species of the same genus); and (3) the things in the same receptive material which differ most are contrary (for the matter is the same for contraries); and (4) of the things which fall under the same faculty the most different are contrary (for one science deals with one class of things, and in these the complete difference is the greatest).

The primary contrariety is that between positive state and privation—not every privation, however (for 'privation' has several meanings), but that which is complete. And the other contraries must be called so with reference to these, some because they possess these, others because they produce or tend to produce them, others because they are acquisitions or losses of these or of other contraries. Now if the kinds of opposition are contradiction and privation and contrariety and relation, and of these the first is contradiction, and contradiction admits of no intermediate, while contraries admit of one, clearly contradiction and contrariety are not the same. But privation is a kind of contradiction; for what suffers privation, either in general or in some determinate way, either that which is quite incapable of having some attribute or that which, being of such a nature as to have it, has it not; here we have already a variety of meanings, which have been distinguished elsewhere. Privation, therefore, is a contradiction or incapacity which is determinate or taken along with the receptive material. This is the reason why, while contradiction does not admit of an intermediate, privation sometimes does; for everything is equal or not equal, but not everything is equal or unequal, or if it is, it is only within the sphere of that which is receptive of equality. If, then, the comings-to-be which happen to the matter start from the contraries, and proceed either from the form and the possession of the form or from a privation of the form or shape, clearly all contrariety must be privation, but presumably not all privation is contrariety (the reason being that that has suffered privation may have suffered it in several ways); for it is only the extremes from which changes proceed that are contraries.

And this is obvious also by induction. For every contrariety involves, as one of its terms, a privation, but not all cases are alike; inequality is the privation of equality and unlikeness of likeness, and on the other hand vice is the privation of virtue. But the cases differ in a way already described; in one case we mean simply that the thing has suffered privation, in another case that it has done so either at a certain time or in a certain part (e.g. at a certain age or in the dominant part), or throughout. This is why in some cases there is a mean (there are men who are neither good nor bad), and in others there is not (a number must be either odd or even). Further, some contraries have their subject defined, others have not. Therefore it is evident that one of the contraries is always privative; but it is enough if this is true of the first—i.e. the generic-contraries, e.g. the one and the many; for the others can be reduced to these.

5

Since one thing has one contrary, we might raise the question how the one is opposed to the many, and the equal to the great and the small. For if we used the word 'whether' only in an antithesis such as 'whether it is white or black', or 'whether it is white or not white' (we do not ask 'whether it is a man or white'), unless we are proceeding on a prior assumption and asking something such as 'whether it was Cleon or Socrates that came'—but this is not a necessary disjunction in any class of things; yet even this is an extension from the case of opposites; for opposites alone cannot be present together; and we assume this incompatibility here too in asking which of the two came; for if they might both have come, the question would have been absurd; but if they might, even so this falls just as much into an antithesis, that of the 'one or many', i.e. 'whether both came or one of the two':—if, then, the question 'whether' is always concerned with opposites, and we can ask 'whether it is greater or less or equal', what is the opposition of the equal to the other two? It is not contrary either to one alone or to both; for why should it be contrary to the greater rather than to the less? Further, the equal is contrary to the unequal. Therefore if it is contrary to the greater and the less, it will be contrary to more things than one. But if the unequal means the same as both the greater and the less together, the equal will be opposite to both (and the difficulty supports those who say the unequal is a 'two'), but it follows that one thing is contrary to two others, which is impossible. Again, the equal is evidently intermediate between the great and the small, but no contrariety is either observed to be intermediate, or, from its definition, can be so; for it would not be complete if it were intermediate between any two things, but rather it always has something intermediate between its own terms.

It remains, then, that it is opposed either as negation or as privation. It cannot be the negation or privation of one of the two; for why of the great rather than of the small? It is, then, the privative negation of both. This is why 'whether' is said with reference to both, not to one of the two (e.g. 'whether it is greater or equal' or 'whether it is equal or less'); there are always three cases. But it is not a necessary privation; for not everything which is not greater or less is equal, but only the things which are of such a nature as to have these attributes.

The equal, then, is that which is neither great nor small but is naturally fitted to be either great or small; and it is opposed to both as a privative negation (and therefore is also intermediate). And that which is neither good nor bad is opposed to both, but has no name; for each of these has several meanings and the recipient subject is not one; but that which is neither white nor black has more claim to unity. Yet even this has not one name, though the colours of which this negation is privatively predicated are in a way limited; for they must be either grey or yellow or something else of the kind. Therefore it is an incorrect criticism that is passed by those who think that all such phrases are used in the same way, so that that which is neither a shoe nor a hand would be intermediate between a shoe and a hand, since that which is neither good nor bad is intermediate between the good and the bad-as if there must be an intermediate in all cases. But this does not necessarily follow. For the one phrase is a joint denial of opposites between which there is an intermediate and a certain natural interval; but between the other two there is no 'difference'; for the things, the denials of which are combined, belong to different classes, so that the *substratum* is not one.

6

We might raise similar questions about the one and the many. For if the many are absolutely opposed to the one, certain impossible results follow. One will then be few, whether few be treated here as singular or plural; for the many are opposed also to the few. Further, two will be many, since the double is multiple and 'double' derives its meaning from 'two'; therefore one will be few; for what is that in comparison with which two are many, except one, which must therefore be few? For there is nothing fewer. Further, if the much and the little are in plurality what the long and the short are in length, and whatever is much is also many, and the many are much (unless, indeed, there is a difference in the case of an easily-bounded *continuum*), the little (or few) will be a plurality. Therefore one is a plurality if it is few; and this it must be, if two are many. But perhaps, while the 'many' are in a sense said to be also 'much', it is with a difference; e.g. water is much but not many. But 'many' is applied to the things that are divisible; in the one sense it means a plurality which is excessive either absolutely or relatively (while 'few' is similarly a plurality which is deficient), and in another sense it means number, in which sense alone it is opposed to the one. For we say 'one or many', just as if one were to say 'one and ones' or 'white thing and white things', or to compare the things that have been measured with the measure. It is in this sense also that multiples are so called. For each number is said to be many because it consists of ones and because each number is measurable by one; and it is 'many' as that which is opposed to one, not to the few. In this sense, then, even two is many—not, however, in the sense of a plurality which is excessive either relatively or absolutely; it is the first plurality. But without qualification two is few; for it is first plurality which is deficient (for this reason Anaxagoras was not right in leaving the subject with the statement that 'all things were together, boundless both in plurality and in smallness'—where for 'and in smallness' he should have said 'and in fewness'; for they could not have been boundless in fewness), since it is not one, as some say, but two, that make a few.

The one is opposed then to the many in numbers as measure to thing measurable; and these are opposed as are the relatives which are not from their very nature relatives. We have distinguished elsewhere the two senses in which relatives are so called:—(1) as contraries; (2) as knowledge to thing known, a term being called relative because another is relative to it. There is nothing to prevent one from being fewer than something, e.g. than two; for if one is fewer, it is not therefore few. Plurality is as it were the class to which number belongs; for number is plurality measurable by one, and one and number are in a sense opposed, not as contrary, but as we have said some relative terms are opposed; for inasmuch as one is measure and the other measurable, they are opposed. This is why not everything that is one is a number; i.e. if the thing is indivisible it is not a number. But though knowledge is similarly spoken of as relative to the knowable, the relation does not work out similarly; for while knowledge might be thought to be the measure, and the knowable the thing measured, the fact that all knowledge is knowable, but not all that is knowable is knowledge, because in a sense knowledge is measured by the knowable.—Plurality is contrary neither to the few (the many being contrary to this as excessive plurality to plurality exceeded), nor to the one in every sense; but in the one sense these are contrary, as has been said, because the former is divisible and the latter indivisible, while in another sense they are relative as knowledge is to knowable, if plurality is number and the one is a measure.

7

Since contraries admit of an intermediate and in some cases have it, intermediates must be composed of the contraries. For (1) all intermediates are in the same genus as the things between which they stand. For we call those things intermediates, into which that which changes must change first; e.g. if we were to pass from the highest string to the lowest by the smallest intervals, we should come sooner to the intermediate notes, and in colours if we were to pass from white to black, we should come sooner to crimson and grey than to black; and similarly in all other cases. But to change from one genus to another genus is not possible except in an incidental way, as from colour to figure. Intermediates, then, must be in the same genus both as one another and as the things they stand between.

But (2) all intermediates stand between opposites of some kind; for only between these can change take place in virtue of their own nature (so that an intermediate is impossible between things which are not opposite; for then there would be change which was not from one opposite towards the other). Of opposites, contradictories admit of no middle term; for this is what contradiction is—an opposition, one or other side of which must attach to anything whatever, i.e. which has no intermediate. Of other opposites, some are relative, others privative, others contrary. Of relative terms, those which are not contrary have no intermediate; the reason is that they are not in the same genus. For what intermediate could there be between knowledge and knowable? But between great and small there is one.

(3) If intermediates are in the same genus, as has been shown, and stand between contraries, they must be composed of these contraries. For either there will be a genus including the contraries or there will be none. And if (a) there is to be a genus in such a way that it is something prior to the contraries, the differentiae which constituted the contrary species-of-a-genus will be contraries prior to the species; for species are composed of the genus and the differentiae. (E.g. if white and black are contraries, and one is a piercing colour and the other a compressing colour, these differentiae—'piercing' and 'compressing'—are prior; so that these are prior contraries of one another.) But, again, the species which differ contrariwise are the more truly contrary species. And the other species, i.e. the intermediates, must be composed of their genus and their differentiae. (E.g. all colours which are between white and black must be said to be composed of the genus, i.e. colour, and certain differentiae. But these differentiae will not be the primary contraries; otherwise every colour would be either white or black. They are different, then, from the primary contraries; and therefore they will be between the primary contraries; the primary differentiae are 'piercing' and 'compressing'.)

Therefore it is (b) with regard to these contraries which do not fall within a genus that we must first ask of what their intermediates are composed. (For things which are in the same genus must be composed of terms in which the genus is not an element, or else be themselves incomposite.) Now contraries do not involve one another in their composition, and are therefore first principles; but the intermediates are either all incomposite, or none of them. But there is something compounded out of the contraries, so that there can be a change from a contrary to it sooner than to the other contrary; for it will have less of the quality in question than the one contrary and more than the other. This also, then, will come between the contraries. All the other intermediates also, therefore, are composite; for that which has more of a quality than one thing and less than another is compounded somehow out of the things than which it is said to have more and less respectively of the quality. And since there are no other things prior to the contraries and homogeneous with the intermediates, all intermediates must be compounded out of the contraries. Therefore also all the inferior classes, both the contraries and their intermediates, will be compounded out of the primary contraries. Clearly, then, intermediates are (1) all in the same genus and (2) intermediate between contraries, and (3) all compounded out of the contraries.

8

That which is other in species is other than something in something, and this must belong to both; e.g. if it is an animal other in species, both are animals. The things, then, which are other in species must be in the same genus. For by genus I mean that one identical thing which is predicated of both and is differentiated in no merely accidental way, whether conceived as matter or otherwise. For not only must the common nature attach to the different things, e.g. not only must both be animals, but this very animality must also be different for each (e.g. in the one case equinity, in the other humanity), and so this common nature is specifically different for each from what it is for the other. One, then, will be in virtue of its own nature one sort of animal, and the other another, e.g. one a horse and the other a man. This difference, then, must be an otherness of the genus. For I give the name of 'difference in the genus' an otherness which makes the genus itself other.

This, then, will be a contrariety (as can be shown also by induction). For all things are divided by opposites, and it has been proved that contraries are in the same genus. For contrariety was seen to be complete difference; and all difference in species is a difference from something in something; so that this is the same for both and is their genus. (Hence also all contraries which are different in species and not in genus are in the same line of predication, and other than one another in the highest degree—for the difference is complete—, and cannot be present along with one another.) The difference, then, is a contrariety.

This, then, is what it is to be 'other in species'—to have a contrariety, being in the same genus and being indivisible (and those things are the same in species which have no contrariety, being indivisible); we say 'being indivisible', for in the process of division contrarieties arise in the intermediate stages before we come to the indivisibles. Evidently, therefore, with reference to that which is called the genus, none of the species-of-a-genus is either the same as it or other than it in species (and this is fitting; for the matter is indicated by negation, and the genus is the matter of that of which it is called the genus, not in the sense in which we speak of the genus or family of the Heraclidae, but in that in which the genus is an element in a thing's nature), nor is it so with reference to things which are not in the same genus, but it will differ in genus from them, and in species from things in the same genus. For a thing's difference from that from which it differs in species must be a contrariety; and this belongs only to things in the same genus.

9

One might raise the question, why woman does not differ from man in species, when female and male are contrary and their difference is a contrariety; and why a female and a male animal are not different in species, though this difference belongs to animal in virtue of its own nature, and not as paleness or darkness does; both 'female' and 'male' belong to it *qua* animal. This question is almost the same as the other, why one contrariety makes things different in species and another does not, e.g. 'with feet' and 'with wings' do, but paleness and darkness do not. Perhaps it is because the former are modifications peculiar to the genus, and the latter are less so. And since one element is definition and one is matter, contrarieties which are in the definition make a difference in species, but those which are in the thing taken as including its matter do not make one. And so paleness in a man, or darkness, does not make one, nor is there a difference in species between the pale man and the dark man, not even if each of them be denoted by one word. For man is here being considered on his material side, and matter does not create a difference; for it does not make individual men species of man, though the flesh and the bones of which this man and that man consist are other. The concrete thing is other, but not other in species, because in the definition there is no contrariety. This is the ultimate indivisible kind. Callias is definition + matter, the pale man, then, is so also, because it is the individual Callias that is pale; man, then, is pale only incidentally. Neither do a brazen and a wooden circle, then, differ in species; and if a brazen triangle and a wooden circle differ in species, it is not because of the matter, but because there is a contrariety in the definition. But does the matter not make things other in species, when it is other in a certain way, or is there a sense in which it does? For why is this horse other than this man in species, although their matter is included with their definitions? Doubtless because there is a contrariety in the definition. For while there is a contrariety also between pale man and dark horse, and it is a contrariety in species, it does not depend on the paleness of the one and the darkness of the other, since even if both had been pale, yet they would have been other in species. But male and female, while they are modifications peculiar to 'animal', are so not in virtue of its essence but in the matter, i.e. the body. This is why the same seed becomes female or male by being acted on in a certain way. We have stated, then, what it is to be other in species, and why some things differ in species and others do not.

10

Since contraries are other in form, and the perishable and the imperishable are contraries (for privation is a determinate incapacity), the perishable and the imperishable must be different in kind.

Now so far we have spoken of the general terms themselves, so that it might be thought not to be necessary that every imperishable thing should be different from every perishable thing in form, just as not every pale thing is different in form from every dark thing. For the same thing can be both, and even at the same time if it is a universal (e.g. man can be both pale and dark), and if it is an individual it can still be both; for the same man can be, though not at the same time, pale and dark. Yet pale is contrary to dark.

But while some contraries belong to certain things by accident (e.g. both those now mentioned and many others), others cannot, and among these are 'perishable' and 'imperishable'. For nothing is by accident perishable. For what is accidental is capable of not being present, but perishableness is one of the attributes that belong of necessity to the things to which they belong; or else one and the same thing may be perishable and imperishable, if perishableness is capable of not belonging to it. Perishableness then must either be the essence or be present in the essence of each perishable thing. The same account holds good for imperishableness also; for both are attributes which are present of necessity. The characteristics, then, in respect of which and in direct consequence of which one thing is perishable and another imperishable, are opposite, so that the things must be different in kind.

Evidently, then, there cannot be Forms such as some maintain, for then one man would be perishable and another imperishable. Yet the Forms are said to be the same in form with the individuals and not merely to have the same name; but things which differ in kind are farther apart than those which differ in form.

Book XI

1

That Wisdom is a science of first principles is evident from the introductory chapters, in which we have raised objections to the statements of others about the first principles; but one might ask the question whether Wisdom is to be conceived as one science or as several. If as one, it may be objected that one science always deals with contraries, but the first principles are not contrary. If it is not one, what sort of sciences are those with which it is to be identified?

Further, is it the business of one science, or of more than one, to examine the first principles of demonstration? If of one, why of this rather than of any other? If of more, what sort of sciences must these be said to be?

Further, does Wisdom investigate all substances or not? If not all, it is hard to say which; but if, being one, it investigates them all, it is doubtful how the same science can embrace several subject-matters.

Further, does it deal with substances only or also with their attributes? If in the case of attributes demonstration is possible, in that of substances it is not. But if the two sciences are different, what is each of them and which is Wisdom? If we think of it as demonstrative, the science of the attributes is Wisdom, but if as dealing with what is primary, the science of substances claims the tide.

But again the science we are looking for must not be supposed to deal with the causes which have been mentioned in the *Physics*. For (A) it does not deal with the final cause (for that is the nature of the good, and this is found in the field of action and movement; and it is the first mover—for that is the nature of the end—but in the case of things unmovable there is nothing that moved them first), and (B) in general it is hard to say whether perchance the science we are now looking for deals with perceptible substances or not with them, but with certain others. If with others, it must deal either with the Forms or with the objects of mathematics. Now (a) evidently the Forms do not exist. (But it is hard to say, even if one suppose them to exist, why in the world the same is not true of the other things of which there are Forms, as of the objects of mathematics. I mean that these thinkers place the objects of mathematics between the Forms and perceptible things, as a kind of third set of things apart both from the Forms and from the things in this world; but there is not a third man or horse besides the ideal and the individuals. If on the other hand it is not as they say, with what sort of things must the mathematician be supposed to deal? Certainly not with the things in this world; for none of these is the sort of thing which the mathematical sciences demand.) Nor (b) does the science which we are now seeking treat of the objects of mathematics; for none of them can exist separately. But again it does not deal with perceptible substances; for they are perishable.

In general one might raise the question, to what kind of science it belongs to discuss the difficulties about the matter of the objects of mathematics. Neither to physics (because the whole inquiry of the physicist is about the things that have in themselves a principle. of movement and rest), nor yet to the science which inquires into demonstration and science; for this is just the subject which it investigates. It remains then that it is the philosophy which we have set before ourselves that treats of those subjects.

One might discuss the question whether the science we are seeking should be said to deal with the principles which are by some called elements; all men suppose these to be present in composite things. But it might be thought that the science we seek should treat rather of universals; for every definition and every science is of universals and not of *infimae species*, so that as far as this goes it would deal with the highest genera. These would turn out to be being and unity; for these might most of all be supposed to contain all things that are, and to be most like principles because they are by nature; for if they perish all other things are destroyed with them; for everything is and is one. But inasmuch as, if one is to suppose them to be genera, they must be predicable of their differentiae, and no genus is predicable of any of its differentiae, in this way it would seem that we should not make them genera nor principles. Further, if the simpler is more of a principle than the less simple, and the ultimate members of the genus are simpler than the genera (for they are indivisible, but the genera are divided into many and differing species), the species might seem to be the principles, rather than the genera. But inasmuch as the species are involved in the destruction of the genera, the genera are more like principles; for that which involves another in its destruction is a principle of it. These and others of the kind are the subjects that involve difficulties.

2

Further, must we suppose something apart from individual things, or is it these that the science we are seeking treats of? But these are infinite in number. Yet the things that are apart from the individuals are genera or species; but the science we now seek treats of neither of these. The reason why this is impossible has been stated. Indeed, it is in general hard to say whether one must assume that there is a separable substance besides the sensible substances (i.e. the substances in this world), or that these are the real things and Wisdom is concerned with them. For we seem to seek another kind of substance, and this is our problem, i.e. to see if there is something which can exist apart by itself and belongs to no sensible thing.—Further, if there is another substance apart from and corresponding to sensible substances, which kinds of sensible substance must be supposed to have this corresponding to them? Why should one suppose men or horses to have it, more than either the other animals or even all lifeless things? On the other hand to set up other and eternal substances equal in number to the sensible and perishable substances would seem to fall beyond the bounds of probability.—But if the principle we now seek is not separable from corporeal things, what has a better claim to the name matter? This, however, does not exist in actuality, but exists in potency. And it would seem rather that the form or shape is a more important principle than this; but the form is perishable, so that there is no eternal substance at all which can exist apart and independent. But this is paradoxical; for such a principle and substance seems to exist and is sought by nearly all the most refined thinkers as something that exists; for how is there to be order unless there is something eternal and independent and permanent?

Further, if there is a substance or principle of such a nature as that which we are now seeking, and if this is one for all things, and the same for eternal and for perishable things, it is hard to say why in the world, if there is the same principle, some of the things that fall under the principle are eternal, and others are not eternal; this is paradoxical. But if there is one principle of perishable and another of eternal things, we shall be in a like difficulty if the principle of perishable things, as well as that of eternal, is eternal; for why, if the principle is eternal, are not the things that fall under the principle also eternal? But if it is perishable another principle is involved to account for it, and another to account for that, and this will go on to infinity.

If on the other hand we are to set up what are thought to be the most unchangeable principles, being and unity, firstly, if each of these does not indicate a 'this' or substance, how will they be separable and independent? Yet we expect the eternal and primary principles to be so. But if each of them does signify a 'this' or substance, all things that are are substances; for being is predicated of all things (and unity also of some); but that all things that are are substance is false. Further, how can they be right who say that the first principle is unity and this is substance, and generate number as the first product from unity and from matter, assert that number is substance? How are we to think of 'two', and each of the other numbers composed of units, as one? On this point neither do they say anything nor is it easy to say anything. But if we are to suppose lines or what comes after these (I mean the primary surfaces) to be principles, these at least are not separable substances, but sections and divisions—the former of surfaces, the latter of bodies (while points are sections and divisions of lines); and further they are limits of these same things; and all these are in other things and none is separable. Further, how are we to suppose that there is a substance of unity and the point? Every substance comes into being by a gradual process, but a point does not; for the point is a division.

A further difficulty is raised by the fact that all knowledge is of universals and of the 'such', but substance is not a universal, but is rather a 'this'—a separable thing, so that if there is knowledge about the first principles, the question arises, how are we to suppose the first principle to be substance?

Further, is there anything apart from the concrete thing (by which I mean the matter and that which is joined with it), or not? If not, we are met by the objection that all things that are in matter are perishable. But if there is something, it must be the form or shape. Now it is hard to determine in which cases this exists apart and in which it does not; for in some cases the form is evidently not separable, e.g. in the case of a house.

Further, are the principles the same in kind or in number? If they are one in number, all things will be the same.

3

Since the science of the philosopher treats of being *qua* being universally and not in respect of a part of it, and 'being' has many senses and is not used in one only, it follows that if the word is used equivocally and in virtue of nothing common to its various uses, being does not fall under one science (for the meanings of an equivocal term do not form one genus); but if the word is used in virtue of something common, being will fall under one science. The term seems to be used in the way we have mentioned, like 'medical' and 'healthy'. For each of these also we use in many senses. Terms are used in this way by virtue of some kind of reference, in the one case to medical science, in the other to health, in others to something else, but in each case to one identical concept. For a discussion and a knife are called medical because the former proceeds from medical science, and the latter is useful to it. And a thing is called healthy in a similar way; one thing because it is indicative of health, another because it is productive of it. And the same is true in the other cases. Everything that is, then, is said to 'be' in this same way; each thing that is is said to 'be' because it is a modification of being *qua* being or a permanent or a transient state or a movement of it, or something else of the sort. And since everything that is may be referred to something single and common, each of the contrarieties also may be referred to the first differences and contrarieties of being, whether the first differences of being are plurality and unity, or likeness and unlikeness, or some other differences; let these be taken as already discussed. It makes no difference whether that which is be referred to being or to unity. For even if they are not the same but different, at least they are convertible; for that which is one is also somehow being, and that which is being is one.

But since every pair of contraries falls to be examined by one and the same science, and in each pair one term is the privative of the other though one might regarding some contraries raise the question, how they can be privately related, viz. those which have an intermediate, e.g. unjust and just—in all such cases one must maintain that the privation is not of the whole definition, but of the *infima species*. if the just man is 'by virtue of some permanent disposition obedient to the laws', the unjust man will not in every case have the whole definition denied of him, but may be merely 'in some respect deficient in obedience to the laws', and in this respect the privation will attach to him; and similarly in all other cases.

As the mathematician investigates abstractions (for before beginning his investigation he strips off all the sensible qualities, e.g. weight and lightness, hardness and its contrary, and also heat and cold and the other sensible contrarieties, and leaves only the quantitative and continuous, sometimes in one, sometimes in two, sometimes in three dimensions, and the attributes of these *qua* quantitative and continuous, and does not consider them in any other respect, and examines the relative positions of some and the attributes of these, and the commensurabilities and incommensurabilities of others, and the ratios of others; but yet we posit one and the same science of all these things—geometry)—the same is true with regard to being. For the attributes of this in so far as it is being, and the contrarieties in it *qua* being, it is the business of no other science than philosophy to investigate; for to physics one would assign the study of things not *qua* being, but rather *qua* sharing in movement; while dialectic and sophistic deal with the attributes of things that are, but not of things *qua* being, and not with being itself in so far as it is being; therefore it remains that it is the philosopher who studies the things we have named, in so far as they are being. Since all that is is to 'be' in virtue of something single and common, though the term has many meanings, and contraries are in the same case (for they are referred to the first contrarieties and differences of being), and things of this sort can fall under one science, the difficulty we stated at the beginning appears to be solved,—I mean the question how there can be a single science of things which are many and different in genus.

4

Since even the mathematician uses the common axioms only in a special application, it must be the business of first philosophy to examine the principles of mathematics also. That when equals are taken from equals the remainders are equal, is common to all quantities, but mathematics studies a part of its proper matter which it has detached, e.g. lines or angles or numbers or some other kind of quantity—not, however, *qua* being but in so far as each of them is continuous in one or two or three dimensions; but philosophy does not inquire about particular subjects in so far as each of them has some attribute or other, but speculates about being, in so far as each particular thing is.— Physics is in the same position as mathematics; for physics studies the attributes and the principles of the things that are, *qua* moving and not *qua* being (whereas the primary science, we have said, deals with these, only in so far as the underlying subjects are existent, and not in virtue of any other character); and so both physics and mathematics must be classed as parts of Wisdom.

5

There is a principle in things, about which we cannot be deceived, but must always, on the contrary recognize the truth,—viz. that the same thing cannot at one and the same time be and not be, or admit any other similar pair of opposites. About such matters there is no proof in the full sense, though there is proof *ad hominem*. For it is not possible to infer this truth itself from a more certain principle, yet this is necessary if there is to be completed proof of it in the full sense. But he who wants to prove to the asserter of opposites that he is wrong must get from him an admission which shall be identical with the principle that the same thing cannot be and not be at one and the same time, but shall not seem to be identical; for thus alone can his thesis be demonstrated to the man who asserts that opposite statements can be truly made about the same subject. Those, then, who are to join in argument with one another must to some extent understand one another; for if this does not happen how are they to join in argument with one another? Therefore every word must be intelligible and indicate something, and not many things but only one; and if it signifies more than one thing, it must be made plain to which of these the word is being applied. He, then, who says 'this is and is not' denies what he affirms, so that what the word signifies, he says it does not signify; and this is impossible. Therefore if 'this is' signifies something, one cannot truly assert its contradictory.

Further, if the word signifies something and this is asserted truly, this connexion must be necessary; and it is not possible that that which necessarily is should ever not be; it is not possible therefore to make the opposed affirmations and negations truly of the same subject. Further, if the affirmation is no more true than the negation, he who says 'man' will be no more right than he who says 'not-man'. It would seem also that in saying the man is not a horse one would be either more or not less right than in saying he is not a man, so that one will also be right in saying that the same person is a horse; for it was assumed to be possible to make opposite statements equally truly. It follows then that the same person is a man and a horse, or any other animal.

While, then, there is no proof of these things in the full sense, there is a proof which may suffice against one who will make these suppositions. And perhaps if one had questioned Heraclitus himself in this way one might have forced him to confess that opposite statements can never be true of the same subjects. But, as it is, he adopted this opinion without understanding what his statement involves. But in any case if what is said by him is true, not even this itself will be true—viz.

that the same thing can at one and the same time both be and not be. For as, when the statements are separated, the affirmation is no more true than the negation, in the same way-the combined and complex statement being like a single affirmation—the whole taken as an affirmation will be no more true than the negation. Further, if it is not possible to affirm anything truly, this itself will be false—the assertion that there is no true affirmation. But if a true affirmation exists, this appears to refute what is said by those who raise such objections and utterly destroy rational discourse.

6

The saying of Protagoras is like the views we have mentioned; he said that man is the measure of all things, meaning simply that that which seems to each man also assuredly is. If this is so, it follows that the same thing both is and is not, and is bad and good, and that the contents of all other opposite statements are true, because often a particular thing appears beautiful to some and the contrary of beautiful to others, and that which appears to each man is the measure. This difficulty may be solved by considering the source of this opinion. It seems to have arisen in some cases from the doctrine of the natural philosophers, and in others from the fact that all men have not the same views about the same things, but a particular thing appears pleasant to some and the contrary of pleasant to others.

That nothing comes to be out of that which is not, but everything out of that which is, is a dogma common to nearly all the natural philosophers. Since, then, white cannot come to be if the perfectly white and in no respect not-white existed before, that which becomes white must come from that which is not white; so that it must come to be out of that which is not (so they argue), unless the same thing was at the beginning white and not-white. But it is not hard to solve this difficulty; for we have said in our works on physics in what sense things that come to be come to be from that which is not, and in what sense from that which is.

But to attend equally to the opinions and the fancies of disputing parties is childish; for clearly one of them must be mistaken. And this is evident from what happens in respect of sensation; for the same thing never appears sweet to some and the contrary of sweet to others, unless in the one case the sense-organ which discriminates the aforesaid flavours has been perverted and injured. And if this is so the one party must be taken to be the measure, and the other must not. And say the same of good and bad, and beautiful and ugly, and all other such qualities. For to maintain the view we are opposing is just like maintaining that the things that appear to people who put their finger under their eye and make the object appear two instead of one must be two (because they appear to be of that number) and again one (for to those who do not interfere with their eye the one object appears one).

In general, it is absurd to make the fact that the things of this earth are observed to change and never to remain in the same state, the basis of our judgement about the truth. For in pursuing the truth one must start from the things that are always in the same state and suffer no change. Such are the heavenly bodies; for these do not appear to be now of one nature and again of another, but are manifestly always the same and share in no change.

Further, if there is movement, there is also something moved, and everything is moved out of something and into something; it follows that that which is moved must first be in that out of which it is to be moved, and then not be in it, and move into the other and come to be in it, and that the contradictory statements are not true at the same time, as these thinkers assert they are.

And if the things of this earth continuously flow and move in respect of quantity—if one were to suppose this, although it is not true—why should they not endure in respect of quality? For the assertion of contradictory statements about the same thing seems to have arisen largely from the belief that the quantity of bodies does not endure, which, our opponents hold, justifies them in saying that the same thing both is and is not four cubits long. But essence depends on quality, and this is of determinate nature, though quantity is of indeterminate.

Further, when the doctor orders people to take some particular food, why do they take it? In what respect is 'this is bread' truer than 'this is not bread'? And so it would make no difference whether one ate or not. But as a matter of fact they take the food which is ordered, assuming that they know the truth about it and that it is bread. Yet they should not, if there were no fixed constant nature in sensible things, but all natures moved and flowed for ever.

Again, if we are always changing and never remain the same, what wonder is it if to us, as to the sick, things never appear the same? (For to them also, because they are not in the same condition as when they were well, sensible qualities do not appear alike; yet, for all that, the sensible things themselves need not share in any change, though they produce different, and not identical, sensations in the sick. And the same must surely happen to the healthy if the afore-said change takes place.) But if we do not change but remain the same, there will be something that endures.

As for those to whom the difficulties mentioned are suggested by reasoning, it is not easy to solve the difficulties to their satisfaction, unless they will posit something and no longer demand a reason for it; for it is only thus that all reasoning and all proof is accomplished; if they posit nothing, they destroy discussion and all reasoning. Therefore with such men there is no reasoning. But as for those who are perplexed by the traditional difficulties, it is easy to meet them and to dissipate the causes of their perplexity. This is evident from what has been said.

It is manifest, therefore, from these arguments that contradictory statements cannot be truly made about the same subject at one time, nor can contrary statements, because every contrariety depends on privation. This is evident if we reduce the definitions of contraries to their principle.

Similarly, no intermediate between contraries can be predicated of one and the same subject, of which one of the contraries is predicated. If the subject is white we shall be wrong in saying it is neither black nor white, for then it follows that it is and is not white; for the second of the two terms we have put together is true of it, and this is the contradictory of white.

We could not be right, then, in accepting the views either of Heraclitus or of Anaxagoras. If we were, it would follow that contraries would be predicated of the same subject; for when Anaxagoras says that in everything there is a part of everything, he says nothing is sweet any more than it is bitter, and so with any other pair of contraries, since in everything everything is present not potentially only, but actually and separately. And similarly all statements cannot be false nor all true, both because of many other difficulties which might be adduced as arising from this position, and because if all are false it will not be true to say even this, and if all are true it will not be false to say all are false.

7

Every science seeks certain principles and causes for each of its objects—e.g. medicine and gymnastics and each of the other sciences, whether productive or mathematical. For each of these marks off a certain class of things for itself and busies itself about this as about something existing and real,—not however *qua* real; the science that does this is another distinct from these. Of the sciences mentioned each gets somehow the 'what' in some class of things and tries to prove the other truths, with more or less precision. Some get the 'what' through perception, others by hypothesis; so that it is clear from an induction of this sort that there is no demonstration. of the substance or 'what'.

There is a science of nature, and evidently it must be different both from practical and from productive science. For in the case of productive science the principle of movement is in the producer and not in the product, and is either an art or some other faculty. And similarly in practical science the movement is not in the thing done, but rather in the doers. But the science of the natural philosopher deals with the things that have in themselves a principle of movement. It is clear from these facts, then, that natural science must be neither practical nor productive, but theoretical (for it must fall into some one of these classes). And since each of the sciences must somehow know the 'what' and use this as a principle, we must not fall to observe how the natural philosopher should define things and how he should state the definition of the essence—whether as akin to 'snub' or rather to 'concave'. For of these the definition of 'snub' includes the matter of the thing, but that of 'concave' is independent of the matter; for snubness is found in a nose, so that we look for its definition without eliminating the nose, for what is snub is a concave nose. Evidently then the definition of flesh also and of the eye and of the other parts must always be stated without eliminating the matter.

Since there is a science of being *qua* being and capable of existing apart, we must consider whether this is to be regarded as the same as physics or rather as different. Physics deals with the things that have a principle of movement in themselves; mathematics is theoretical, and is a science that deals with things that are at rest, but its subjects cannot exist apart. Therefore about that which can exist apart and is unmovable there is a science different from both of these, if there is a substance of this nature (I mean separable and unmovable), as we shall try to prove there is. And if there is such a kind of thing in the world, here must surely be the divine, and this must be the first and most dominant principle. Evidently, then, there are three kinds of theoretical sciences—physics, mathematics, theology. The class of theoretical sciences is the best, and of these themselves the last named is best; for it deals with the highest of existing things, and each science is called better or worse in virtue of its proper object.

One might raise the question whether the science of being *qua* being is to be regarded as universal or not. Each of the mathematical sciences deals with some one determinate class of things, but universal mathematics applies alike to all. Now if natural substances are the first of existing things, physics must be the first of sciences; but if there is another entity and substance, separable and unmovable, the knowledge of it must be different and prior to physics and universal because it is prior.

8

Since 'being' in general has several senses, of which one is 'being by accident', we must consider first that which 'is' in this sense. Evidently none of the traditional sciences busies itself about the accidental. For neither does architecture consider what will happen to those who are to use the house (e.g. whether they have a painful life in it or not), nor does weaving, or shoemaking, or the confectioner's art, do the like; but each of these sciences considers only what is peculiar to it, i.e. its proper end. And as for the argument that 'when he who is musical becomes lettered he'll be both at once, not having been both before; and that which is, not always having been, must have come to be; therefore he must have at once become musical and lettered',—this none of the recognized sciences considers, but only sophistic; for this alone busies itself about the accidental, so that Plato is not far wrong when he says that the sophist spends his time on non-being.

That a science of the accidental is not even possible will be evident if we try to see what the accidental really is. We say that everything either is always and of necessity (necessity not in the sense of violence, but that which we appeal to in demonstrations), or is for the most part, or is neither for the most part, nor always and of necessity, but merely as it chances; e.g. there might be cold in the dog-days, but this occurs neither always and of necessity, nor for the most part, though it might happen sometimes. The accidental, then, is what occurs, but not always nor of necessity, nor for the most part. Now we have said what the accidental is, and it is obvious why there is no science of such a thing; for all science is of that which is always or for the most part, but the accidental is in neither of these classes.

Evidently there are not causes and principles of the accidental, of the same kind as there are of the essential; for if there were, everything would be of necessity. If A is when B is, and B is when C is, and if C exists not by chance but of necessity, that also of which C was cause will exist of necessity, down to the last *causatum* as it is called (but this was supposed to be accidental). Therefore all things will be of necessity, and chance and the possibility of a thing's either occurring or not occurring are removed entirely from the range of events. And if the cause be supposed not to exist but to be coming to be, the same results will follow; everything will occur of necessity. For to-morrow's eclipse will occur if A occurs, and A if B occurs, and B if C occurs; and in this way if we subtract time from the limited time between now and to-morrow we shall come sometime to the already existing condition. Therefore since this exists, everything after this will occur of necessity, so that all things occur of necessity.

As to that which 'is' in the sense of being true or of being by accident, the former depends on a combination in thought and is an affection of thought (which is the reason why it is the principles, not of that which 'is' in this sense, but of that which is outside and can exist apart, that are sought); and the latter is not necessary but indeterminate (I mean the accidental); and of such a thing the causes are unordered and indefinite.

Adaptation to an end is found in events that happen by nature or as the result of thought. It is 'luck' when one of these events happens by accident. For as a thing may exist, so it may be a cause, either by its own nature or by accident. Luck is an accidental cause at work in such events adapted to an end as are usually effected in accordance with purpose. And so luck and thought are concerned with the same sphere; for purpose cannot exist without thought. The causes from which lucky results might happen are indeterminate; and so luck is obscure to human calculation and is a cause by accident, but in the unqualified sense a cause of nothing. It is good or bad luck when the result is good or evil; and prosperity or misfortune when the scale of the results is large.

Since nothing accidental is prior to the essential, neither are accidental causes prior. If, then, luck or spontaneity is a cause of the material universe, reason and nature are causes before it.

9

Some things are only actually, some potentially, some potentially and actually, what they are, viz. in one case a particular reality, in another, characterized by a particular quantity, or the like. There is no movement apart from things; for change is always according to the categories of being, and there is nothing common to these and in no one category. But each of the categories belongs to all its subjects in either of two ways (e.g. 'this-ness'—for one kind of it is 'positive form', and the other is 'privation'; and as regards quality one kind is 'white' and the other 'black', and as regards quantity one kind is 'complete' and the other 'incomplete', and as regards spatial movement one is 'upwards' and the other 'downwards', or one thing is 'light' and another 'heavy'); so that there are as many kinds of movement and change as of being. There being a distinction in each class of things between the potential and the completely real, I call the actuality of the potential as such, movement. That what we say is true, is plain from the following facts. When the 'buildable', in so far as it is what we mean by 'buildable', exists actually, it is being built, and this is the process of building. Similarly with learning, healing, walking, leaping, ageing, ripening. Movement takes when the complete reality itself exists, and neither earlier nor later. The complete reality, then, of that which exists potentially, when it is completely real and actual, not *qua* itself, but *qua* movable, is movement. By *qua* I mean this: bronze is potentially a statue; but yet it is not the complete reality of bronze *qua* bronze that is movement. For it is not the same thing to be bronze and to be a certain potency. If it were absolutely the same in its definition, the complete reality of bronze would have been a movement. But it is not the same. (This is evident in the case of contraries; for to be capable of being well and to be capable of being ill are not the same—for if they were, being well and being ill would have been the same—it is that which underlies and is healthy or diseased, whether it is moisture or blood, that is one and the same.) And since it is not the same, as colour and the visible are not the same, it is the complete reality of the potential, and as potential, that is movement. That it is this, and that movement takes place when the complete reality itself exists, and neither earlier nor later, is evident. For each thing is capable of being sometimes actual, sometimes not, e.g. the buildable *qua* buildable; and the actuality of the buildable *qua* buildable is building. For the actuality is either this—the act of building—or the house. But when the house exists, it is no longer buildable; the buildable is what is being built. The actuality, then, must be the act of building, and this is a movement. And the same account applies to all other movements.

That what we have said is right is evident from what all others say about movement, and from the fact that it is not easy to define it otherwise. For firstly one cannot put it in any class. This is evident from what people say. Some call it otherness and inequality and the unreal; none of these, however, is necessarily moved, and further, change is not either to these or from these any more than from their opposites. The reason why people put movement in these classes is that it is thought to be something indefinite, and the principles in one of the two 'columns of contraries' are indefinite because they are privative, for none of them is either a 'this' or a 'such' or in any of the other categories. And the reason why movement is thought to be indefinite is that it cannot be classed either with the potency of things or with their actuality; for neither that which is capable of being of a certain quantity, nor that which is actually of a certain quantity, is of necessity moved, and movement is thought to be an actuality, but incomplete; the reason is that the potential, whose actuality it is, is incomplete. And therefore it is hard to grasp what movement is; for it must be classed either under privation or under potency or under absolute actuality, but evidently none of these is possible. Therefore what remains is that it must be what we said—both actuality and the actuality we have described—which is hard to detect but capable of existing.

And evidently movement is in the movable; for it is the complete realization of this by that which is capable of causing movement. And the actuality of that which is capable of causing movement is no other than that of the movable. For it must be the complete reality of both. For while a thing is capable of causing movement because it can do this, it is a mover because it is active; but it is on the movable that it is capable of acting, so that the actuality of both is one, just as there is the same interval from one to two as from two to one, and as the steep ascent and the steep descent are one, but the being of them is not one; the case of the mover and the moved is similar.

10

The infinite is either that which is incapable of being traversed because it is not its nature to be traversed (this corresponds to the sense in which the voice is 'invisible'), or that which admits only of incomplete traverse or scarcely admits of traverse, or that which, though it naturally admits of traverse, is not traversed or limited; further, a thing may be infinite in respect of addition or of subtraction, or both. The infinite cannot be a separate, independent thing. For if it is neither a spatial magnitude nor a plurality, but infinity itself is its substance and not an accident of it, it will be indivisible; for the divisible is either magnitude or plurality. But if indivisible, it is not infinite, except as the voice is invisible; but people do not mean this, nor are we examining this sort of infinite, but the infinite as untraversable. Further, how can an infinite exist by itself, unless number and magnitude also exist by themselves,—since infinity is an attribute of these? Further, if the infinite is an accident of something else, it cannot be *qua* infinite an element in things, as the invisible is not an element in speech, though the voice is invisible. And evidently the infinite cannot exist actually. For then any part of it that might be taken would be infinite (for 'to be infinite' and 'the infinite' are the same, if the infinite is substance and not predicated of a subject). Therefore it is either indivisible, or if it is partible, it is divisible into infinites; but the same thing cannot be many infinites (as a part of air is air, so a part of the infinite would be infinite, if the infinite is substance and a principle). Therefore it must be impartible and indivisible. But the actually infinite cannot be indivisible; for it must be of a certain quantity. Therefore infinity belongs to its subject incidentally. But if so, then (as we have said) it cannot be it that is a principle, but that of which it is an accident—the air or the even number.

This inquiry is universal; but that the infinite is not among sensible things, is evident from the following argument. If the definition of a body is 'that which is bounded by planes', there cannot be an infinite body either sensible or intelligible; nor a separate and infinite number, for number or that which has a number is numerable. Concretely, the truth is evident from the following argument. The infinite can neither be composite nor simple. For (a) it cannot be a composite body, since the elements are limited in multitude. For the contraries must be equal and no one of them must be infinite; for if one of the two bodies falls at all short of the other in potency, the finite will be destroyed by the infinite. And that each should be infinite is impossible. For body is that which has extension in all directions, and the infinite is the boundlessly extended, so that if the infinite is a body it will be infinite in every direction. Nor (b) can the infinite body be one and simple—neither, as some say, something apart from the elements, from which they generate these (for there is no such body apart from the elements; for everything can be resolved into that of which it consists, but no such product of analysis is observed except the simple bodies), nor fire nor any other of the elements. For apart from the question how any of them could be infinite, the All, even if it is finite, cannot either be or become any one of them, as Heraclitus says all things sometime become fire. The same argument applies to this as to the One which the natural philosophers posit besides the elements. For everything changes from contrary to contrary, e.g. from hot to cold.

Further, a sensible body is somewhere, and whole and part have the same proper place, e.g. the whole earth and part of the earth. Therefore if (a) the infinite body is homogeneous, it will be unmovable or it will be always moving. But this is impossible; for why should it rather rest, or move, down, up, or anywhere, rather than anywhere else? E.g. if there were a clod which were part of an infinite body, where will this move or rest? The proper place of the body which is homogeneous with it is infinite. Will the clod occupy the whole place, then? And how? (This is impossible.) What then is its rest or its movement? It will either rest everywhere, and then it cannot move; or it will move everywhere, and then it cannot be still. But (b) if the All has unlike parts, the proper places of the parts are unlike also, and, firstly, the body of the All is not one except by contact, and, secondly, the parts will be either finite or infinite in variety of kind. Finite they cannot be; for then those of one kind will be infinite in quantity and those of another will not (if the All is infinite), e.g. fire or water would be infinite, but such an infinite element would be destruction to the contrary elements. But if the parts are infinite and simple, their places also are infinite and there will be an infinite number of elements; and if this is impossible, and the places are finite, the All also must be limited.

In general, there cannot be an infinite body and also a proper place for bodies, if every sensible body has either weight or lightness. For it must move either towards the middle or upwards, and the infinite— either the whole or the half of it—cannot do either; for how will you divide it? Or how will part of the infinite be down and part up, or part extreme and part middle? Further, every sensible body is in a place, and there are six kinds of place, but these cannot exist in an infinite body. In general, if there cannot be an infinite place, there cannot be an infinite body; (and there cannot be an infinite place,) for that which is in a place is somewhere, and this means either up or down or in one of the other directions, and each of these is a limit.

The infinite is not the same in the sense that it is a single thing whether exhibited in distance or in movement or in time, but the posterior among these is called infinite in virtue of its relation to the prior; i.e. a movement is called infinite in virtue of the distance covered by the spatial movement or alteration or growth, and a time is called infinite because of the movement which occupies it.

11

Of things which change, some change in an accidental sense, like that in which 'the musical' may be said to walk, and others are said, without qualification, to change, because something in them changes, i.e. the things that change in parts; the body becomes healthy, because the eye does. But there is something which is by its own nature moved directly, and this is the essentially movable. The same distinction is found in the case of the mover; for it causes movement either in an accidental sense or in respect of a part of itself or essentially. There is something that directly causes movement; and there is something that is moved, also the time in which it is moved, and that from which and that into which it is moved. But the forms and the affections and the place, which are the terminals of the movement of moving things, are unmovable, e.g. knowledge or heat; it is not heat that is a movement, but heating. Change which is not accidental is found not in all things, but between contraries, and their intermediates, and between contradictories. We may convince ourselves of this by induction.

That which changes changes either from positive into positive, or from negative into negative, or from positive into negative, or from negative into positive. (By positive I mean that which is expressed by an affirmative term.) Therefore there must be three changes; that from negative into negative is not change, because (since the terms are neither contraries nor contradictories) there is no opposition. The change from the negative into the positive which is its contradictory is generation—absolute change absolute generation, and partial change partial generation; and the change from positive to negative is destruction—absolute change absolute destruction, and partial change partial destruction. If, then, 'that which is not' has several senses, and movement can attach neither to that which implies putting together or separating, nor to that which implies potency and is opposed to that which is in the full sense (true, the not-white or not-good can be moved incidentally, for the not-white might be a man; but that which is not a particular thing at all can in no wise be moved), that which is not cannot be moved (and if this is so, generation cannot be movement; for that which is not is generated; for even if we admit to the full that its generation is accidental, yet it is true to say that 'not-being' is predicable of that which is generated absolutely). Similarly rest cannot be long to that which is not. These consequences, then, turn out to be awkward, and also this, that everything that is moved is in a place, but that which is not is not in a place; for then it would be somewhere. Nor is destruction movement; for the contrary of movement is rest, but the contrary of destruction is generation. Since every movement is a change, and the kinds of change are the three named above, and of these those in the way of generation and destruction are not movements, and these are the changes from a thing to its contradictory, it follows that only the change from positive into positive is movement. And the positives are either contrary or intermediate (for even privation must be regarded as contrary), and are expressed by an affirmative term, e.g. 'naked' or 'toothless' or 'black'.

12

If the categories are classified as substance, quality, place, acting or being acted on, relation, quantity, there must be three kinds of movement—of quality, of quantity, of place. There is no movement in respect of substance (because there is nothing contrary to substance), nor of relation (for it is possible that if one of two things in relation changes, the relative term which was true of the other thing ceases to be true, though this other does not change at all,—so that their movement is accidental), nor of agent and patient, or mover and moved, because there is no movement of movement nor generation of generation, nor, in general, change of change. For there might be movement of movement in two senses; (1) movement might be the subject moved, as a man is moved because he changes from pale to dark,—so that on this showing movement, too, may be either heated or cooled or change its place or increase. But this is impossible; for change is not a subject. Or (2) some other subject might change from change into some other form of existence (e.g. a man from disease into health). But this also is not possible except incidentally. For every movement is change from something into something. (And so are generation and destruction; only, these are changes into things opposed in certain ways while the other, movement, is into things opposed in another way.) A thing changes, then, at the same time from health into illness, and from this change itself into another. Clearly, then, if it has become ill, it will have changed into whatever may be the other change concerned (though it may be at rest), and, further, into a determinate change each time; and that new change will be from something definite into some other definite thing; therefore it will be the opposite change, that of growing well. We answer that this happens only incidentally; e.g. there is a change from the process of recollection to that of forgetting, only because that to which the process attaches is changing, now into a state of knowledge, now into one of ignorance.

Further, the process will go on to infinity, if there is to be change of change and coming to be of coming to be. What is true of the later, then, must be true of the earlier; e.g. if the simple coming to be was once coming to be, that which comes to be something was also once coming to be; therefore that which simply comes to be something was not yet in existence, but something which was coming to be coming to be something was already in existence. And this was once coming to be, so that at that time it was not yet coming to be something else. Now since of an infinite number of terms there is not a first, the first in this series will not exist, and therefore no following term exist. Nothing, then, can either come to be or move or change. Further, that which is capable of a movement is also capable of the contrary movement and rest, and that which comes to be also ceases to be. Therefore that which is coming to be is ceasing to be when it has come to be coming to be; for it cannot cease to be as soon as it is coming to be coming to be, nor after it has come to be; for that which is ceasing to be must be. Further, there must be a matter underlying that which comes to be and changes. What will this be, then,—what is it that becomes movement or becoming, as body or soul is that which suffers alteration? And; again, what is it that they move into? For it must be the movement or becoming of something from something into something. How, then, can this condition be fulfilled? There can be no learning of learning, and therefore no becoming of becoming. Since there is not movement either of substance or of relation or of activity and passivity, it remains that movement is in respect of quality and quantity and place; for each of these admits of contrariety. By quality I mean not that which is in the substance (for even the differentia is a quality), but the passive quality, in virtue of which a thing is said to be acted on or to be incapable of being acted on. The immobile is either that which is wholly incapable of being moved, or that which is moved with difficulty in a long time or begins slowly, or that which is of a nature to be moved and can be moved but is not moved when and where and as it would naturally be moved. This alone among immobiles I describe as being at rest; for rest is contrary to movement, so that it must be a privation in that which is receptive of movement.

Things which are in one proximate place are together in place, and things which are in different places are apart: things whose extremes are together touch: that at which a changing thing, if it changes continuously according to its nature, naturally arrives before it arrives at the extreme into which it is changing, is between. That which is most distant in a straight line is contrary in place. That is successive which is after the beginning (the order being determined by position or form or in some other way) and has nothing of the same class between it and that which it succeeds, e.g. lines in the case of a line, units in that of a unit, or a house in that of a house. (There is nothing to prevent a thing of some other class from being between.) For the successive succeeds something and is something later; 'one' does not succeed 'two', nor the first day of the month the second. That which, being successive, touches, is contiguous. (Since all change is between opposites, and these are either contraries or contradictories, and there is no middle term for contradictories, clearly that which is between is between contraries.) The continuous is a species of the contiguous. I call two things continuous when the limits of each, with which they touch and by which they are kept together, become one and the same, so that plainly the continuous is found in the things out of which a unity naturally arises in virtue of their contact. And plainly the successive is the first of these concepts (for the successive does not necessarily touch, but that which touches is successive; and if a thing is continuous, it touches, but if it touches, it is not necessarily continuous; and in things in which there is no touching, there is no organic unity); therefore a point is not the same as a unit; for contact belongs to points, but not to units, which have only succession; and there is something between two of the former, but not between two of the latter.

Book XII

1

The subject of our inquiry is substance; for the principles and the causes we are seeking are those of substances. For if the universe is of the nature of a whole, substance is its first part; and if it coheres merely by virtue of serial succession, on this view also substance is first, and is succeeded by quality, and then by quantity. At the same time these latter are not even being in the full sense, but are qualities and movements of it,—or else even the not-white and the not-straight would be being; at least we say even these are, e.g. 'there is a not-white'. Further, none of the categories other than substance can exist apart. And the early philosophers also in practice testify to the primacy of substance; for it was of substance that they sought the principles and elements and causes. The thinkers of the present day tend to rank universals as substances (for genera are universals, and these they tend to describe as principles and substances, owing to the abstract nature of their inquiry); but the thinkers of old ranked particular things as substances, e.g. fire and earth, not what is common to both, body.

There are three kinds of substance—one that is sensible (of which one subdivision is eternal and another is perishable; the latter is recognized by all men, and includes e.g. plants and animals), of which we must grasp the elements, whether one or many; and another that is immovable, and this certain thinkers assert to be capable of existing apart, some dividing it into two, others identifying the Forms and the objects of mathematics, and others positing, of these two, only the objects of mathematics. The former two kinds of substance are the subject of physics (for they imply movement); but the third kind belongs to another science, if there is no principle common to it and to the other kinds.

2

Sensible substance is changeable. Now if change proceeds from opposites or from intermediates, and not from all opposites (for the voice is not-white, (but it does not therefore change to white)), but from the contrary, there must be something underlying which changes into the contrary state; for the contraries do not change. Further, something persists, but the contrary does not persist; there is, then, some third thing besides the contraries, viz. the matter. Now since changes are of four kinds—either in respect of the 'what' or of the quality or of the quantity or of the place, and change in respect of 'thisness' is simple generation and destruction, and change in quantity is increase and diminution, and change in respect of an affection is alteration, and change of place is motion, changes will be from given states into those contrary to them in these several respects. The matter, then, which changes must be capable of both states. And since that which 'is' has two senses, we must say that everything changes from that which is potentially to that which is actually, e.g. from potentially white to actually white, and similarly in the case of increase and diminution. Therefore not only can a thing come to be, incidentally, out of that which is not, but also all things come to be out of that which is, but is potentially, and is not actually. And this is the 'One' of Anaxagoras; for instead of 'all things were together'—and the 'Mixture' of Empedocles and Anaximander and the account given by Democritus—it is better to say 'all things were together potentially but not actually'. Therefore these thinkers seem to have had some notion of matter. Now all things that change have matter, but different matter; and of eternal things those which are not generable but are movable in space have matter—not matter for generation, however, but for motion from one place to another.

One might raise the question from what sort of non-being generation proceeds; for 'non-being' has three senses. If, then, one form of non-being exists potentially, still it is not by virtue of a potentiality for any and every thing, but different things come from different things; nor is it satisfactory to say that 'all things were together'; for they differ in their matter, since otherwise why did an infinity of things come to be, and not one thing? For 'reason' is one, so that if matter also were one, that must have come to be in actuality which the matter was in potency. The causes and the principles, then, are three, two being the pair of contraries of which one is definition and form and the other is privation, and the third being the matter.

3

Note, next, that neither the matter nor the form comes to be—and I mean the last matter and form. For everything that changes is something and is changed by something and into something. That by which it is changed is the immediate mover; that which is changed, the matter; that into which it is changed, the form. The process, then, will go on to infinity, if not only the bronze comes to be round but also the round or the bronze comes to be; therefore there must be a stop.

Note, next, that each substance comes into being out of something that shares its name. (Natural objects and other things both rank as substances.) For things come into being either by art or by nature or by luck or by spontaneity. Now art is a principle of movement in something other than the thing moved, nature is a principle in the thing itself (for man begets man), and the other causes are privations of these two.

There are three kinds of substance—the matter, which is a 'this' in appearance (for all things that are characterized by contact and not, by organic unity are matter and *substratum*, e.g. fire, flesh, head; for these are all matter, and the last matter is the matter of that which is in the full sense substance); the nature, which is a 'this' or positive state towards which movement takes place; and again, thirdly, the particular substance which is composed of these two, e.g. Socrates or Callias. Now in some cases the 'this' does not exist apart from the composite substance, e.g. the form of house does not so exist, unless the art of building exists apart (nor is there generation and destruction of these forms, but it is in another way that the house apart from its matter, and health, and all ideals of art, exist and do not exist); but if the 'this' exists apart from the concrete thing, it is only in the case of natural objects. And so Plato was not far wrong when he said that there are as many Forms as there are kinds of natural object (if there are Forms distinct from the things of this earth). The moving causes exist as things preceding the effects, but causes in the sense of definitions are simultaneous with their effects. For when a man is healthy, then health also exists; and the shape of a bronze sphere exists at the same time as the bronze sphere. (But we must examine whether any form also survives afterwards. For in some cases there is nothing to prevent this; e.g. the soul may be of this sort—not all soul but the reason; for presumably it is impossible that all soul should survive.) Evidently then there is no necessity, on this ground at least, for the existence of the Ideas. For man is begotten by man, a given man by an individual father; and similarly in the arts; for the medical art is the formal cause of health.

4

The causes and the principles of different things are in a sense different, but in a sense, if one speaks universally and analogically, they are the same for all. For one might raise the question whether the principles and elements are different or the same for substances and for relative terms, and similarly in the case of each of the categories. But it would be paradoxical if they were the same for all. For then from the same elements will proceed relative terms and substances. What then will this common element be? For (1) (a) there is nothing common to and distinct from substance and the other categories, viz. those which are predicated; but an element is prior to the things of which it is an element. But again (b) substance is not an element in relative terms, nor is any of these an element in substance. Further, (2) how can all things have the same elements? For none of the elements can be the same as that which is composed of elements, e.g. b or a cannot be the same as ba. (None, therefore, of the intelligibles, e.g. being or unity, is an element; for these are predicable of each of the compounds as well.) None of the elements, then, will be either a substance or a relative term; but it must be one or other. All things, then, have not the same elements.

Or, as we are wont to put it, in a sense they have and in a sense they have not; e.g. perhaps the elements of perceptible bodies are, as form, the hot, and in another sense the cold, which is the privation; and, as matter, that which directly and of itself potentially has these attributes; and substances comprise both these and the things composed of these, of which these are the principles, or any unity which is produced out of the hot and the cold, e.g. flesh or bone; for the product must be different from the elements. These things then have the same elements and principles (though specifically different things have specifically different elements); but all things have not the same elements in this sense, but only analogically; i.e. one might say that there are three principles—the form, the privation, and the matter. But each of these is different for each class; e.g. in colour they are white, black, and surface, and in day and night they are light, darkness, and air.

Since not only the elements present in a thing are causes, but also something external, i.e. the moving cause, clearly while 'principle' and 'element' are different both are causes, and 'principle' is divided into these two kinds; and that which acts as producing movement or rest is a principle and a substance. Therefore analogically there are three elements, and four causes and principles; but the elements are different in different things, and the proximate moving cause is different for different things. Health, disease, body; the moving cause is the medical art. Form, disorder of a particular kind, bricks; the moving cause is the building art. And since the moving cause in the case of natural things is—for man, for instance, man, and in the products of thought the form or its contrary, there will be in a sense three causes, while in a sense there are four. For the medical art is in some sense health, and the building art is the form of the house, and man begets man; further, besides these there is that which as first of all things moves all things.

5

Some things can exist apart and some cannot, and it is the former that are substances. And therefore all things have the same causes, because, without substances, modifications and movements do not exist. Further, these causes will probably be soul and body, or reason and desire and body.

And in yet another way, analogically identical things are principles, i.e. actuality and potency; but these also are not only different for different things but also apply in different ways to them. For in some cases the same thing exists at one time actually and at another potentially, e.g. wine or flesh or man does so. (And these too fall under the above-named causes. For the form exists actually, if it can exist apart, and so does the complex of form and matter, and the privation, e.g. darkness or disease; but the matter exists potentially; for this is that which can become qualified either by the form or by the privation.) But the distinction of actuality and potentiality applies in another way to cases where the matter of cause and of effect is not the same, in some of which cases the form is not the same but different; e.g. the cause of man is (1) the elements in man (viz. fire and earth as matter, and the peculiar form), and further (2) something else outside, i.e. the father, and (3) besides these the sun and its oblique course, which are neither matter nor form nor privation of man nor of the same species with him, but moving causes.

Further, one must observe that some causes can be expressed in universal terms, and some cannot. The proximate principles of all things are the 'this' which is proximate in actuality, and another which is proximate in potentiality. The universal causes, then, of which we spoke do not exist. For it is the individual that is the originative principle of the individuals. For while man is the originative principle of man universally, there is no universal man, but Peleus is the originative principle of Achilles, and your father of you, and this particular *b* of this particular *ba*, though *b* in general is the originative principle of *ba* taken without qualification.

Further, if the causes of substances are the causes of all things, yet different things have different causes and elements, as was said; the causes of things that are not in the same class, e.g. of colours and sounds, of substances and quantities, are different except in an analogical sense; and those of things in the same species are different, not in species, but in the sense that the causes of different individuals are different, your matter and form and moving cause being different from mine, while in their universal definition they are the same. And if we inquire what are the principles or elements of substances and relations and qualities—whether they are the same or different—clearly when the names of the causes are used in several senses the causes of each are the same, but when the senses are distinguished the causes are not the same but different, except that in the following senses the causes of all are the same. They are (1) the same or analogous in this sense, that matter, form, privation, and the moving cause are common to all things; and (2) the causes of substances may be treated as causes of all things in this sense, that when substances are removed all things are removed; further, (3) that which is first in respect of complete reality is the cause of all things. But in another sense there are different first causes, viz. all the contraries which are neither generic nor ambiguous terms; and, further, the matters of different things are different. We have stated, then, what are the principles of sensible things and how many they are, and in what sense they are the same and in what sense different.

6

Since there were three kinds of substance, two of them physical and one unmovable, regarding the latter we must assert that it is necessary that there should be an eternal unmovable substance. For substances are the first of existing things, and if they are all destructible, all things are destructible. But it is impossible that movement should either have come into being or cease to be (for it must always have existed), or that time should. For there could not be a before and an after if time did not exist. Movement also is continuous, then, in the sense in which time is; for time is either the same thing as movement or an attribute of movement. And there is no continuous movement except movement in place, and of this only that which is circular is continuous.

But if there is something which is capable of moving things or acting on them, but is not actually doing so, there will not necessarily be movement; for that which has a potency need not exercise it. Nothing, then, is gained even if we suppose eternal substances, as the believers in the Forms do, unless there is to be in them some principle which can cause change; nay, even this is not enough, nor is another substance besides the Forms enough; for if it is not to act, there will be no movement. Further even if it acts, this will not be enough, if its essence is potency; for there will not be eternal movement, since that which is potentially may possibly not be. There must, then, be such a principle, whose very essence is actuality. Further, then, these substances must be without matter; for they must be eternal, if anything is eternal. Therefore they must be actuality.

Yet there is a difficulty; for it is thought that everything that acts is able to act, but that not everything that is able to act acts, so that the potency is prior. But if this is so, nothing that is need be; for it is possible for all things to be capable of existing but not yet to exist.

Yet if we follow the theologians who generate the world from night, or the natural philosophers who say that 'all things were together', the same impossible result ensues. For how will there be movement, if there is no actually existing cause? Wood will surely not move itself—the carpenter's art must act on it; nor will the menstrual blood nor the earth set themselves in motion, but the seeds must act on the earth and the semen on the menstrual blood.

This is why some suppose eternal actuality—e.g. Leucippus and Plato; for they say there is always movement. But why and what this movement is they do say, nor, if the world moves in this way or that, do they tell us the cause of its doing so. Now nothing is moved at random, but there must always be something present to move it; e.g. as a matter of fact a thing moves in one way by nature, and in another by force or through the influence of reason or something else. (Further, what sort of movement is primary? This makes a vast difference.) But again for Plato, at least, it is not permissible to name here that which he sometimes supposes to be the source of movement—that which moves itself; for the soul is later, and coeval with the heavens, according to his account. To suppose potency prior to actuality, then, is in a sense right, and in a sense not; and we have specified these senses. That actuality is prior is testified by Anaxagoras (for his 'reason' is actuality) and by Empedocles in his doctrine of love and strife, and by those who say that there is always movement, e.g. Leucippus. Therefore chaos or night did not exist for an infinite time, but the same things have always existed (either passing through a cycle of changes or obeying some other law), since actuality is prior to potency. If, then, there is a constant cycle, something must always remain, acting in the same way. And if there is to be generation and destruction, there must be something else which is always acting in different ways. This must, then, act in one way in virtue of itself, and in another in virtue of something else—either of a third agent, therefore, or of the first. Now it must be in virtue of the first. For otherwise this again causes the motion both of the second agent and of the third. Therefore it is better to say 'the first'. For it was the cause of eternal uniformity; and something else is the cause of variety, and evidently both together are the cause of eternal variety. This, accordingly, is the character which the motions actually exhibit. What need then is there to seek for other principles?

7

Since (1) this is a possible account of the matter, and (2) if it were not true, the world would have proceeded out of night and 'all things together' and out of non-being, these difficulties may be taken as solved. There is, then, something which is always moved with an unceasing motion, which is motion in a circle; and this is plain not in theory only but in fact. Therefore the first heaven must be eternal. There is therefore also something which moves it. And since that which moves and is moved is intermediate, there is something which moves without being moved, being eternal, substance, and actuality. And the object of desire and the object of thought move in this way; they move without being moved. The primary objects of desire and of thought are the same. For the apparent good is the object of appetite, and the real good is the primary object of rational wish. But desire is consequent on opinion rather than opinion on desire; for the thinking is the starting-point. And thought is moved by the object of thought, and one of the two columns of opposites is in itself the object of thought; and in this, substance is first, and in substance, that which is simple and exists actually. (The one and the simple are not the same; for 'one' means a measure, but 'simple' means that the thing itself has a certain nature.) But the beautiful, also, and that which is in itself desirable are in the same column; and the first in any class is always best, or analogous to the best.

That a final cause may exist among unchangeable entities is shown by the distinction of its meanings. For the final cause is (a) some being for whose good an action is done, and (b) something at which the action aims; and of these the latter exists among unchangeable entities though the former does not. The final cause, then, produces motion as being loved, but all other things move by being moved. Now if something is moved it is capable of being otherwise than as it is. Therefore if its actuality is the primary form of spatial motion, then in so far as it is subject to change, in this respect it is capable of being otherwise,—in place, even if not in substance. But since there is something which moves while itself unmoved, existing actually, this can in no way be otherwise than as it is. For motion in space is the first of the kinds of change, and motion in a circle the first kind of spatial motion; and this the first mover produces. The first mover, then, exists of necessity; and in so far as it exists by necessity, its mode of being is good, and it is in this sense a first principle. For the necessary has all these senses—that which is necessary perforce because it is contrary to the natural impulse, that without which the good is impossible, and that which cannot be otherwise but can exist only in a single way.

On such a principle, then, depend the heavens and the world of nature. And it is a life such as the best which we enjoy, and enjoy for but a short time (for it is ever in this state, which we cannot be), since its actuality is also pleasure. (And for this reason are waking, perception, and thinking most pleasant, and hopes and memories are so on account of these.) And thinking in itself deals with that which is best in itself, and that which is thinking in the fullest sense with that which is best in the fullest sense. And thought thinks on itself because it shares the nature of the object of thought; for it becomes an object of thought in coming into contact with and thinking its objects, so that thought and object of thought are the same. For that which is capable of receiving the object of thought, i.e. the essence, is thought. But it is active when it possesses this object. Therefore the possession rather than the receptivity is the divine element which thought seems to contain, and the act of contemplation is what is most pleasant and best. If, then, God is always in that good state in which we sometimes are, this compels our wonder; and if in a better this compels it yet more. And God is in a better state. And life also belongs to God; for the actuality of thought is life, and God is that actuality; and God's self-dependent actuality is life most good and eternal. We say therefore that God is a living being, eternal, most good, so that life and duration continuous and eternal belong to God; for this is God.

Those who suppose, as the Pythagoreans and Speusippus do, that supreme beauty and goodness are not present in the beginning, because the beginnings both of plants and of animals are causes, but beauty and completeness are in the effects of these, are wrong in their opinion. For the seed comes from other individuals which are prior and complete, and the first thing is not seed but the complete being; e.g. we must say that before the seed there is a man,—not the man produced from the seed, but another from whom the seed comes.

It is clear then from what has been said that there is a substance which is eternal and unmovable and separate from sensible things. It has been shown also that this substance cannot have any magnitude, but is without parts and indivisible (for it produces movement through infinite time, but nothing finite has infinite power; and, while every magnitude is either infinite or finite, it cannot, for the above reason, have finite magnitude, and it cannot have infinite magnitude because there is no infinite magnitude at all). But it has also been shown that it is impassive and unalterable; for all the other changes are posterior to change of place.

8

It is clear, then, why these things are as they are. But we must not ignore the question whether we have to suppose one such substance or more than one, and if the latter, how many; we must also mention, regarding the opinions expressed by others, that they have said nothing about the number of the substances that can even be clearly stated. For the theory of Ideas has no special discussion of the subject; for those who speak of Ideas say the Ideas are numbers, and they speak of numbers now as unlimited, now as limited by the number 10; but as for the reason why there should be just so many numbers, nothing is said with any demonstrative exactness. We however must discuss the subject, starting from the presuppositions and distinctions we have mentioned. The first principle or primary being is not movable either in itself or accidentally, but produces the primary eternal and single movement. But since that which is moved must be moved by something, and the first mover must be in itself unmovable, and eternal movement must be produced by something eternal and a single movement by a single thing, and since we see that besides the simple spatial movement of the universe, which we say the first and unmovable substance produces, there are other spatial movements— those of the planets—which are eternal (for a body which moves in a circle is eternal and unresting; we have proved these points in the physical treatises), each of these movements also must be caused by a substance both unmovable in itself and eternal. For the nature of the stars is eternal just because it is a certain kind of substance, and the mover is eternal and prior to the moved, and that which is prior to a substance must be a substance. Evidently, then, there must be substances which are of the same number as the movements of the stars, and in their nature eternal, and in themselves unmovable, and without magnitude, for the reason before mentioned. That the movers are substances, then, and that one of these is first and another second according to the same order as the movements of the stars, is evident. But in the number of the movements we reach a problem which must be treated from the standpoint of that one of the mathematical sciences which is most akin to philosophy—viz. of astronomy; for this science speculates about substance which is perceptible but eternal, but the other mathematical sciences, i.e. arithmetic and geometry, treat of no substance. That the movements are more numerous than the bodies that are moved is evident to those who have given even moderate attention to the matter; for each of the planets has more than one movement. But as to the actual number of these movements, we now—to give some notion of the subject—quote what some of the mathematicians say, that our thought may have some definite number to grasp; but, for the rest, we must partly investigate for ourselves, Partly learn from other investigators, and if those who study this subject form an opinion contrary to what we have now stated, we must esteem both parties indeed, but follow the more accurate.

Eudoxus supposed that the motion of the sun or of the moon involves, in either case, three spheres, of which the first is the sphere of the fixed stars, and the second moves in the circle which runs along the middle of the zodiac, and the third in the circle which is inclined across the breadth of the zodiac; but the circle in which the moon moves is inclined at a greater angle than that in which the sun moves. And the motion of the planets involves, in each case, four spheres, and of these also the first and second are the same as the first two mentioned above (for the sphere of the fixed stars is that which moves all the other spheres, and that which is placed beneath this and has its movement in the circle which bisects the zodiac is common to all), but the poles of the third sphere of each planet are in the circle which bisects the zodiac, and the motion of the fourth sphere is in the circle which is inclined at an angle to the equator of the third sphere; and the poles of the third sphere are different for each of the other planets, but those of Venus and Mercury are the same.

Callippus made the position of the spheres the same as Eudoxus did, but while he assigned the same number as Eudoxus did to Jupiter and to Saturn, he thought two more spheres should be added to the sun and two to the moon, if one is to explain the observed facts; and one more to each of the other planets.

But it is necessary, if all the spheres combined are to explain the observed facts, that for each of the planets there should be other spheres (one fewer than those hitherto assigned) which counteract those already mentioned and bring back to the same position the outermost sphere of the star which in each case is situated below the star in question; for only thus can all the forces at work produce the observed motion of the planets. Since, then, the spheres involved in the movement of the planets themselves are—eight for Saturn and Jupiter and twenty-five for the others, and of these only those involved in the movement of the lowest-situated planet need not be counteracted the spheres which counteract those of the outermost two planets will be six in number, and the spheres which counteract those of the next four planets will be sixteen; therefore the number of all the spheres—both those which move the planets and those which counteract these—will be fifty-five. And if one were not to add to the moon and to the sun the movements we mentioned, the whole set of spheres will be forty-seven in number.

Let this, then, be taken as the number of the spheres, so that the unmovable substances and principles also may probably be taken as just so many; the assertion of necessity must be left to more powerful thinkers. But if there can be no spatial movement which does not conduce to the moving of a star, and if further every being and every substance which is immune from change and in virtue of itself has attained to the best must be considered an end, there can be no other being apart from these we have named, but this must be the number of the substances. For if there are others, they will cause change as being a final cause of movement; but there cannot he other movements besides those mentioned. And it is reasonable to infer this from a consideration of the bodies that are moved; for if everything that moves is for the sake of that which is moved, and every movement belongs to something that is moved, no movement can be for the sake of itself or of another movement, but all the movements must be for the sake of the stars. For if there is to be a movement for the sake of a movement, this latter also will have to be for the sake of something else; so that since there cannot be an infinite regress, the end of every movement will be one of the divine bodies which move through the heaven.

(Evidently there is but one heaven. For if there are many heavens as there are many men, the moving principles, of which each heaven will have one, will be one in form but in number many. But all things that are many in number have matter; for one and the same definition, e.g. that of man, applies to many things, while Socrates is one. But the primary essence has not matter; for it is complete reality. So the unmovable first mover is one both in definition and in number; so too, therefore, is that which is moved always and continuously; therefore there is one heaven alone.) Our forefathers in the most remote ages have handed down to their posterity a tradition, in the form of a myth, that these bodies are gods, and that the divine encloses the whole of nature. The rest of the tradition has been added later in mythical form with a view to the persuasion of the multitude and to its legal and utilitarian expediency; they say these gods are in the form of men or like some of the other animals, and they say other things consequent on and similar to these which we have mentioned. But if one were to separate the first point from these additions and take it alone—that they thought the first substances to be gods, one must regard this as an inspired utterance, and reflect that, while probably each art and each science has often been developed as far as possible and has again perished, these opinions, with others, have been preserved until the present like relics of the ancient treasure. Only thus far, then, is the opinion of our ancestors and of our earliest predecessors clear to us.

9

The nature of the divine thought involves certain problems; for while thought is held to be the most divine of things observed by us, the question how it must be situated in order to have that character involves difficulties. For if it thinks of nothing, what is there here of dignity? It is just like one who sleeps. And if it thinks, but this depends on something else, then (since that which is its substance is not the act of thinking, but a potency) it cannot be the best substance; for it is through thinking that its value belongs to it. Further, whether its substance is the faculty of thought or the act of thinking, what does it think of? Either of itself or of something else; and if of something else, either of the same thing always or of something different. Does it matter, then, or not, whether it thinks of the good or of any chance thing? Are there not some things about which it is incredible that it should think? Evidently, then, it thinks of that which is most divine and precious, and it does not change; for change would be change for the worse, and this would be already a movement. First, then, if 'thought' is not the act of thinking but a potency, it would be reasonable to suppose that the continuity of its thinking is wearisome to it. Secondly, there would evidently be something else more precious than thought, viz. that which is thought of. For both thinking and the act of thought will belong even to one who thinks of the worst thing in the world, so that if this ought to be avoided (and it ought, for there are even some things which it is better not to see than to see), the act of thinking cannot be the best of things. Therefore it must be of itself that the divine thought thinks (since it is the most excellent of things), and its thinking is a thinking on thinking.

But evidently knowledge and perception and opinion and understanding have always something else as their object, and themselves only by the way. Further, if thinking and being thought of are different, in respect of which does goodness belong to thought? For to be an act of thinking and to be an object of thought are not the same thing. We answer that in some cases the knowledge is the object. In the productive sciences it is the substance or essence of the object, matter omitted, and in the theoretical sciences the definition or the act of thinking is the object. Since, then, thought and the object of thought are not different in the case of things that have not matter, the divine thought and its object will be the same, i.e. the thinking will be one with the object of its thought.

A further question is left—whether the object of the divine thought is composite; for if it were, thought would change in passing from part to part of the whole. We answer that everything which has not matter is indivisible—as human thought, or rather the thought of composite beings, is in a certain period of time (for it does not possess the good at this moment or at that, but its best, being something different from it, is attained only in a whole period of time), so throughout eternity is the thought which has itself for its object.

10

We must consider also in which of two ways the nature of the universe contains the good, and the highest good, whether as something separate and by itself, or as the order of the parts. Probably in both ways, as an army does; for its good is found both in its order and in its leader, and more in the latter; for he does not depend on the order but it depends on him. And all things are ordered together somehow, but not all alike,—both fishes and fowls and plants; and the world is not such that one thing has nothing to do with another, but they are connected. For all are ordered together to one end, but it is as in a house, where the freemen are least at liberty to act at random, but all things or most things are already ordained for them, while the slaves and the animals do little for the common good, and for the most part live at random; for this is the sort of principle that constitutes the nature of each. I mean, for instance, that all must at least come to be dissolved into their elements, and there are other functions similarly in which all share for the good of the whole.

We must not fail to observe how many impossible or paradoxical results confront those who hold different views from our own, and what are the views of the subtler thinkers, and which views are attended by fewest difficulties. All make all things out of contraries. But neither 'all things' nor 'out of contraries' is right; nor do these thinkers tell us how all the things in which the contraries are present can be made out of the contraries; for contraries are not affected by one another. Now for us this difficulty is solved naturally by the fact that there is a third element. These thinkers however make one of the two contraries matter; this is done for instance by those who make the unequal matter for the equal, or the many matter for the one. But this also is refuted in the same way; for the one matter which underlies any pair of contraries is contrary to nothing. Further, all things, except the one, will, on the view we are criticizing, partake of evil; for the bad itself is one of the two elements. But the other school does not treat the good and the bad even as principles; yet in all things the good is in the highest degree a principle. The school we first mentioned is right in saying that it is a principle, but how the good is a principle they do not say—whether as end or as mover or as form.

Empedocles also has a paradoxical view; for he identifies the good with love, but this is a principle both as mover (for it brings things together) and as matter (for it is part of the mixture). Now even if it happens that the same thing is a principle both as matter and as mover, still the being, at least, of the two is not the same. In which respect then is love a principle? It is paradoxical also that strife should be imperishable; the nature of his 'evil' is just strife.

Anaxagoras makes the good a motive principle; for his 'reason' moves things. But it moves them for an end, which must be something other than it, except according to our way of stating the case; for, on our view, the medical art is in a sense health. It is paradoxical also not to suppose a contrary to the good, i.e. to reason. But all who speak of the contraries make no use of the contraries, unless we bring their views into shape. And why some things are perishable and others imperishable, no one tells us; for they make all existing things out of the same principles. Further, some make existing things out of the nonexistent; and others to avoid the necessity of this make all things one.

Further, why should there always be becoming, and what is the cause of becoming?—this no one tells us. And those who suppose two principles must suppose another, a superior principle, and so must those who believe in the Forms; for why did things come to participate, or why do they participate, in the Forms? And all other thinkers are confronted by the necessary consequence that there is something contrary to Wisdom, i.e. to the highest knowledge; but we are not. For there is nothing contrary to that which is primary; for all contraries have matter, and things that have matter exist only potentially; and the ignorance which is contrary to any knowledge leads to an object contrary to the object of the knowledge; but what is primary has no contrary.

Again, if besides sensible things no others exist, there will be no first principle, no order, no becoming, no heavenly bodies, but each principle will have a principle before it, as in the accounts of the theologians and all the natural philosophers. But if the Forms or the numbers are to exist, they will be causes of nothing; or if not that, at least not of movement. Further, how is extension, i.e. a *continuum*, to be produced out of unextended parts? For number will not, either as mover or as form, produce a *continuum*. But again there cannot be any contrary that is also essentially a productive or moving principle; for it would be possible for it not to be. Or at least its action would be posterior to its potency. The world, then, would not be eternal. But it is; one of these premises, then, must be denied. And we have said how this must be done. Further, in virtue of what the numbers, or the soul and the body, or in general the form and the thing, are one—of this no one tells us anything; nor can any one tell, unless he says, as we do, that the mover makes them one. And those who say mathematical number is first and go on to generate one kind of substance after another and give different principles for each, make the substance of the universe a mere series of episodes (for one substance has no influence on another by its existence or nonexistence), and they give us many governing principles; but the world refuses to be governed badly.

'The rule of many is not good; one ruler let there be.'

Book XIII

1

We have stated what is the substance of sensible things, dealing in the treatise on physics with matter, and later with the substance which has actual existence. Now since our inquiry is whether there is or is not besides the sensible substances any which is immovable and eternal, and, if there is, what it is, we must first consider what is said by others, so that, if there is anything which they say wrongly, we may not be liable to the same objections, while, if there is any opinion common to them and us, we shall have no private grievance against ourselves on that account; for one must be content to state some points better than one's predecessors, and others no worse.

Two opinions are held on this subject; it is said that the objects of mathematics—i.e. numbers and lines and the like—are substances, and again that the Ideas are substances. And (1) since some recognize these as two different classes—the Ideas and the mathematical numbers, and (2) some recognize both as having one nature, while (3) some others say that the mathematical substances are the only substances, we must consider first the objects of mathematics, not qualifying them by any other characteristic—not asking, for instance, whether they are in fact Ideas or not, or whether they are the principles and substances of existing things or not, but only whether as objects of mathematics they exist or not, and if they exist, how they exist. Then after this we must separately consider the Ideas themselves in a general way, and only as far as the accepted mode of treatment demands; for most of the points have been repeatedly made even by the discussions outside our school, and, further, the greater part of our account must finish by throwing light on that inquiry, viz. when we examine whether the substances and the principles of existing things are numbers and Ideas; for after the discussion of the Ideas this remains as a third inquiry.

If the objects of mathematics exist, they must exist either in sensible objects, as some say, or separate from sensible objects (and this also is said by some); or if they exist in neither of these ways, either they do not exist, or they exist only in some special sense. So that the subject of our discussion will be not whether they exist but how they exist.

2

That it is impossible for mathematical objects to exist in sensible things, and at the same time that the doctrine in question is an artificial one, has been said already in our discussion of difficulties we have pointed out that it is impossible for two solids to be in the same place, and also that according to the same argument the other powers and characteristics also should exist in sensible things and none of them separately. This we have said already. But, further, it is obvious that on this theory it is impossible for any body whatever to be divided; for it would have to be divided at a plane, and the plane at a line, and the line at a point, so that if the point cannot be divided, neither can the line, and if the line cannot, neither can the plane nor the solid. What difference, then, does it make whether sensible things are such indivisible entities, or, without being so themselves, have indivisible entities in them? The result will be the same; if the sensible entities are divided the others will be divided too, or else not even the sensible entities can be divided.

But, again, it is not possible that such entities should exist separately. For if besides the sensible solids there are to be other solids which are separate from them and prior to the sensible solids, it is plain that besides the planes also there must be other and separate planes and points and lines; for consistency requires this. But if these exist, again besides the planes and lines and points of the mathematical solid there must be others which are separate. (For incomposites are prior to compounds; and if there are, prior to the sensible bodies, bodies which are not sensible, by the same argument the planes which exist by themselves must be prior to those which are in the motionless solids. Therefore these will be planes and lines other than those that exist along with the mathematical solids to which these thinkers assign separate existence; for the latter exist along with the mathematical solids, while the others are prior to the mathematical solids.) Again, therefore, there will be, belonging to these planes, lines, and prior to them there will have to be, by the same argument, other lines and points; and prior to these points in the prior lines there will have to be other points, though there will be no others prior to these. Now (1) the accumulation becomes absurd; for we find ourselves with one set of solids apart from the sensible solids; three sets of planes apart from the sensible planes—those which exist apart from the sensible planes, and those in the mathematical solids, and those which exist apart from those in the mathematical solids; four sets of lines, and five sets of points. With which of these, then, will the mathematical sciences deal? Certainly not with the planes and lines and points in the motionless solid; for science always deals with what is prior. And (the same account will apply also to numbers; for there will be a different set of units apart from each set of points, and also apart from each set of realities, from the objects of sense and again from those of thought; so that there will be various classes of mathematical numbers.

Again, how is it possible to solve the questions which we have already enumerated in our discussion of difficulties? For the objects of astronomy will exist apart from sensible things just as the objects of geometry will; but how is it possible that a heaven and its parts—or anything else which has movement—should exist apart? Similarly also the objects of optics and of harmonics will exist apart; for there will be both voice and sight besides the sensible or individual voices and sights. Therefore it is plain that the other senses as well, and the other objects of sense, will exist apart; for why should one set of them do so and another not? And if this is so, there will also be animals existing apart, since there will be senses.

Again, there are certain mathematical theorems that are universal, extending beyond these substances. Here then we shall have another intermediate substance separate both from the Ideas and from the intermediates,—a substance which is neither number nor points nor spatial magnitude nor time. And if this is impossible, plainly it is also impossible that the former entities should exist separate from sensible things.

And, in general, conclusion contrary alike to the truth and to the usual views follow, if one is to suppose the objects of mathematics to exist thus as separate entities. For because they exist thus they must be prior to sensible spatial magnitudes, but in truth they must be posterior; for the incomplete spatial magnitude is in the order of generation prior, but in the order of substance posterior, as the lifeless is to the living.

Again, by virtue of what, and when, will mathematical magnitudes be one? For things in our perceptible world are one in virtue of soul, or of a part of soul, or of something else that is reasonable enough; when these are not present, the thing is a plurality, and splits up into parts. But in the case of the subjects of mathematics, which are divisible and are quantities, what is the cause of their being one and holding together?

Again, the modes of generation of the objects of mathematics show that we are right. For the dimension first generated is length, then comes breadth, lastly depth, and the process is complete. If, then, that which is posterior in the order of generation is prior in the order of substantiality, the solid will be prior to the plane and the line. And in this way also it is both more complete and more whole, because it can become animate. How, on the other hand, could a line or a plane be animate? The supposition passes the power of our senses.

Again, the solid is a sort of substance; for it already has in a sense completeness. But how can lines be substances? Neither as a form or shape, as the soul perhaps is, nor as matter, like the solid; for we have no experience of anything that can be put together out of lines or planes or points, while if these had been a sort of material substance, we should have observed things which could be put together out of them.

Grant, then, that they are prior in definition. Still not all things that are prior in definition are also prior in substantiality. For those things are prior in substantiality which when separated from other things surpass them in the power of independent existence, but things are prior in definition to those whose definitions are compounded out of their definitions; and these two properties are not coextensive. For if attributes do not exist apart from the substances (e.g. a 'mobile' or a pale'), pale is prior to the pale man in definition, but not in substantiality. For it cannot exist separately, but is always along with the concrete thing; and by the concrete thing I mean the pale man. Therefore it is plain that neither is the result of abstraction prior nor that which is produced by adding determinants posterior; for it is by adding a determinant to pale that we speak of the pale man.

It has, then, been sufficiently pointed out that the objects of mathematics are not substances in a higher degree than bodies are, and that they are not prior to sensibles in being, but only in definition, and that they cannot exist somewhere apart. But since it was not possible for them to exist in sensibles either, it is plain that they either do not exist at all or exist in a special sense and therefore do not 'exist' without qualification. For 'exist' has many senses.

3

For just as the universal propositions of mathematics deal not with objects which exist separately, apart from extended magnitudes and from numbers, but with magnitudes and numbers, not however *qua* such as to have magnitude or to be divisible, clearly it is possible that there should also be both propositions and demonstrations about sensible magnitudes, not however *qua* sensible but *qua* possessed of certain definite qualities. For as there are many propositions about things merely considered as in motion, apart from what each such thing is and from their accidents, and as it is not therefore necessary that there should be either a mobile separate from sensibles, or a distinct mobile entity in the sensibles, so too in the case of mobiles there will be propositions and sciences, which treat them however not *qua* mobile but only *qua* bodies, or again only *qua* planes, or only *qua* lines, or *qua* divisibles, or *qua* indivisibles having position, or only *qua* indivisibles. Thus since it is true to say without qualification that not only things which are separable but also things which are inseparable exist (for instance, that mobiles exist), it is true also to say without qualification that the objects of mathematics exist, and with the character ascribed to them by mathematicians. And as it is true to say of the other sciences too, without qualification, that they deal with such and such a subject—not with what is accidental to it (e.g. not with the pale, if the healthy thing is pale, and the science has the healthy as its subject), but with that which is the subject of each science—with the healthy if it treats its object *qua* healthy, with man if *qua* man:—so too is it with geometry; if its subjects happen to be sensible, though it does not treat them *qua* sensible, the mathematical sciences will not for that reason be sciences of sensibles-nor, on the other hand, of other things separate from sensibles. Many properties attach to things in virtue of their own nature as possessed of each such character; e.g. there are attributes peculiar to the animal *qua* female or *qua* male (yet there is no 'female' nor 'male' separate from animals); so that there are also attributes which belong to things merely as lengths or as planes. And in proportion as we are dealing with things which are prior in definition and simpler, our knowledge has more accuracy, i.e. simplicity. Therefore a science which abstracts from spatial magnitude is more precise than one which takes it into account; and a science is most precise if it abstracts from movement, but if it takes account of movement, it is most precise if it deals with the primary movement, for this is the simplest; and of this again uniform movement is the simplest form.

The same account may be given of harmonics and optics; for neither considers its objects *qua* sight or *qua* voice, but *qua* lines and numbers; but the latter are attributes proper to the former. And mechanics too proceeds in the same way. Therefore if we suppose attributes separated from their fellow attributes and make any inquiry concerning them as such, we shall not for this reason be in error, any more than when one draws a line on the ground and calls it a foot long when it is not; for the error is not included in the premisses.

Each question will be best investigated in this way—by setting up by an act of separation what is not separate, as the arithmetician and the geometer do. For a man *qua* man is one indivisible thing; and the arithmetician supposed one indivisible thing, and then considered whether any attribute belongs to a man *qua* indivisible. But the geometer treats him neither *qua* man nor *qua* indivisible, but as a solid. For evidently the properties which would have belonged to him even if perchance he had not been indivisible, can belong to him even apart from these attributes. Thus, then, geometers speak correctly; they talk about existing things, and their subjects do exist; for being has two forms—it exists not only in complete reality but also materially.

Now since the good and the beautiful are different (for the former always implies conduct as its subject, while the beautiful is found also in motionless things), those who assert that the mathematical sciences say nothing of the beautiful or the good are in error. For these sciences say and prove a great deal about them; if they do not expressly mention them, but prove attributes which are their results or their definitions, it is not true to say that they tell us nothing about them. The chief forms of beauty are order and symmetry and definiteness, which the mathematical sciences demonstrate in a special degree. And since these (e.g. order and definiteness) are obviously causes of many things, evidently these sciences must treat this sort of causative principle also (i.e. the beautiful) as in some sense a cause. But we shall speak more plainly elsewhere about these matters.

4

So much then for the objects of mathematics; we have said that they exist and in what sense they exist, and in what sense they are prior and in what sense not prior. Now, regarding the Ideas, we must first examine the ideal theory itself, not connecting it in any way with the nature of numbers, but treating it in the form in which it was originally understood by those who first maintained the existence of the Ideas. The supporters of the ideal theory were led to it because on the question about the truth of things they accepted the Heraclitean sayings which describe all sensible things as ever passing away, so that if knowledge or thought is to have an object, there must be some other and permanent entities, apart from those which are sensible; for there could be no knowledge of things which were in a state of flux. But when Socrates was occupying himself with the excellences of character, and in connexion with them became the first to raise the problem of universal definition (for of the physicists Democritus only touched on the subject to a small extent, and defined, after a fashion, the hot and the cold; while the Pythagoreans had before this treated of a few things, whose definitions—e.g. those of opportunity, justice, or marriage— they connected with numbers; but it was natural that Socrates should be seeking the essence, for he was seeking to syllogize, and 'what a thing is' is the starting-point of syllogisms; for there was as yet none of the dialectical power which enables people even without knowledge of the essence to speculate about contraries and inquire whether the same science deals with contraries; for two things may be fairly ascribed to Socrates—inductive arguments and universal definition, both of which are concerned with the starting-point of science):—but Socrates did not make the universals or the definitions exist apart: they, however, gave them separate existence, and this was the kind of thing they called Ideas. Therefore it followed for them, almost by the same argument, that there must be Ideas of all things that are spoken of universally, and it was almost as if a man wished to count certain things, and while they were few thought he would not be able to count them, but made more of them and then counted them; for the Forms are, one may say, more numerous than the particular sensible things, yet it was in seeking the causes of these that they proceeded from them to the Forms. For to each thing there answers an entity which has the same name and exists apart from the substances, and so also in the case of all other groups there is a one over many, whether these be of this world or eternal.

Again, of the ways in which it is proved that the Forms exist, none is convincing; for from some no inference necessarily follows, and from some arise Forms even of things of which they think there are no Forms. For according to the arguments from the sciences there will be Forms of all things of which there are sciences, and according to the argument of the 'one over many' there will be Forms even of negations, and according to the argument that thought has an object when the individual object has perished, there will be Forms of perishable things; for we have an image of these. Again, of the most accurate arguments, some lead to Ideas of relations, of which they say there is no independent class, and others introduce the 'third man'.

And in general the arguments for the Forms destroy things for whose existence the believers in Forms are more zealous than for the existence of the Ideas; for it follows that not the dyad but number is first, and that prior to number is the relative, and that this is prior to the absolute—besides all the other points on which certain people, by following out the opinions held about the Forms, came into conflict with the principles of the theory.

Again, according to the assumption on the belief in the Ideas rests, there will be Forms not only of substances but also of many other things; for the concept is single not only in the case of substances, but also in that of non-substances, and there are sciences of other things than substance; and a thousand other such difficulties confront them. But according to the necessities of the case and the opinions about the Forms, if they can be shared in there must be Ideas of substances only. For they are not shared in incidentally, but each Form must be shared in as something not predicated of a subject. (By 'being shared in incidentally' I mean that if a thing shares in 'double itself', it shares also in 'eternal', but incidentally; for 'the double' happens to be eternal.) Therefore the Forms will be substance. But the same names indicate substance in this and in the ideal world (or what will be the meaning of saying that there is something apart from the particulars—the one over many?). And if the Ideas and the things that share in them have the same form, there will be something common: for why should '2' be one and the same in the perishable 2's, or in the 2's which are many but eternal, and not the same in the '2 itself' as in the individual 2? But if they have not the same form, they will have only the name in common, and it is as if one were to call both Callias and a piece of wood a 'man', without observing any community between them.

But if we are to suppose that in other respects the common definitions apply to the Forms, e.g. that 'plane figure' and the other parts of the definition apply to the circle itself, but 'what really is' has to be added, we must inquire whether this is not absolutely meaningless. For to what is this to be added? To 'centre' or to 'plane' or to all the parts of the definition? For all the elements in the essence are Ideas, e.g. 'animal' and 'two-footed'. Further, there must be some Ideal answering to 'plane' above, some nature which will be present in all the Forms as their genus.

5

Above all one might discuss the question what in the world the Forms contribute to sensible things, either to those that are eternal or to those that come into being and cease to be; for they cause neither movement nor any change in them. But again they help in no wise either towards the knowledge of other things (for they are not even the substance of these, else they would have been in them), or towards their being, if they are not in the individuals which share in them; though if they were, they might be thought to be causes, as white causes whiteness in a white object by entering into its composition. But this argument, which was used first by Anaxagoras, and later by Eudoxus in his discussion of difficulties and by certain others, is very easily upset; for it is easy to collect many and insuperable objections to such a view.

But, further, all other things cannot come from the Forms in any of the usual senses of 'from'. And to say that they are patterns and the other things share in them is to use empty words and poetical metaphors. For what is it that works, looking to the Ideas? And any thing can both be and come into being without being copied from something else, so that, whether Socrates exists or not, a man like Socrates might come to be. And evidently this might be so even if Socrates were eternal. And there will be several patterns of the same thing, and therefore several Forms; e.g. 'animal' and 'two-footed', and also 'man-himself', will be Forms of man. Again, the Forms are patterns not only of sensible things, but of Forms themselves also; i.e. the genus is the pattern of the various forms-of-a-genus; therefore the same thing will be pattern and copy.

Again, it would seem impossible that substance and that whose substance it is should exist apart; how, therefore, could the Ideas, being the substances of things, exist apart?

In the *Phaedo* the case is stated in this way—that the Forms are causes both of being and of becoming. Yet though the Forms exist, still things do not come into being, unless there is something to originate movement; and many other things come into being (e.g. a house or a ring) of which they say there are no Forms. Clearly therefore even the things of which they say there are Ideas can both be and come into being owing to such causes as produce the things just mentioned, and not owing to the Forms. But regarding the Ideas it is possible, both in this way and by more abstract and accurate arguments, to collect many objections like those we have considered.

6

Since we have discussed these points, it is well to consider again the results regarding numbers which confront those who say that numbers are separable substances and first causes of things. If number is an entity and its substance is nothing other than just number, as some say, it follows that either (1) there is a first in it and a second, each being different in species,—and either (a) this is true of the units without exception, and any unit is inassociable with any unit, or (b) they are all without exception successive, and any of them are associable with any, as they say is the case with mathematical number; for in mathematical number no one unit is in any way different from another. Or (c) some units must be associable and some not; e.g. suppose that 2 is first after 1, and then comes 3 and then the rest of the number series, and the units in each number are associable, e.g. those in the first 2 are associable with one another, and those in the first 3 with one another, and so with the other numbers; but the units in the '2-itself' are inassociable with those in the '3-itself'; and similarly in the case of the other successive numbers. And so while mathematical number is counted thus—after 1, 2 (which consists of another 1 besides the former 1), and 3 which consists of another 1 besides these two), and the other numbers similarly, ideal number is counted thus—after 1, a distinct 2 which does not include the first 1, and a 3 which does not include the 2 and the rest of the number series similarly. Or (2) one kind of number must be like the first that was named, one like that which the mathematicians speak of, and that which we have named last must be a third kind.

Again, these kinds of numbers must either be separable from things, or not separable but in objects of perception (not however in the way which we first considered, in the sense that objects of perception consists of numbers which are present in them)—either one kind and not another, or all of them.

These are of necessity the only ways in which the numbers can exist. And of those who say that the 1 is the beginning and substance and element of all things, and that number is formed from the 1 and something else, almost every one has described number in one of these ways; only no one has said all the units are inassociable. And this has happened reasonably enough; for there can be no way besides those mentioned. Some say both kinds of number exist, that which has a before and after being identical with the Ideas, and mathematical number being different from the Ideas and from sensible things, and both being separable from sensible things; and others say mathematical number alone exists, as the first of realities, separate from sensible things. And the Pythagoreans, also, believe in one kind of number—the mathematical; only they say it is not separate but sensible substances are formed out of it. For they construct the whole universe out of numbers—only not numbers consisting of abstract units; they suppose the units to have spatial magnitude. But how the first 1 was constructed so as to have magnitude, they seem unable to say.

Another thinker says the first kind of number, that of the Forms, alone exists, and some say mathematical number is identical with this.

The case of lines, planes, and solids is similar. For some think that those which are the objects of mathematics are different from those which come after the Ideas; and of those who express themselves otherwise some speak of the objects of mathematics and in a mathematical way—viz. those who do not make the Ideas numbers nor say that Ideas exist; and others speak of the objects of mathematics, but not mathematically; for they say that neither is every spatial magnitude divisible into magnitudes, nor do any two units taken at random make 2. All who say the 1 is an element and principle of things suppose numbers to consist of abstract units, except the Pythagoreans; but they suppose the numbers to have magnitude, as has been said before. It is clear from this statement, then, in how many ways numbers may be described, and that all the ways have been mentioned; and all these views are impossible, but some perhaps more than others.

7

First, then, let us inquire if the units are associable or inassociable, and if inassociable, in which of the two ways we distinguished. For it is possible that any unity is inassociable with any, and it is possible that those in the 'itself' are inassociable with those in the 'itself', and, generally, that those in each ideal number are inassociable with those in other ideal numbers. Now (1) all units are associable and without difference, we get mathematical number—only one kind of number, and the Ideas cannot be the numbers. For what sort of number will man-himself or animal-itself or any other Form be? There is one Idea of each thing e.g. one of man-himself and another one of animal-itself; but the similar and undifferentiated numbers are infinitely many, so that any particular 3 is no more man-himself than any other 3. But if the Ideas are not numbers, neither can they exist at all. For from what principles will the Ideas come? It is number that comes from the 1 and the indefinite dyad, and the principles or elements are said to be principles and elements of number, and the Ideas cannot be ranked as either prior or posterior to the numbers.

But (2) if the units are inassociable, and inassociable in the sense that any is inassociable with any other, number of this sort cannot be mathematical number; for mathematical number consists of undifferentiated units, and the truths proved of it suit this character. Nor can it be ideal number. For 2 will not proceed immediately from 1 and the indefinite dyad, and be followed by the successive numbers, as they say '2, 3, 4'—for the units in the ideal are generated at the same time, whether, as the first holder of the theory said, from unequals (coming into being when these were equalized) or in some other way—since, if one unit is to be prior to the other, it will be prior also to 2 the composed of these; for when there is one thing prior and another posterior, the resultant of these will be prior to one and posterior to the other. Again, since the 1-itself is first, and then there is a particular 1 which is first among the others and next after the 1-itself, and again a third which is next after the second and next but one after the first 1,-so the units must be prior to the numbers after which they are named when we count them; e.g. there will be a third unit in 2 before 3 exists, and a fourth and a fifth in 3 before the numbers 4 and 5 exist.—Now none of these thinkers has said the units are inassociable in this way, but according to their principles it is reasonable that they should be so even in this way, though in truth it is impossible. For it is reasonable both that the units should have priority and posteriority if there is a first unit or first 1, and also that the 2's should if there is a first 2; for after the first it is reasonable and necessary that there should be a second, and if a second, a third, and so with the others successively. (And to say both things at the same time, that a unit is first and another unit is second after the ideal 1, and that a 2 is first after it, is impossible.) But they make a first unit or 1, but not also a second and a third, and a first 2, but not also a second and a third. Clearly, also, it is not possible, if all the units are inassociable, that there should be a 2-itself and a 3-itself; and so with the other numbers. For whether the units are undifferentiated or different each from each, number must be counted by addition, e.g. 2 by adding another 1 to the one, 3 by adding another 1 to the two, and similarly. This being so, numbers cannot be generated as they generate them, from the 2 and the 1; for 2 becomes part of 3 and 3 of 4 and the same happens in the case of the succeeding numbers, but they say 4 came from the first 2 and the indefinite 2,—which makes it two 2's other than the 2-itself; if not, the 2-itself will be a part of 4 and one other 2 will be added. And similarly 2 will consist of the 1-itself and another 1; but if this is so, the other element cannot be an indefinite 2; for it generates one unit, not, as the indefinite 2 does, a definite 2.

Again, besides the 3-itself and the 2-itself how can there be other 3's and 2's? And how do they consist of prior and posterior units? All this is absurd and fictitious, and there cannot be a first 2 and then a 3-itself. Yet there must, if the 1 and the indefinite dyad are to be the elements. But if the results are impossible, it is also impossible that these are the generating principles.

If the units, then, are differentiated, each from each, these results and others similar to these follow of necessity. But (3) if those in different numbers are differentiated, but those in the same number are alone undifferentiated from one another, even so the difficulties that follow are no less. E.g. in the 10-itself their are ten units, and the 10 is composed both of them and of two 5's. But since the 10-itself is not any chance number nor composed of any chance 5's—or, for that matter, units—the units in this 10 must differ. For if they do not differ, neither will the 5's of which the 10 consists differ; but since these differ, the units also will differ. But if they differ, will there be no other 5's in the 10 but only these two, or will there be others? If there are not, this is paradoxical; and if there are, what sort of 10 will consist of them? For there is no other in the 10 but the 10 itself. But it is actually necessary on their view that the 4 should not consist of any chance 2's; for the indefinite as they say, received the definite 2 and made two 2's; for its nature was to double what it received.

Again, as to the 2 being an entity apart from its two units, and the 3 an entity apart from its three units, how is this possible? Either by one's sharing in the other, as 'pale man' is different from 'pale' and 'man' (for it shares in these), or when one is a differentia of the other, as 'man' is different from 'animal' and 'two-footed'.

Again, some things are one by contact, some by intermixture, some by position; none of which can belong to the units of which the 2 or the 3 consists; but as two men are not a unity apart from both, so must it be with the units. And their being indivisible will make no difference to them; for points too are indivisible, but yet a pair of them is nothing apart from the two.

But this consequence also we must not forget, that it follows that there are prior and posterior 2 and similarly with the other numbers. For let the 2's in the 4 be simultaneous; yet these are prior to those in the 8 and as the 2 generated them, they generated the 4's in the 8-itself. Therefore if the first 2 is an Idea, these 2's also will be Ideas of some kind. And the same account applies to the units; for the units in the first 2 generate the four in 4, so that all the units come to be Ideas and an Idea will be composed of Ideas. Clearly therefore those things also of which these happen to be the Ideas will be composite, e.g. one might say that animals are composed of animals, if there are Ideas of them.

In general, to differentiate the units in any way is an absurdity and a fiction; and by a fiction I mean a forced statement made to suit a hypothesis. For neither in quantity nor in quality do we see unit differing from unit, and number must be either equal or unequal—all number but especially that which consists of abstract units—so that if one number is neither greater nor less than another, it is equal to it; but things that are equal and in no wise differentiated we take to be the same when we are speaking of numbers. If not, not even the 2 in the 10-itself will be undifferentiated, though they are equal; for what reason will the man who alleges that they are not differentiated be able to give?

Again, if every unit + another unit makes two, a unit from the 2-itself and one from the 3-itself will make a 2. Now (a) this will consist of differentiated units; and will it be prior to the 3 or posterior? It rather seems that it must be prior; for one of the units is simultaneous with the 3 and the other is simultaneous with the 2. And we, for our part, suppose that in general 1 and 1, whether the things are equal or unequal, is 2, e.g. the good and the bad, or a man and a horse; but those who hold these views say that not even two units are 2.

If the number of the 3-itself is not greater than that of the 2, this is surprising; and if it is greater, clearly there is also a number in it equal to the 2, so that this is not different from the 2-itself. But this is not possible, if there is a first and a second number.

Nor will the Ideas be numbers. For in this particular point they are right who claim that the units must be different, if there are to be Ideas; as has been said before. For the Form is unique; but if the units are not different, the 2's and the 3's also will not be different. This is also the reason why they must say that when we count thus—'1, 2'—we do not proceed by adding to the given number; for if we do, neither will the numbers be generated from the indefinite dyad, nor can a number be an Idea; for then one Idea will be in another, and all Forms will be parts of one Form. And so with a view to their hypothesis their statements are right, but as a whole they are wrong; for their view is very destructive, since they will admit that this question itself affords some difficulty—whether, when we count and say '1, 2, 3' we count by addition or by separate portions. But we do both; and so it is absurd to reason back from this problem to so great a difference of essence.

8

First of all it is well to determine what is the differentia of a number—and of a unit, if it has a differentia. Units must differ either in quantity or in quality; and neither of these seems to be possible. But number *qua* number differs in quantity. And if the units also did differ in quantity, number would differ from number, though equal in number of units. Again, are the first units greater or smaller, and do the later ones increase or diminish? All these are irrational suppositions. But neither can they differ in quality. For no attribute can attach to them; for even to numbers quality is said to belong after quantity. Again, quality could not come to them either from the 1 or the dyad; for the former has no quality, and the latter gives quantity; for this entity is what makes things to be many. If the facts are really otherwise, they should state this quite at the beginning and determine if possible, regarding the differentia of the unit, why it must exist, and, failing this, what differentia they mean.

Evidently then, if the Ideas are numbers, the units cannot all be associable, nor can they be inassociable in either of the two ways. But neither is the way in which some others speak about numbers correct. These are those who do not think there are Ideas, either without qualification or as identified with certain numbers, but think the objects of mathematics exist and the numbers are the first of existing things, and the 1-itself is the starting-point of them. It is paradoxical that there should be a 1 which is first of 1's, as they say, but not a 2 which is first of 2's, nor a 3 of 3's; for the same reasoning applies to all. If, then, the facts with regard to number are so, and one supposes mathematical number alone to exist, the 1 is not the starting-point (for this sort of 1 must differ from the-other units; and if this is so, there must also be a 2 which is first of 2's, and similarly with the other successive numbers). But if the 1 is the starting-point, the truth about the numbers must rather be what Plato used to say, and there must be a first 2 and 3 and numbers must not be associable with one another. But if on the other hand one supposes this, many impossible results, as we have said, follow. But either this or the other must be the case, so that if neither is, number cannot exist separately.

It is evident, also, from this that the third version is the worst,—the view ideal and mathematical number is the same. For two mistakes must then meet in the one opinion. (1) Mathematical number cannot be of this sort, but the holder of this view has to spin it out by making suppositions peculiar to himself. And (2) he must also admit all the consequences that confront those who speak of number in the sense of 'Forms'.

The Pythagorean version in one way affords fewer difficulties than those before named, but in another way has others peculiar to itself. For not thinking of number as capable of existing separately removes many of the impossible consequences; but that bodies should be composed of numbers, and that this should be mathematical number, is impossible. For it is not true to speak of indivisible spatial magnitudes; and however much there might be magnitudes of this sort, units at least have not magnitude; and how can a magnitude be composed of indivisibles? But arithmetical number, at least, consists of units, while these thinkers identify number with real things; at any rate they apply their propositions to bodies as if they consisted of those numbers.

If, then, it is necessary, if number is a self-subsistent real thing, that it should exist in one of these ways which have been mentioned, and if it cannot exist in any of these, evidently number has no such nature as those who make it separable set up for it.

Again, does each unit come from the great and the small,

equalized, or one from the small, another from the great? (a) If the latter, neither does each thing contain all the elements, nor are the units without difference; for in one there is the great and in another the small, which is contrary in its nature to the great. Again, how is it with the units in the 3-itself? One of them is an odd unit. But perhaps it is for this reason that they give 1-itself the middle place in odd numbers. (b) But if each of the two units consists of both the great and the small, equalized, how will the 2 which is a single thing, consist of the great and the small? Or how will it differ from the unit? Again, the unit is prior to the 2; for when it is destroyed the 2 is destroyed. It must, then, be the Idea of an Idea since it is prior to an Idea, and it must have come into being before it. From what, then? Not from the indefinite dyad, for its function was to double.

Again, number must be either infinite or finite; for these thinkers think of number as capable of existing separately, so that it is not possible that neither of those alternatives should be true. Clearly it cannot be infinite; for infinite number is neither odd nor even, but the generation of numbers is always the generation either of an odd or of an even number; in one way, when 1 operates on an even number, an odd number is produced; in another way, when 2 operates, the numbers got from 1 by doubling are produced; in another way, when the odd numbers operate, the other even numbers are produced. Again, if every Idea is an Idea of something, and the numbers are Ideas, infinite number itself will be an Idea of something, either of some sensible thing or of something else. Yet this is not possible in view of their thesis any more than it is reasonable in itself, at least if they arrange the Ideas as they do.

But if number is finite, how far does it go? With regard to this not only the fact but the reason should be stated. But if number goes only up to 10 as some say, firstly the Forms will soon run short; e.g. if 3 is man-himself, what number will be the horse-itself? The series of the numbers which are the several things-themselves goes up to 10. It must, then, be one of the numbers within these limits; for it is these that are substances and Ideas. Yet they will run short; for the various forms of animal will outnumber them. At the same time it is clear that if in this way the 3 is man-himself, the other 3's are so also (for those in identical numbers are similar), so that there will be an infinite number of men; if each 3 is an Idea, each of the numbers will be man-himself, and if not, they will at least be men. And if the smaller number is part of the greater (being number of such a sort that the units in the same number are associable), then if the 4-itself is an Idea of something, e.g. of 'horse' or of 'white', man will be a part of horse, if man is It is paradoxical also that there should be an Idea of 10 but not of 11, nor of the succeeding numbers. Again, there both are and come to be certain things of which there are no Forms; why, then, are there not Forms of them also? We infer that the Forms are not causes. Again, it is paradoxical-if the number series up to 10 is more of a real thing and a Form than 10 itself. There is no generation of the former as one thing, and there is of the latter. But they try to work on the assumption that the series of numbers up to 10 is a complete series. At least they generate the derivatives—e.g. the void, proportion, the odd, and the others of this kind—within the decade. For some things, e.g. movement and rest, good and bad, they assign to the originative principles, and the others to the numbers. This is why they identify the odd with 1; for if the odd implied 3 how would 5 be odd? Again, spatial magnitudes and all such things are explained without going beyond a definite number; e.g. the first, the indivisible, line, then the 2 &c.; these entities also extend only up to 10.

Again, if number can exist separately, one might ask which is prior—1, or 3 or 2? Inasmuch as the number is composite, 1 is prior, but inasmuch as the universal and the form is prior, the number is prior; for each of the units is part of the number as its matter, and the number acts as form. And in a sense the right angle is prior to the acute, because it is determinate and in virtue of its definition; but in a sense the acute is prior, because it is a part and the right angle is divided into acute angles. As matter, then, the acute angle and the element and the unit are prior, but in respect of the form and of the substance as expressed in the definition, the right angle, and the whole consisting of the matter and the form, are prior; for the concrete thing is nearer to the form and to what is expressed in the definition, though in generation it is later. How then is 1 the starting-point? Because it is not divisible, they say; but both the universal, and the particular or the element, are indivisible. But they are starting-points in different ways, one in definition and the other in time. In which way, then, is 1 the starting-point? As has been said, the right angle is thought to be prior to the acute, and the acute to the right, and each is one. Accordingly they make 1 the starting-point in both ways. But this is impossible. For the universal is one as form or substance, while the element is one as a part or as matter. For each of the two is in a sense one—in truth each of the two units exists potentially (at least if the number is a unity and not like a heap, i.e. if different numbers consist of differentiated units, as they say), but not in complete reality; and the cause of the error they fell into is that they were conducting their inquiry at the same time from the standpoint of mathematics and from that of universal definitions, so that (1) from the former standpoint they treated unity, their first principle, as a point; for the unit is a point without position. They put things together out of the smallest parts, as some others also have done. Therefore the unit becomes the matter of numbers and at the same time prior to 2; and again posterior, 2 being treated as a whole, a unity, and a form. But (2) because they were seeking the universal they treated the unity which can be predicated of a number, as in this sense also a part of the number. But these characteristics cannot belong at the same time to the same thing.

If the 1-itself must be unitary (for it differs in nothing from other 1's except that it is the starting-point), and the 2 is divisible but the unit is not, the unit must be liker the 1-itself than the 2 is. But if the unit is liker it, it must be liker to the unit than to the 2; therefore each of the units in 2 must be prior to the 2. But they deny this; at least they generate the 2 first. Again, if the 2-itself is a unity and the 3-itself is one also, both form a 2. From what, then, is this 2 produced?

9

Since there is not contact in numbers, but succession, viz. between the units between which there is nothing, e.g. between those in 2 or in 3 one might ask whether these succeed the 1-itself or not, and whether, of the terms that succeed it, 2 or either of the units in 2 is prior.

Similar difficulties occur with regard to the classes of things posterior to number,—the line, the plane, and the solid. For some construct these out of the species of the 'great and small'; e.g. lines from the 'long and short', planes from the 'broad and narrow', masses from the 'deep and shallow'; which are species of the 'great and small'. And the originative principle of such things which answers to the 1 different thinkers describe in different ways, And in these also the impossibilities, the fictions, and the contradictions of all probability are seen to be innumerable. For (i) geometrical classes are severed from one another, unless the principles of these are implied in one another in such a way that the 'broad and narrow' is also 'long and short' (but if this is so, the plane will be line and the solid a plane; again, how will angles and figures and such things be explained?). And (ii) the same happens as in regard to number; for 'long and short', &c., are attributes of magnitude, but magnitude does not consist of these, any more than the line consists of 'straight and curved', or solids of 'smooth and rough'.

(All these views share a difficulty which occurs with regard to species-of-a-genus, when one posits the universals, viz. whether it is animal-itself or something other than animal-itself that is in the particular animal. True, if the universal is not separable from sensible things, this will present no difficulty; but if the 1 and the numbers are separable, as those who express these views say, it is not easy to solve the difficulty, if one may apply the words 'not easy' to the impossible. For when we apprehend the unity in 2, or in general in a number, do we apprehend a thing-itself or something else?).

Some, then, generate spatial magnitudes from matter of this sort, others from the point—and the point is thought by them to be not 1 but something like 1—and from other matter like plurality, but not identical with it; about which principles none the less the same difficulties occur. For if the matter is one, line and plane and solid will be the same; for from the same elements will come one and the same thing. But if the matters are more than one, and there is one for the line and a second for the plane and another for the solid, they either are implied in one another or not, so that the same results will follow even so; for either the plane will not contain a line or it will be a line.

Again, how number can consist of the one and plurality, they make no attempt to explain; but however they express themselves, the same objections arise as confront those who construct number out of the one and the indefinite dyad. For the one view generates number from the universally predicated plurality, and not from a particular plurality; and the other generates it from a particular plurality, but the first; for 2 is said to be a 'first plurality'. Therefore there is practically no difference, but the same difficulties will follow,—is it intermixture or position or blending or generation? and so on. Above all one might press the question 'if each unit is one, what does it come from?' Certainly each is not the one-itself. It must, then, come from the one itself and plurality, or a part of plurality. To say that the unit is a plurality is impossible, for it is indivisible; and to generate it from a part of plurality involves many other objections; for (a) each of the parts must be indivisible (or it will be a plurality and the unit will be divisible) and the elements will not be the one and plurality; for the single units do not come from plurality and the one. Again, (,the holder of this view does nothing but presuppose another number; for his plurality of indivisibles is a number. Again, we must inquire, in view of this theory also, whether the number is infinite or finite. For there was at first, as it seems, a plurality that was itself finite, from which and from the one comes the finite number of units. And there is another plurality that is plurality-itself and infinite plurality; which sort of plurality, then, is the element which co-operates with the one? One might inquire similarly about the point, i.e. the element out of which they make spatial magnitudes. For surely this is not the one and only point; at any rate, then, let them say out of what each of the points is formed. Certainly not of some distance + the point-itself. Nor again can there be indivisible parts of a distance, as the elements out of which the units are said to be made are indivisible parts of plurality; for number consists of indivisibles, but spatial magnitudes do not.

All these objections, then, and others of the sort make it evident that number and spatial magnitudes cannot exist apart from things. Again, the discord about numbers between the various versions is a sign that it is the incorrectness of the alleged facts themselves that brings confusion into the theories. For those who make the objects of mathematics alone exist apart from sensible things, seeing the difficulty about the Forms and their fictitiousness, abandoned ideal number and posited mathematical. But those who wished to make the Forms at the same time also numbers, but did not see, if one assumed these principles, how mathematical number was to exist apart from ideal, made ideal and mathematical number the same—in words, since in fact mathematical number has been destroyed; for they state hypotheses peculiar to themselves and not those of mathematics. And he who first supposed that the Forms exist and that the Forms are numbers and that the objects of mathematics exist, naturally separated the two. Therefore it turns out that all of them are right in some respect, but on the whole not right. And they themselves confirm this, for their statements do not agree but conflict. The cause is that their hypotheses and their principles are false. And it is hard to make a good case out of bad materials, according to Epicharmus: 'as soon as 'tis said, 'tis seen to be wrong.'

But regarding numbers the questions we have raised and the conclusions we have reached are sufficient (for while he who is already convinced might be further convinced by a longer discussion, one not yet convinced would not come any nearer to conviction); regarding the first principles and the first causes and elements, the views expressed by those who discuss only sensible substance have been partly stated in our works on nature, and partly do not belong to the present inquiry; but the views of those who assert that there are other substances besides the sensible must be considered next after those we have been mentioning. Since, then, some say that the Ideas and the numbers are such substances, and that the elements of these are elements and principles of real things, we must inquire regarding these what they say and in what sense they say it.

Those who posit numbers only, and these mathematical, must be considered later; but as regards those who believe in the Ideas one might survey at the same time their way of thinking and the difficulty into which they fall. For they at the same time make the Ideas universal and again treat them as separable and as individuals. That this is not possible has been argued before. The reason why those who described their substances as universal combined these two characteristics in one thing, is that they did not make substances identical with sensible things. They thought that the particulars in the sensible world were a state of flux and none of them remained, but that the universal was apart from these and something different. And Socrates gave the impulse to this theory, as we said in our earlier discussion, by reason of his definitions, but he did not separate universals from individuals; and in this he thought rightly, in not separating them. This is plain from the results; for without the universal it is not possible to get knowledge, but the separation is the cause of the objections that arise with regard to the Ideas. His successors, however, treating it as necessary, if there are to be any substances besides the sensible and transient substances, that they must be separable, had no others, but gave separate existence to these universally predicated substances, so that it followed that universals and individuals were almost the same sort of thing. This in itself, then, would be one difficulty in the view we have mentioned.

10

Let us now mention a point which presents a certain difficulty both to those who believe in the Ideas and to those who do not, and which was stated before, at the beginning, among the problems. If we do not suppose substances to be separate, and in the way in which individual things are said to be separate, we shall destroy substance in the sense in which we understand 'substance'; but if we conceive substances to be separable, how are we to conceive their elements and their principles?

If they are individual and not universal, (a) real things will be just of the same number as the elements, and (b) the elements will not be knowable. For (a) let the syllables in speech be substances, and their elements elements of substances; then there must be only one *ba* and one of each of the syllables, since they are not universal and the same in form but each is one in number and a 'this' and not a kind possessed of a common name (and again they suppose that the 'just what a thing is' is in each case one). And if the syllables are unique, so too are the parts of which they consist; there will not, then, be more *a*'s than one, nor more than one of any of the other elements, on the same principle on which an identical syllable cannot exist in the plural number. But if this is so, there will not be other things existing besides the elements, but only the elements.

(b) Again, the elements will not be even knowable; for they are not universal, and knowledge is of universals. This is clear from demonstrations and from definitions; for we do not conclude that this triangle has its angles equal to two right angles, unless every triangle has its angles equal to two right angles, nor that this man is an animal, unless every man is an animal.

But if the principles are universal, either the substances composed of them are also universal, or non-substance will be prior to substance; for the universal is not a substance, but the element or principle is universal, and the element or principle is prior to the things of which it is the principle or element.

All these difficulties follow naturally, when they make the Ideas out of elements and at the same time claim that apart from the substances which have the same form there are Ideas, a single separate entity. But if, e.g. in the case of the elements of speech, the a's and the b's may quite well be many and there need be no a-itself and b-itself besides the many, there may be, so far as this goes, an infinite number of similar syllables. The statement that an knowledge is universal, so that the principles of things must also be universal and not separate substances, presents indeed, of all the points we have mentioned, the greatest difficulty, but yet the statement is in a sense true, although in a sense it is not. For knowledge, like the verb 'to know', means two things, of which one is potential and one actual. The potency, being, as matter, universal and indefinite, deals with the universal and indefinite; but the actuality, being definite, deals with a definite object,—being a 'this', it deals with a 'this'. But *per accidens* sight sees universal colour, because this individual colour which it sees is colour; and this individual a which the grammarian investigates is an a. For if the principles must be universal, what is derived from them must also be universal, as in demonstrations; and if this is so, there will be nothing capable of separate existence—i.e. no substance. But evidently in a sense knowledge is universal, and in a sense it is not.

Book XIV

1

Regarding this kind of substance, what we have said must be taken as sufficient. All philosophers make the first principles contraries: as in natural things, so also in the case of unchangeable substances. But since there cannot be anything prior to the first principle of all things, the principle cannot be the principle and yet be an attribute of something else. To suggest this is like saying that the white is a first principle, not *qua* anything else but *qua* white, but yet that it is predicable of a subject, i.e. that its being white presupposes its being something else; this is absurd, for then that subject will be prior. But all things which are generated from their contraries involve an underlying subject; a subject, then, must be present in the case of contraries, if anywhere. All contraries, then, are always predicable of a subject, and none can exist apart, but just as appearances suggest that there is nothing contrary to substance, argument confirms this. No contrary, then, is the first principle of all things in the full sense; the first principle is something different.

But these thinkers make one of the contraries matter, some making the unequal which they take to be the essence of plurality—matter for the One, and others making plurality matter for the One. (The former generate numbers out of the dyad of the unequal, i.e. of the great and small, and the other thinker we have referred to generates them out of plurality, while according to both it is generated by the essence of the One.) For even the philosopher who says the unequal and the One are the elements, and the unequal is a dyad composed of the great and small, treats the unequal, or the great and the small, as being one, and does not draw the distinction that they are one in definition, but not in number. But they do not describe rightly even the principles which they call elements, for some name the great and the small with the One and treat these three as elements of numbers, two being matter, one the form; while others name the many and few, because the great and the small are more appropriate in their nature to magnitude than to number; and others name rather the universal character common to these—'that which exceeds and that which is exceeded'. None of these varieties of opinion makes any difference to speak of, in view of some of the consequences; they affect only the abstract objections, which these thinkers take care to avoid because the demonstrations they themselves offer are abstract,—with this exception, that if the exceeding and the exceeded are the principles, and not the great and the small, consistency requires that number should come from the elements before does; for number is more universal than as the exceeding and the exceeded are more universal than the great and the small. But as it is, they say one of these things but do not say the other. Others oppose the different and the other to the One, and others oppose plurality to the One. But if, as they claim, things consist of contraries, and to the One either there is nothing contrary, or if there is to be anything it is plurality, and the unequal is contrary to the equal, and the different to the same, and the other to the thing itself, those who oppose the One to plurality have most claim to plausibility, but even their view is inadequate, for the One would on their view be a few; for plurality is opposed to fewness, and the many to the few.

'The one' evidently means a measure. And in every case there is some underlying thing with a distinct nature of its own, e.g. in the scale a quarter-tone, in spatial magnitude a finger or a foot or something of the sort, in rhythms a beat or a syllable; and similarly in gravity it is a definite weight; and in the same way in all cases, in qualities a quality, in quantities a quantity (and the measure is indivisible, in the former case in kind, and in the latter to the sense); which implies that the one is not in itself the substance of anything. And this is reasonable; for 'the one' means the measure of some plurality, and 'number' means a measured plurality and a plurality of measures. (Thus it is natural that one is not a number; for the measure is not measures, but both the measure and the one are starting-points.) The measure must always be some identical thing predicable of all the things it measures, e.g. if the things are horses, the measure is 'horse', and if they are men, 'man'. If they are a man, a horse, and a god, the measure is perhaps 'living being', and the number of them will be a number of living beings. If the things are 'man' and 'pale' and 'walking', these will scarcely have a number, because all belong to a subject which is one and the same in number, yet the number of these will be a number of 'kinds' or of some such term.

Those who treat the unequal as one thing, and the dyad as an indefinite compound of great and small, say what is very far from being probable or possible. For (a) these are modifications and accidents, rather than substrata, of numbers and magnitudes—the many and few of number, and the great and small of magnitude—like even and odd, smooth and rough, straight and curved. Again, (b) apart from this mistake, the great and the small, and so on, must be relative to something; but what is relative is least of all things a kind of entity or substance, and is posterior to quality and quantity; and the relative is an accident of quantity, as was said, not its matter, since something with a distinct nature of its own must serve as matter both to the relative in general and to its parts and kinds. For there is nothing either great or small, many or few, or, in general, relative to something else, which without having a nature of its own is many or few, great or small, or relative to something else. A sign that the relative is least of all a substance and a real thing is the fact that it alone has no proper generation or destruction or movement, as in respect of quantity there is increase and diminution, in respect of quality alteration, in respect of place locomotion, in respect of substance simple generation and destruction. In respect of relation there is no proper change; for, without changing, a thing will be now greater and now less or equal, if that with which it is compared has changed in quantity. And (c) the matter of each thing, and therefore of substance, must be that which is potentially of the nature in question; but the relative is neither potentially nor actually substance. It is strange, then, or rather impossible, to make not-substance an element in, and prior to, substance; for all the categories are posterior to substance. Again, (d) elements are not predicated of the things of which they are elements, but many and few are predicated both apart and together of number, and long and short of the line, and both broad and narrow apply to the plane. If there is a plurality, then, of which the one term, viz. few, is always predicated, e.g. 2 (which cannot be many, for if it were many, 1 would be few), there must be also one which is absolutely many, e.g. 10 is many (if there is no number which is greater than 10), or 10,000. How then, in view of this, can number consist of few and many? Either both ought to be predicated of it, or neither; but in fact only the one or the other is predicated.

2

We must inquire generally, whether eternal things can consist of elements. If they do, they will have matter; for everything that consists of elements is composite. Since, then, even if a thing exists for ever, out of that of which it consists it would necessarily also, if it had come into being, have come into being, and since everything comes to be what it comes to be out of that which is it potentially (for it could not have come to be out of that which had not this capacity, nor could it consist of such elements), and since the potential can be either actual or not,- this being so, however everlasting number or anything else that has matter is, it must be capable of not existing, just as that which is any number of years old is as capable of not existing as that which is a day old; if this is capable of not existing, so is that which has lasted for a time so long that it has no limit. They cannot, then, be eternal, since that which is capable of not existing is not eternal, as we had occasion to show in another context. If that which we are now saying is true universally—that no substance is eternal unless it is actuality—and if the elements are matter that underlies substance, no eternal substance can have elements present in it, of which it consists.

There are some who describe the element which acts with the One as an indefinite dyad, and object to 'the unequal', reasonably enough, because of the ensuing difficulties; but they have got rid only of those objections which inevitably arise from the treatment of the unequal, i.e. the relative, as an element; those which arise apart from this opinion must confront even these thinkers, whether it is ideal number, or mathematical, that they construct out of those elements.

There are many causes which led them off into these explanations, and especially the fact that they framed the difficulty in an obsolete form. For they thought that all things that are would be one (viz. Being itself), if one did not join issue with and refute the saying of Parmenides:

'For never will this be proved, that things that are not are.'

They thought it necessary to prove that that which is not is; for only thus—of that which is and something else-could the things that are be composed, if they are many.

But, first, if 'being' has many senses (for it means sometimes substance, sometimes that it is of a certain quality, sometimes that it is of a certain quantity, and at other times the other categories), what sort of 'one', then, are all the things that are, if non-being is to be supposed not to be? Is it the substances that are one, or the affections and similarly the other categories as well, or all together—so that the 'this' and the 'such' and the 'so much' and the other categories that indicate each some one class of being will all be one? But it is strange, or rather impossible, that the coming into play of a single thing should bring it about that part of that which is is a 'this', part a 'such', part a 'so much', part a 'here'.

Secondly, of what sort of non-being and being do the things that are consist? For 'non-being' also has many senses, since 'being' has; and 'not being a man' means not being a certain substance, 'not being straight' not being of a certain quality, 'not being three cubits long' not being of a certain quantity. What sort of being and non-being, then, by their union pluralize the things that are? This thinker means by the non-being the union of which with being pluralizes the things that are, the false and the character of falsity. This is also why it used to be said that we must assume something that is false, as geometers assume the line which is not a foot long to be a foot long. But this cannot be so. For neither do geometers assume anything false (for the enunciation is extraneous to the inference), nor is it non-being in this sense that the things that are are generated from or resolved into. But since 'non-being' taken in its various cases has as many senses as there are categories, and besides this the false is said not to be, and so is the potential, it is from this that generation proceeds, man from that which is not man but potentially man, and white from that which is not white but potentially white, and this whether it is some one thing that is generated or many.

The question evidently is, how being, in the sense of 'the substances', is many; for the things that are generated are numbers and lines and bodies. Now it is strange to inquire how being in the sense of the 'what' is many, and not how either qualities or quantities are many. For surely the indefinite dyad or 'the great and the small' is not a reason why there should be two kinds of white or many colours or flavours or shapes; for then these also would be numbers and units. But if they had attacked these other categories, they would have seen the cause of the plurality in substances also; for the same thing or something analogous is the cause. This aberration is the reason also why in seeking the opposite of being and the one, from which with being and the one the things that are proceed, they posited the relative term (i.e. the unequal), which is neither the contrary nor the contradictory of these, and is one kind of being as 'what' and quality also are.

They should have asked this question also, how relative terms are many and not one. But as it is, they inquire how there are many units besides the first 1, but do not go on to inquire how there are many unequals besides the unequal. Yet they use them and speak of great and small, many and few (from which proceed numbers), long and short (from which proceeds the line), broad and narrow (from which proceeds the plane), deep and shallow (from which proceed solids); and they speak of yet more kinds of relative term. What is the reason, then, why there is a plurality of these?

It is necessary, then, as we say, to presuppose for each thing that which is it potentially; and the holder of these views further declared what that is which is potentially a 'this' and a substance but is not in itself being—viz. that it is the relative (as if he had said 'the qualitative'), which is neither potentially the one or being, nor the negation of the one nor of being, but one among beings. And it was much more necessary, as we said, if he was inquiring how beings are many, not to inquire about those in the same category—how there are many substances or many qualities—but how beings as a whole are many; for some are substances, some modifications, some relations. In the categories other than substance there is yet another problem involved in the existence of plurality. Since they are not separable from substances, qualities and quantities are many just because their *substratum* becomes and is many; yet there ought to be a matter for each category; only it cannot be separable from substances. But in the case of 'thises', it is possible to explain how the 'this' is many things, unless a thing is to be treated as both a 'this' and a general character. The difficulty arising from the facts about substances is rather this, how there are actually many substances and not one.

But further, if the 'this' and the quantitative are not the same, we are not told how and why the things that are are many, but how quantities are many. For all 'number' means a quantity, and so does the 'unit', unless it means a measure or the quantitatively indivisible. If, then, the quantitative and the 'what' are different, we are not told whence or how the 'what' is many; but if any one says they are the same, he has to face many inconsistencies.

One might fix one's attention also on the question, regarding the numbers, what justifies the belief that they exist. To the believer in Ideas they provide some sort of cause for existing things, since each number is an Idea, and the Idea is to other things somehow or other the cause of their being; for let this supposition be granted them. But as for him who does not hold this view because he sees the inherent objections to the Ideas (so that it is not for this reason that he posits numbers), but who posits mathematical number, why must we believe his statement that such number exists, and of what use is such number to other things? Neither does he who says it exists maintain that it is the cause of anything (he rather says it is a thing existing by itself), nor is it observed to be the cause of anything; for the theorems of arithmeticians will all be found true even of sensible things, as was said before.

3

As for those, then, who suppose the Ideas to exist and to be numbers, by their assumption—in virtue of the method of setting out each term apart from its instances—of the unity of each general term they try at least to explain somehow why number must exist. Since their reasons, however, are neither conclusive nor in themselves possible, one must not, for these reasons at least, assert the existence of number. Again, the Pythagoreans, because they saw many attributes of numbers belonging to sensible bodies, supposed real things to be numbers—not separable numbers, however, but numbers of which real things consist. But why? Because the attributes of numbers are present in a musical scale and in the heavens and in many other things. Those, however, who say that mathematical number alone exists cannot according to their hypotheses say anything of this sort, but it used to be urged that these sensible things could not be the subject of the sciences. But we maintain that they are, as we said before. And it is evident that the objects of mathematics do not exist apart; for if they existed apart their attributes would not have been present in bodies. Now the Pythagoreans in this point are open to no objection; but in that they construct natural bodies out of numbers, things that have lightness and weight out of things that have not weight or lightness, they seem to speak of another heaven and other bodies, not of the sensible. But those who make number separable assume that it both exists and is separable because the axioms would not be true of sensible things, while the statements of mathematics are true and 'greet the soul'; and similarly with the spatial magnitudes of mathematics. It is evident, then, both that the rival theory will say the contrary of this, and that the difficulty we raised just now, why if numbers are in no way present in sensible things their attributes are present in sensible things, has to be solved by those who hold these views.

There are some who, because the point is the limit and extreme of the line, the line of the plane, and the plane of the solid, think there must be real things of this sort. We must therefore examine this argument too, and see whether it is not remarkably weak. For (i) extremes are not substances, but rather all these things are limits. For even walking, and movement in general, has a limit, so that on their theory this will be a 'this' and a substance. But that is absurd. Not but what (ii) even if they are substances, they will all be the substances of the sensible things in this world; for it is to these that the argument applied. Why then should they be capable of existing apart?

Again, if we are not too easily satisfied, we may, regarding all number and the objects of mathematics, press this difficulty, that they contribute nothing to one another, the prior to the posterior; for if number did not exist, none the less spatial magnitudes would exist for those who maintain the existence of the objects of mathematics only, and if spatial magnitudes did not exist, soul and sensible bodies would exist. But the observed facts show that nature is not a series of episodes, like a bad tragedy. As for the believers in the Ideas, this difficulty misses them; for they construct spatial magnitudes out of matter and number, lines out of the number 2, planes doubtless out of 3, solids out of 4,—or they use other numbers, which makes no difference. But will these magnitudes be Ideas, or what is their manner of existence, and what do they contribute to things? These contribute nothing, as the objects of mathematics contribute nothing. But not even is any theorem true of them, unless we want to change the objects of mathematics and invent doctrines of our own. But it is not hard to assume any random hypotheses and spin out a long string of conclusions. These thinkers, then, are wrong in this way, in wanting to unite the objects of mathematics with the Ideas. And those who first posited two kinds of number, that of the Forms and that which is mathematical, neither have said nor can say how mathematical number is to exist and of what it is to consist. For they place it between ideal and sensible number. If (i) it consists of the great and small, it will be the same as the other-ideal-number (he makes spatial magnitudes out of some other small and great). And if (ii) he names some other element, he will be making his elements rather many. And if the principle of each of the two kinds of number is a 1, unity will be something common to these, and we must inquire how the one is these many things, while at the same time number, according to him, cannot be generated except from one and an indefinite dyad.

All this is absurd, and conflicts both with itself and with the probabilities, and we seem to see in it Simonides 'long rigmarole' for the long rigmarole comes into play, like those of slaves, when men have nothing sound to say. And the very elements—the great and the small—seem to cry out against the violence that is done to them; for they cannot in any way generate numbers other than those got from 1 by doubling.

It is strange also to attribute generation to things that are eternal, or rather this is one of the things that are impossible. There need be no doubt whether the Pythagoreans attribute generation to them or not; for they say plainly that when the one had been constructed, whether out of planes or of surface or of seed or of elements which they cannot express, immediately the nearest part of the unlimited began to be constrained and limited by the limit. But since they are constructing a world and wish to speak the language of natural science, it is fair to make some examination of their physical theories, but to let them off from the present inquiry; for we are investigating the principles at work in unchangeable things, so that it is numbers of this kind whose genesis we must study.

4

These thinkers say there is no generation of the odd number, which evidently implies that there is generation of the even; and some present the even as produced first from unequals—the great and the small—when these are equalized. The inequality, then, must belong to them before they are equalized. If they had always been equalized, they would not have been unequal before; for there is nothing before that which is always. Therefore evidently they are not giving their account of the generation of numbers merely to assist contemplation of their nature.

A difficulty, and a reproach to any one who finds it no difficulty, are contained in the question how the elements and the principles are related to the good and the beautiful; the difficulty is this, whether any of the elements is such a thing as we mean by the good itself and the best, or this is not so, but these are later in origin than the elements. The theologians seem to agree with some thinkers of the present day, who answer the question in the negative, and say that both the good and the beautiful appear in the nature of things only when that nature has made some progress. (This they do to avoid a real objection which confronts those who say, as some do, that the one is a first principle. The objection arises not from their ascribing goodness to the first principle as an attribute, but from their making the one a principle—and a principle in the sense of an element—and generating number from the one.) The old poets agree with this inasmuch as they say that not those who are first in time, e.g. Night and Heaven or Chaos or Ocean, reign and rule, but Zeus. These poets, however, are led to speak thus only because they think of the rulers of the world as changing; for those of them who combine the two characters in that they do not use mythical language throughout, e.g. Pherecydes and some others, make the original generating agent the Best, and so do the Magi, and some of the later sages also, e.g. both Empedocles and Anaxagoras, of whom one made love an element, and the other made reason a principle. Of those who maintain the existence of the unchangeable substances some say the One itself is the good itself; but they thought its substance lay mainly in its unity.

This, then, is the problem,—which of the two ways of speaking is right. It would be strange if to that which is primary and eternal and most self-sufficient this very quality—self-sufficiency and self-maintenance—belongs primarily in some other way than as a good. But indeed it can be for no other reason indestructible or self-sufficient than because its nature is good. Therefore to say that the first principle is good is probably correct; but that this principle should be the One or, if not that, at least an element, and an element of numbers, is impossible. Powerful objections arise, to avoid which some have given up the theory (viz. those who agree that the One is a first principle and element, but only of mathematical number). For on this view all the units become identical with species of good, and there is a great profusion of goods. Again, if the Forms are numbers, all the Forms are identical with species of good. But let a man assume Ideas of anything he pleases. If these are Ideas only of goods, the Ideas will not be substances; but if the Ideas are also Ideas of substances, all animals and plants and all individuals that share in Ideas will be good.

These absurdities follow, and it also follows that the contrary element, whether it is plurality or the unequal, i.e. the great and small, is the bad-itself. (Hence one thinker avoided attaching the good to the One, because it would necessarily follow, since generation is from contraries, that badness is the fundamental nature of plurality; while others say inequality is the nature of the bad.) It follows, then, that all things partake of the bad except one—the One itself, and that numbers partake of it in a more undiluted form than spatial magnitudes, and that the bad is the space in which the good is realized, and that it partakes in and desires that which tends to destroy it; for contrary tends to destroy contrary. And if, as we were saying, the matter is that which is potentially each thing, e.g. that of actual fire is that which is potentially fire, the bad will be just the potentially good.

All these objections, then, follow, partly because they make every principle an element, partly because they make contraries principles, partly because they make the One a principle, partly because they treat the numbers as the first substances, and as capable of existing apart, and as Forms.

5

If, then, it is equally impossible not to put the good among the first principles and to put it among them in this way, evidently the principles are not being correctly described, nor are the first substances. Nor does any one conceive the matter correctly if he compares the principles of the universe to that of animals and plants, on the ground that the more complete always comes from the indefinite and incomplete—which is what leads this thinker to say that this is also true of the first principles of reality, so that the One itself is not even an existing thing. This is incorrect, for even in this world of animals and plants the principles from which these come are complete; for it is a man that produces a man, and the seed is not first.

It is out of place, also, to generate place simultaneously with the mathematical solids (for place is peculiar to the individual things, and hence they are separate in place; but mathematical objects are nowhere), and to say that they must be somewhere, but not say what kind of thing their place is.

Those who say that existing things come from elements and that the first of existing things are the numbers, should have first distinguished the senses in which one thing comes from another, and then said in which sense number comes from its first principles.

By intermixture? But (1) not everything is capable of intermixture, and (2) that which is produced by it is different from its elements, and on this view the one will not remain separate or a distinct entity; but they want it to be so.

By juxtaposition, like a syllable? But then (1) the elements must have position; and (2) he who thinks of number will be able to think of the unity and the plurality apart; number then will be this—a unit and plurality, or the one and the unequal.

Again, coming from certain things means in one sense that these are still to be found in the product, and in another that they are not; which sense does number come from these elements? Only things that are generated can come from elements which are present in them. Does number come, then, from its elements as from seed? But nothing can be excreted from that which is indivisible. Does it come from its contrary, its contrary not persisting? But all things that come in this way come also from something else which does persist. Since, then, one thinker places the 1 as contrary to plurality, and another places it as contrary to the unequal, treating the 1 as equal, number must be being treated as coming from contraries. There is, then, something else that persists, from which and from one contrary the compound is or has come to be. Again, why in the world do the other things that come from contraries, or that have contraries, perish (even when all of the contrary is used to produce them), while number does not? Nothing is said about this. Yet whether present or not present in the compound the contrary destroys it, e.g. 'strife' destroys the 'mixture' (yet it should not; for it is not to that that is contrary).

Once more, it has not been determined at all in which way numbers are the causes of substances and of being-whether (1) as boundaries (as points are of spatial magnitudes). This is how Eurytus decided what was the number of what (e.g. one of man and another of horse), viz. by imitating the figures of living things with pebbles, as some people bring numbers into the forms of triangle and square. Or (2) is it because harmony is a ratio of numbers, and so is man and everything else? But how are the attributes—white and sweet and hot—numbers? Evidently it is not the numbers that are the essence or the causes of the form; for the ratio is the essence, while the number the causes of the form; for the ratio is the essence, while the number is the matter. E.g. the essence of flesh or bone is number only in this way, 'three parts of fire and two of earth'. And a number, whatever number it is, is always a number of certain things, either of parts of fire or earth or of units; but the essence is that there is so much of one thing to so much of another in the mixture; and this is no longer a number but a ratio of mixture of numbers, whether these are corporeal or of any other kind.

Number, then, whether it be number in general or the number which consists of abstract units, is neither the cause as agent, nor the matter, nor the ratio and form of things. Nor, of course, is it the final cause.

6

One might also raise the question what the good is that things get from numbers because their composition is expressible by a number, either by one which is easily calculable or by an odd number. For in fact honey-water is no more wholesome if it is mixed in the proportion of three times three, but it would do more good if it were in no particular ratio but well diluted than if it were numerically expressible but strong. Again, the ratios of mixtures are expressed by the adding of numbers, not by mere numbers; e.g. it is 'three parts to two', not 'three times two'. For in any multiplication the genus of the things multiplied must be the same; therefore the product $1 \times 2 \times 3$ must be measurable by 1, and $4 \times 5 \times 6$ by 4 and therefore all products into which the same factor enters must be measurable by that factor. The number of fire, then, cannot be $2 \times 5 \times 3 \times 6$ and at the same time that of water 2×3.

If all things must share in number, it must follow that many things are the same, and the same number must belong to one thing and to another. Is number the cause, then, and does the thing exist because of its number, or is this not certain? E.g. the motions of the sun have a number, and again those of the moon,—yes, and the life and prime of each animal. Why, then, should not some of these numbers be squares, some cubes, and some equal, others double? There is no reason why they should not, and indeed they must move within these limits, since all things were assumed to share in number. And it was assumed that things that differed might fall under the same number. Therefore if the same number had belonged to certain things, these would have been the same as one another, since they would have had the same form of number; e.g. sun and moon would have been the same. But why need these numbers be causes? There are seven vowels, the scale consists of seven strings, the Pleiades are seven, at seven animals lose their teeth (at least some do, though some do not), and the champions who fought against Thebes were seven. Is it then because the number is the kind of number it is, that the champions were seven or the Pleiad consists of seven stars? Surely the champions were seven because there were seven gates or for some other reason, and the Pleiad we count as seven, as we count the Bear as twelve, while other peoples count more stars in both. Nay they even say that Ξ, Ψ and Z are concords and that because there are three concords, the double consonants also are three. They quite neglect the fact that there might be a thousand such letters; for one symbol might be assigned to ΓΡ. But if they say that each of these three is equal to two of the other letters, and no other is so, and if the cause is that there are three parts of the mouth and one letter is in each applied to sigma, it is for this reason that there are only three, not because the concords are three; since as a matter of fact the concords are more than three, but of double consonants there cannot be more.

These people are like the old-fashioned Homeric scholars, who see small resemblances but neglect great ones. Some say that there are many such cases, e.g. that the middle strings are represented by nine and eight, and that the epic verse has seventeen syllables, which is equal in number to the two strings, and that the scansion is, in the right half of the line nine syllables, and in the left eight. And they say that the distance in the letters from alpha to omega is equal to that from the lowest note of the flute to the highest, and that the number of this note is equal to that of the whole choir of heaven. It may be suspected that no one could find difficulty either in stating such analogies or in finding them in eternal things, since they can be found even in perishable things.

But the lauded characteristics of numbers, and the contraries of these, and generally the mathematical relations, as some describe them, making them causes of nature, seem, when we inspect them in this way, to vanish; for none of them is a cause in any of the senses that have been distinguished in reference to the first principles. In a sense, however, they make it plain that goodness belongs to numbers, and that the odd, the straight, the square, the potencies of certain numbers, are in the column of the beautiful. For the seasons and a particular kind of number go together; and the other agreements that they collect from the theorems of mathematics all have this meaning. Hence they are like coincidences. For they are accidents, but the things that agree are all appropriate to one another, and one by analogy. For in each category of being an analogous term is found—as the straight is in length, so is the level in surface, perhaps the odd in number, and the white in colour.

Again, it is not the ideal numbers that are the causes of musical phenomena and the like (for equal ideal numbers differ from one another in form; for even the units do); so that we need not assume Ideas for this reason at least.

These, then, are the results of the theory, and yet more might be brought together. The fact that our opponents have much trouble with the generation of numbers and can in no way make a system of them, seems to indicate that the objects of mathematics are not separable from sensible things, as some say, and that they are not the first principles.

THE END